A FIELD GUIDE TO THE
STREET NAMES
······· OF ·······
CENTRAL CAIRO

A FIELD GUIDE TO THE
STREET NAMES
·························· O F ··························
CENTRAL CAIRO

HUMPHREY DAVIES   LESLEY LABABIDI

The American University in Cairo Press
Cairo   New York

First published in 2018 by
The American University in Cairo Press
113 Sharia Kasr el Aini, Cairo, Egypt
420 Fifth Avenue, New York, NY 10018
www.aucpress.com

Exclusive distribution outside Egypt and North America by I.B.Tauris & Co Ltd.,
6 Salem Road, London, W4 2BU

Dar el Kutub No. 10118/17
ISBN 978 977 416 856 7

Dar el Kutub Cataloging-in-Publication Data

Davies, Humphrey and Lababidi, Lesley
        A Field Guide to the Street Names of Central Cairo / Humphrey Davies
    and Lesley Lababidi.—Cairo: The American University in Cairo Press, 2018.
        p.   cm.
        ISBN 978 977 416 856 7
        1. Egypt—Description and Travel
        2. Street Names—Egypt—Cairo
        388.411025

1   2   3   4   5   22   21   20   19   18

Maps by Cherif Abdullah
Designed by Adam el-Sehemy
Printed in the United States of America

CONTENTS

INTRODUCTION

This is not a guidebook, or at least not one that will help the reader to get from A to B (let alone from A to Z). It sets out, rather, to help him or her to get from now to then or vice versa within those parts of the city that lie east of the Nile and west of medieval Cairo, from Midan Ramsis in the north to Midan Fumm el-Khalig in the south, as well as on the island of el-Gezira. In order to do so, it presents an alphabetical list of current street names, each with its former or alternative names, if any, in reverse chronological order, and provides, where possible, short descriptions of who or what each street is named for and the dates at which street names changed. An index at the end of the book links the former and alternative names to the current name of the street used in the main entries. The definite article *el-* and the letter *'* (*'ayn*) are ignored in the alphabetization of entries.

It has been our aim to provide information for every officially-recognized thoroughfare or public space, be it a *share'* (street), *hara* (lane), *'atfa* (alley), *darb* (formerly, side street), *sekka* (connecting street), *zuqaq* (cul-de-sac), *midan* (square), or *kubri* (bridge), as well as a representative sample of passageways.[1] The list contains 607 current street names and some 377 former and alternative names. Street names are transliterated (*see below*), and translated when they consist of more than a simple personal name, without title. Names that begin with a title are listed under that title but a cross-reference is provided, as titles are often dropped in casual references (for example, Share' el-Shahid Zakariya Rezq is listed under el-Shahid with a cross-reference from Zakariya). Cross-references are also provided for foreign names (for example, Share' Shambuliyon is cross-referenced from Champollion).

Before turning to the city as it is today, we should note three types of watery body, that though today absent or greatly changed, have exerted a ghostly influence over its development and are referred to in the text. These are the River Nile, the canals, and the lakes.

The course of the Nile at the time of the Arab conquest of Egypt ran about a kilometer and a half to the east of its present bed, if the distance is measured at its greatest. From the mosque of 'Amr ebn el-'As, which was built on its bank, the river ran along today's Share' Sidi Hasan el-Anwar to west of Midan el-Sayyeda Zeinab, from there to Share' Mustafa Kamel, from there to Share' Muhammad Farid, from there to Share' 'Emad el-Din, and from there to Midan Ramsis; thereafter, it veered west to meet its present channel at Shubra. The river's slow shift to the west—accelerating during the twelfth and thirteenth centuries and only coming to an end with the engineering works of the nineteenth century—left behind a plain of alluvial soil (the *luq* of Bab el-Luq) dotted with swamps and ponds. This was originally given over, to the extent possible, to agriculture (hence the frequent occurrence of *bustan*, or 'plantation,' in street names). In addition, the occasional settlement grew up, either in the form of a *hekr* (an estate granted on a long lease to a member of the establishment, on which suburban communities often arose) or a *manshiya* (a housing compound for the elite); these have left their mark among the city's street names. Other areas were turned into grounds dedicated to equestrian sports and military exercises.

At the start of the nineteenth century, the lands on which Cairo now stands were also traversed by two large canals.

El-Khalig el-Masri (the Egyptian Canal), or el-Khalig el-Kebir (the Great Canal), whose origins go back to at least the Romans and probably to the pharaohs, was dug to provide a navigable channel between the Nile and the Red Sea. Much given to silting even in antiquity, it was re-dug by 'Amr ebn el-'As (c.585–664), Egypt's first Muslim governor, at which point it became known as Khalig Amir el-Mu'menin (the Canal of the Commander of the Faithful). Neglected by the Umayads, it was dug again under the Fatimids, under whom it seems to have acquired its present name, though it was also sometimes referred to as el-Khalig el-Hakimi, after the Fatimid caliph el-Hakim be-Amrillah, or as Khalig Lu'lu'a, after a bridge over the canal named for a Fatimid governor, or, in a map produced by the French in 1800, as "Canal el-Soultany" (i.e., el-Khalig el-Sultani, or the Royal Canal). In Fatimid times, it defined the city's western edge; by the mid-nineteenth century it traversed the center of the city, the quarters to its west having grown up under Mamluk rule. Before the river's retreat to the west, its intake point had been located to the east of its present site, at a point some 300 meters west of today's Midan el-Sayyeda Zeinab; it was extended from there to Midan Fumm el-Khalig (Mouth of the Canal Sq.) on the river in 1241. In its course toward the north, it followed that of the street that would replace it, originally known as Share' el-Khalig el-Masri, now called Share' Bur Said, and passed through the city walls at Bab el-Sha'riya before continuing to the area of el-Daher, after which it crossed the desert to debouch into the lake system at the northern end of the Red Sea; by the nineteenth century, however, it no longer extended beyond el-Daher.

El-Khalig el-Naseri was dug by Mamluk ruler el-Malek el-Naser Muhammad ebn Qalawun in 1325. It provided water to el-Khalig el-Masri, at that time silted up along its initial stretch, as well as to el-Malek el-Naser's new resort at Siryaqus, north of the city near Birket el-Huggag. It also formed a navigable route for commodities, irrigated lands exposed by the river's westward retreat, and allowed the seasonal refilling of certain lakes (such as those of el-Azbakiya and el-Nasriya) that had become magnets for urban development. El-Khalig el-Naseri started at Qasr el-'Eini, not far north of the intake of el-Khalig el-Masri, and ran more or less parallel to el-Khalig el-Masri a little less than a kilometer to its west, prefiguring and facilitating the building of today's Share' Qasr el-'Eini, Share' Tal'at Harb, and Share' 'Urabi, as well as the northern end of Share' Ramsis. At a point about two hundred meters west of Midan Ramsis, it swung to the northeast to meet and merge with el-Khalig el-Masri just west of the mosque of el-Daher, about five kilometers from where it started. Stretches of the canal have been known by different names at different times. That most commonly used in what is now the Downtown area was Khalig el-Maghrabi, or el-Maghrabi's Canal, after Sheikh Salah el-Din Yusef el-Maghrabi (d.1355), a Sufi saint whose tomb once stood close to its bank on today's Share' 'Adli. A branch, Khalig el-Khor, survives in the form of a street name. Bridges over these canals, of which there were some twenty-four at the end of the nineteenth century, were called *qanater*, singular *qantara*. These survive today in street names such as Qantaret Qadadar and Qantaret el-Dekka.

At the beginning of the nineteenth century, the area covered by this book contained at least six lakes, several of them known by more than one name. These were depressions exposed by the westward retreat of the Nile that filled only during the river's annual flood. By the end of the century all of them had been filled in, some leaving a visible impression on the city landscape, such as the best known, Berket el-Azbakiya, from which the celebrated el-Azbakiya Gardens were created, and Berket el-Farrayin, which occupied what is now Midan el-Gumhuriya in ʿAbdin. Others, such as el-Berka el-Nasriya, survive only in the name of a street.

This plain to the west of the city created by the retreat of the Nile, with its canals and lakes, became, from approximately 1867, the canvas on which Cairo's planners would seek to implement their vision. The "Esmaʿiliya project"—the term we use to denote the developments that took place in and around downtown Cairo beginning in the last quarter of the nineteenth century and whose momentum later led to the appearance of districts such as el-Zamalek and Garden City—has traditionally been described as the brainchild of two men. The first was Khedive Esmaʿil (r.1863–79), who is supposed to have been inspired by what he had seen of post-Haussmann Paris, and above all by a visit he made to the Exposition Universelle in 1867, to issue an order for the creation of a "Paris on the Nile." This aggressive project extended to the west of the existing medieval city and included the upgrading of the el-Azbakiya area, then the modern city center. The second man was ʿAli Mubarak (1823–93), Esmaʿil's minister of public works, who joined the khedive on his visit to Paris and was charged with overseeing the project's implementation, a process that he described twenty years later in his twenty-volume *al-Khitat al-Tawfiqiya al-Jadida* (The New Tawfiqian Topography).

The above account emphasizes the radical nature of the break with past city-planning practice and the centrality of a foreign urban model. It asserts that the Esmaʿiliya project divided Cairo into two cities, one 'oriental' and almost entirely composed, as a description written in 1800 has it, "of extremely short, broken, zig-zag streets with innumerable dead ends,"[2] and another that was 'western,' with open spaces and straight streets.

But this model has been challenged. Jean-Luc Arnaud, in his *Le Caire, mise en place d'une ville modern, 1867–1907*, has pointed to urban improvements made before the Esma'iliya project and questioned the central role of 'Ali Mubarak, drawing attention to other, lesser known, but equally influential, players. Khaled Fahmy, in "Modernizing Cairo: A Revisionist Narrative," has detailed those earlier efforts, going back to the first Tanzim (literally, 'Organization') Council, created in 1844 by the governor of Cairo (and later viceroy of Egypt) 'Abbas Helmi (r.1848–54), whose task was to regulate and improve street planning, issue building and renovation permits, and implement public hygiene, and which was also entrusted with the task of naming streets, numbering houses, and installing street signs. Further important decrees followed in 1859 and 1866. Fahmy attributes these efforts not to a desire to imitate Europe but to a determination, on the one hand, to implement *'umariya*, a term that covered 'construction,' 'urban development,' and even 'civilization,' and, on the other, to improve public health and hygiene. Rulers of the time believed (to the point of "obsession") in the then accepted theory that "miasmas," or "thick air," resulting from decomposing matter, caused disease and thought that these could be prevented by removing their causes and improving air circulation.[3] As an acknowledgment of the importance of these earlier efforts to transform the city, we have included in this book two streets conceived before the Esma'iliya project and falling outside its area: both Share' el-Qal'a/Share' Muhammad 'Ali and Share' Kulut (Clot) Beih run through the heart of the old city and both were planned under Muhammad 'Ali Basha (r.1805–48), though neither was completed until 1875.

Notwithstanding this adjustment to our understanding of the historical context of the Esma'iliya project, it remains a fact that "the outlines of Cairo . . . were roughly the same in 1848 as they had been in 1798."[4] During the first half of the nineteenth century, the lakes and swamps to its west had been drained and the eastern riverbank stabilized by the planting of fast-growing figs, oranges, and banyans. New palaces had been built along the Nile. As early as 1864, Khedive Esma'il had taken steps to improve the city's infrastructure by establishing a department of public works. This was followed in 1865 by the creation of the Cairo Water Company and the Cairo Gas Company. Plans for a project of wider scope were also being formulated. This envisaged the transformation of the city by refurbishing the el-Azbakiya district, then the city's modern center, by creating a network of traffic circles and radiating streets that would penetrate even the older part of the city,[5] and, yet more ambitiously, by creating an entirely new quarter, in which, according to ʿAli Mubarak's description, "all streets and lanes would be planned to follow straight lines, with most of them intersecting at right angles, and whose houses would be separate from one another; whose streets and lanes would be laid with crushed limestone and on either side of which there would be sidewalks for pedestrians, the middle of the roads being set aside for vehicles and animals; where each street would be provided with piped water with which to lay the dust and irrigate the gardens, and gas lamps would be erected to light each street, so that it might become Cairo's finest and most flourishing district, to be inhabited by the princes and notables of the Muslims, and others."[6] It would seem, therefore, that the 1867 Exposition Universelle in Paris was, for Esmaʿil, an opportunity rather than a moment of revelation—an opportunity that Esmaʿil seized to gather the players (gardeners, landscapers, engineers, and architects) needed to put this grander vision into effect. The timetable was determined by the khedive's desire to show off his new city at the upcoming opening of the Suez Canal, slated for 1869, to which he had invited most of the crowned heads of Europe. In fact, the frantic activity over the next two years failed to produce much more, outside el-Azbakiya, than a street grid (an observer in 1871 writing that "the Viceroy has here . . . laid out broad macadamized roads . . . *as if he were contemplating an European city*"[7]), and a part of the plan, namely, the creation of new traffic circles and streets in the old city, was abandoned. By 1867 work had, however, begun, and it is this date that we shall use, only slightly arbitrarily, as that of the start of the "Esmaʿiliya project."

The boundaries of the area slated for development were surprisingly wide and ran, according to Mubarak's account, from today's Shareʿ Setta w-ʿEshrin Yulyu in the north to the complex of buildings known as Qasr el-ʿEini in the south, and from Bab el-Luq in the east to the Nile in the west,[8] thus embracing not only the central portions of downtown Cairo that Cairenes generally have in mind today when they speak of the Esmaʿiliya Quarter, but also the districts of Garden City, el-Munira, ʿAbdin, and Fumm el-Khalig. It is this 'Greater Esmaʿiliya' that we have taken as our coverage area, adding to it, however, the district of el-Tawfiqiya, north of Shareʿ Setta w-ʿEshrin Yulyu, and the island of el-Gezira, on the grounds that these both developed under the momentum and within the same broad time-frame as the areas listed by Mubarak.

To help readers orientate themselves, we have divided the area outlined above into ten districts (*see* maps). While these do not necessarily follow administrative boundaries, they do, we believe, reflect popular usage:

el-Tawfiqiya (after Khedive Muhammad Tawfiq, r.1879–92) is located between Shareʿ Setta w-ʿEshrin Yulyu and Midan Ramsis and consisted, before its development, of ponds and irrigation and drainage canals, along with a few palaces and their grounds; it was sparsely populated. The digging of the el-Esmaʿiliya Canal on its western border, completed in 1866, made the land more accessible, and draining, leveling, and subdivision were completed during the rule of its eponym. It received its greatest boost, however, from the collaboration of the families of ʿAli Galal Basha (d.1892) and Saʿid Halim Basha (1865–1921), whose large land holdings in the northwest of the district and to the west of el-Azbakiya, respectively, were unified in 1881, a development that was clinched in 1894 and 1895 by double intermarriage between them.[9] This allowed for a concerted and coherent development of the area, and el-Tawfiqiya came into effective existence in the decade that followed.

el-Azbakiya (after Azbak min Tutukh, d.1498 or 1499) was an affluent suburb by the time of the French invasion. It was subdivided around 1867 and saw during the immediately following years more rapid growth than any other area within the Esmaʿiliya project, because of the availability of lands on its periphery. It remained the center of the modern city until the first decades of the twentieth century, and the site of most of its modern hotels and upmarket retailing, which by then had moved to Midan el-Ubera and surrounding streets from Shareʿ el-Muski (out of area). With the Downtown building boom of the late nineteenth and early twentieth century, however, the city's center of gravity moved west and el-Azbakiya stagnated.

Downtown (*West el-Balad*) came into existence on the soft, alluvial lands (*ard el-luq*) between the western wall of the old city and the Nile that had been exposed by the river's withdrawal to the west in the late thirteenth century. Along its eastern border, defined by a wall that Edward Lane, writing around 1828, described as "more like the walls of a garden than those of a great city,"[10] it blended into the fringe of unplanned neighborhoods that had arisen as Cairo expanded in the early nineteenth century. Development plans were drawn up, probably in 1867, and plots offered free to those with sufficient funds to build villas. Uptake, however, was slow (though lower-grade building probably continued strongly in already established areas such as Bab el-Luq) and was further delayed by Ahmad 'Urabi's movement and the British occupation of 1882. Growth surged from 1897 to 1917, here and throughout Cairo's new areas, on the back of a strong economy, aided by the completion of the first Aswan Dam in 1902, which allowed the banks of the Nile to be stabilized, and continued, in fits and starts, up to the Second World War. The second half of the twentieth century saw a gradual exodus of the area's affluent residents (el-Zamalek excepted) and the increased domination of commerce, with large apartments divided into sweat shops or rented cheaply as storerooms, while others were closed, or simply abandoned, the resulting dilapidation plain from the glassless windows and shutters hanging askew. Today, there is a movement to reverse the decline, with repainting and perhaps even renovation proceeding apace, in the hope of valorizing modern Cairo's 'historic heritage' and raising property values. The prospect of revitalization hovers, while the threat of gentrification looms.

'Abdin (after either 'Abdin Beih, a seventeenth-century Ottoman general, or 'Abdin Basha el-Arnauti (1780–1827), one of Muhammad 'Ali Basha's generals) was, in the mid-nineteenth century, an area of ponds and unplanned neighborhoods spilling over from the older city to its east. It became a center of development in the wake of the construction by Khedive Esma'il in 1874 of 'Abdin Palace, the monarch's new residence after the abandonment of Salah el-Din's Citadel as home of the ruler and seat of government. New neighborhoods sprang up around the palace to accommodate staff and servants, many of them reproducing the patterns of the old city with its *hara*s, or semi-self-contained quarters, and relics of these remain to this day, alongside Europeanized residential and commercial neighborhoods.

Qasr el-Dubara (after the palace of that name built on the Nile by Muhammad ʿAli Basha for his wives) is located between Shareʿ el-Tahrir to the north and Garden City to the south. The district surrounding the palace was subdivided in 1880, many of the lots being purchased by the British Residence, now the British Embassy, in 1892; other embassies, many of which remain, followed suit. In the 1940s, the palace and its grounds were sold and subdivided, leading to the creation of more streets. In the thick of things during the events of 2011 and their aftermath, the district today remains something of an enclave, with many streets closed to through traffic.

Garden City, on the Nile between Qasr el-Dubara on the north and the Qasr el-ʿEini hospital complex in the south, was designed in accordance with the 'garden suburb' planning theories of English architect Ebenezer Howard and was built on the former grounds of a complex of palaces belonging to Ebrahim Basha, whose oldest components were constructed in 1835 and which was known collectively as el-Qasr el-ʿAli, or the High Palace (demolished 1906). Some street names here, such as Shareʿ el-Tulumbat (Pump Street) and Shareʿ el-Nabatat (Nursery Street), recall installations associated with the palace. Though the street plan—virtually unchanged until today—was designed by real estate developer Charles Bacos and surveyor José Lamba in 1906, the suburb grew slowly, and many lots remained unused until the late 1920s, when it saw a rapid increase in the number of villas, and soon became one of the most sought-after residential districts in the city. From the 1940s, apartment blocks began to replace villas, and the amount of green space shrank. Despite this, it retains something of its former cachet.

el-Munira (meaning 'the Radiant,' so called because of the brilliance of the lights at the celebration of the simultaneous 1873 marriage in the adjacent grounds of el-Qasr el-ʿAli palace of four of Khedive Esmaʿil's children) runs from Shareʿ el-Sheikh Rihan on the north to Shareʿ el-Duktur ʿAli Ebrahim on the south and from Shareʿ Qasr el-ʿEini on the west to Shareʿ Nubar, Shareʿ Kheirat, and Shareʿ Bur Saʿid on the east. During the first half of the nineteenth century, the district consisted of plantations belonging to Ebrahim Pasha. The district includes, at its northern end, the former subdistricts of el-Dawawin ('government offices') and el-Ensha ('construction'), names that are no longer widely used but that allude to the development there during the reign of Khedive Esma'il, and following the descent of government from the Citadel, of an administrative zone around which government buildings and residential accommodations were constructed for civil servants and staff. Today, the district is largely residential.

Fumm el-Khalig ('the Mouth of the Canal,' after the intake point of el-Khalig el-Masri) is located between Share' el-Duktur 'Ali Ebrahim on the north and the starting point of the aqueduct of Magra el-'Eyun on the Nile on the south. The district was best known, from the Mamluk era to the nineteenth century, as the site of the celebrations at the breaking of the dam that admitted water into el-Khalig el-Masri at the height of the Nile flood. Its modern development began in 1865 when land there was granted to the Société des Eaux du Caire to install a pumping station to provide drinking water to the Citadel and the district of el-'Abbasiya. In 1874, the station was relocated to a site near the el-Esma'iliya Canal. Ownership of much of the land was initially in dispute and it could not therefore be subdivided or sold; this led to the springing up of unplanned low-grade housing, some of which remains, and to its use for industrial purposes. Some of the land belongs to the Coptic Church, which uses it for cemeteries.

el-Gezira ('the Island') is located on an island in the Nile, and runs from Share' el-Gezira on the north to the island's southern end. The island itself, whose northern third now goes under the name of el-Zamalek, did not take on its final shape until the middle of the nineteenth century, when three separate islands completed a process of coalescence that had begun in the fourteenth century. The district saw the construction of occasional palaces over the centuries, of which only the Saray el-Gezira, built by Khedive Esma'il in 1869 to house guests attending the opening of the Suez Canal, survives (as part of the Marriott Hotel). To this day, el-Gezira continues to consist largely of open land, the preserve of sporting clubs, military facilities, and exhibition grounds.

el-Zamalek (whose etymology is hotly debated and, in our opinion, unresolved) occupies el-Gezira island north of Share' el-Gezira. El-Zamalek first saw residential development when part of the grounds of the old Saray el-Gezira, by then a hotel, were sold in the 1890s. At this time, the area north of the hotel grounds was subdivided, its streets later to be named after royal princes, and the district's main street, now part of Share' Setta w-'Eshrin Yulyu, came into existence. The pace of construction picked up in 1907, when real estate companies bought much of the island. By 1910, the area northwest of the palace grounds had also been laid out; here the choice of names, equally systematic but perhaps less obviously relevant, favored Ayyubid princes and their followers. Development northward was slow, keeping pace largely with the raising of the Aswan Dam and the stabilization of the island's banks; not surprisingly, many of central el-Zamalek's original street names commemorate hydraulic engineers. Though facing challenges from Cairo's newer affluent suburbs, el-Zamalek remains arguably the city's most prestigious neighborhood.

To compile the list of current street names within the above districts on which this guide is based we initially walked the area, noting names. The resulting list was compared with published street guides[11] and with maps (ranging in date from 1800 to 2006), including Google Earth. Anomalies (of which many emerged) were resolved (where possible) by further research on the ground. However, no inventory made by a pedestrian in a city as complex as Cairo is likely to capture every thoroughfare, especially as many streets have no sign. Likewise, almost no map even aims to draw, let alone name, every street. We must, therefore, have failed to take note of some streets, and the smaller the street the greater the possibility of its having been overlooked. Despite this, we feel confident that we have listed the great majority of streets in our coverage area.

Name changes are more the rule than the exception for Cairo's streets. Writing in 1941, an English resident noted of a favorite street of his that "the name . . . has recently been changed, in accordance with an invidious innovation, that causes endless complication, distorts local history (a great pity in Cairo, where the names of streets, and places, were full of significance), and raises delicate problems."[12] Against this practice, a tenacious attachment to at least some old names ensures that they are not forgotten. Thus Share' Fu'ad, for example, may still be heard for Share' Setta w-'Eshrin Yulyu, Midan 'Abdin for Midan el-Gumhuriya, and Share' Seliman Basha for Share'Tal'at Harb, decades after these names were officially abolished. In some cases, such as Mamarr Behlar (now Share' el-Muhandes 'Ali Labib Gabr) and Share' el-Bustan (now Share' el-Ra'is 'Abd el-Salam 'Aref), popular preference for the older name seems to threaten the survival of the newer, and even the authorities appear to be of two minds, with signs for both names still in evidence. To add a further layer of richness, some streets have popular names that have persisted as tenaciously as those former official names. Thus Midan el-Falaki is a name unknown to many, who call the square Midan Bab el-Luq, simply, no doubt, because it is the center of the neigh-borhood of that name (and despite the fact that Midan Muhammad Farid close by has a better claim to it). That same Midan Muham-mad Farid is known to some as Midan Abu Zarifa, for a famous ful and falafel restaurant formerly located just off the square.

Tracing the evolution of these names is not always easy. In a few instances, a street's former name is given on its sign. Where this is not the case (and it is in fact rare and can at best only take us back one generation), we consulted maps. Gaps exist in the record, however, in terms of both date and area: one may find a map of central Cairo for 1926, for example, but not one of the same date of el-Munira or el-Tawfiqiya, and vice versa. Even some official maps show street names that are at odds with the dates written on them, a map that claims to have been last revised in 1948 showing, for example, Midan el-Tahrir, which did not exist before 1954. Issues of the *Journal Officiel* and *el-Waqa'e'el-Misriya*, official gazettes in which decrees mandating name changes should, by law, be published, were also searched, though not every issue was available to us; these were useful not only for the decrees but also for the incidental mentions of streets in, for example, lists of those where begging was to be banned, or that were to be set aside for residential use only. The records of the Streets Naming Committee of the Cairo Governorate were indispensable for the period after 1960, when they begin. Finally, we were helped by studies already conducted. Outstanding among these are the works of Fathi Hafiz el-Hadidi and Muhammad Kamal el-Sayyid Muhammad, although neither is focused primarily on street names and neither

discusses more than a limited number of streets. Certain specialized online resources were also vital, most notably, for Garden City
and el-Zamalek, Samir Raafat's egy.com. Works of history, commercial and professional directories, and even telephone directories
were all also used, in addition, of course, to the resources of the
Internet and, inevitably but with caution, local lore. A complete list
of sources is provided at the back of the book.

Surprising gaps exist in the sources. There is no comprehen-
sive listing, for example, of the *shahid*s ('martyrs')—members of the
armed forces who gave their lives for their country—to whose memory many streets are dedicated. There is no 'Big Book of Sheikhs' to
provide us with more than just the name of many of these ubiquitous
figures of whom nothing remains but the memory of their piety, nor
is there a list of minor Mamluks and their exploits, though these
doughty warriors have captured a fair share of the city's street names.
Other street names resist analysis, bearing generic names such as
Tarboosh Maker's Lane or Butcher's Lane and evading any more
specificity than that provided by their translation. Many streets are
named for some local feature such as a mound or a pond, now disappeared, or the name of an early resident or shopkeeper, knowledge
of whose identity has faded with time. It may be that we shall never
know to what or to whom such names refer, and approximately ten
percent of the names in this book have been classed as 'unidentified.'

Determining the date at which a name came into use is also
often difficult. It is usually assumed that streets are given names by
local authorities according to an established procedure and at the
time of their creation. This is not what usually happens, in Cairo or
elsewhere. Rather, for practical reasons, thoroughfares acquire names
before—sometimes long before—official procedures can come into
play. Thereafter, it is up to the naming authority to play catch-up by
ratifying, or sometimes quashing, names already in use. This can lead
to striking anomalies. To cite but one example, Share' el-Sheikh 'Abd
el-'Aziz Gawish, in 'Abdin, has been known as such since at least
1973, when the name appears in a telephone directory, and, if the
weathered state of its signs is any indication, for much longer; the
name was only officially recognized and ratified, however, in 2013.[13]
The majority of decrees relating to streets in our area are in fact ratifi-
cations of pre-existing traditional names, rendering moot the question
of when the name in fact first appeared. In the case of many streets,

and especially before 1960, no official mention, either of the assignment of a new name or the ratification of an old one, can be found.

It follows from this that the date we give for a street name is that for which we have plausible documentation, either in the form of a decree assigning a new name, or, and this is more frequent, in the form of its appearance on a map, or in any other written material. It is not necessarily the date at which the street in question was actually first called by that name. For example, while common sense dictates that Share' el-'Ashmawi was probably so called from the time that the popular Sufi saint after whom it is named and who died in 1831 took up residence there, or soon after, we are obliged to give its date as 1913, which is that of the earliest reference to it that we have found, in the *Journal Officiel*.[14] If we say that a street has borne a particular name "since" a certain date, this means that we have solid evidence of that. In most cases, however, we have been obliged to say that a name was in place "by" a certain date, meaning that the name is documented for that date but almost certainly appeared earlier, or to hedge our bets with "probably" and "*circa*." In other cases, where no documentation of any sort exists, we have been obliged to provide only tentative dates, based on analogy to dateable nearby streets, or even to provide no date at all.

Such ambiguities are not universal. A minority of streets, usually those of symbolic importance, have received their names in the full light of bureaucratic procedure. Thus, as is well known, the renaming of fifteen streets and three squares originally named for members of the royal family took place all at one go in September 1954 (a few had been changed earlier, and one was missed); thus, from that date on, in place of Share' Fu'ad el-Awwal we find Share' Setta w-'Eshrin Yulyu, in place of Midan Tawfiq we find Midan 'Urabi, and in place of Share' el-Amir Tusun we find Share' el-Shahid Eshaq Ya'qub. Earlier, ideological pressures of a different stripe had also led to the renaming of certain streets. For example, the series of aligned streets that today are known by the name Share' el-Gumhuriya lost their original names in 1933, when they were united for the first time under the name of Share' Ebrahim Basha, after the son of the founder of Egypt's modern monarchy, and this fact is duly noted in the official gazette.[15]

Sometimes, as in the preceding example, the owner of the abolished name was too important simply to confine to oblivion, and such cases resulted in the common phenomenon of street name reassignment. Thus, in 1933, the name Share' Nubar, formerly that of today's Share' el-Gumhuriya between former Midan Qantaret el-Dekka and Midan Ramsis and named for a critical figure in late nineteenth-century Egyptian history whose mansion once stood on that street, was reassigned to another street, traversing Downtown and el-Munira, that had until then been called Share' el-Dawawin. Authorities sometimes preferred less drastic relocations, and a form of reassignment that we may call 'the pivot' was followed. For example, when, in 1904, the street formerly known as Share' Qantaret el-Dekka was displaced by Share' Nubar (the name that would itself be displaced in 1933 by Share' Ebrahim), the former was reassigned to a street at right angles to, and connecting with, the original street (today's Share' Nagib el-Rihani), as though the street had performed a 180-degree westward pivot to the south. Similarly, Share' Seliman Basha, now Share' Muhammad Sabri Abu 'Alam, was reassigned in 1900 to today's Share' Tal'at Harb, pivoting in this case on the point at which it connects to Midan Tal'at Harb. Nor is it unknown for a favored name to be moved over time from one street to another—being promoted, as it were, as opportunity allowed. Thus, Tal'at Harb, founder of Bank Misr and the father of 'national capitalism,' was first commemorated, from 1944, in the name of today's Share' Gawad Husni, a relatively small downtown street on which Bank Misr's first headquarters stood; in 1961, the name Share' Tal'at Harb was reassigned to one of the city's best-known streets, namely Share' Seliman Basha (in its post-1900 position).

In choosing names, the authorities, especially in the first half of the twentieth century, often sought inspiration in the past: the streets of an entire section of el-Zamalek, are, as already noted, named after Ayyubid rulers and their followers, and more Ayyubids, and Mamluks, are to be found in Downtown and elsewhere. The cogency and appropriateness of these choices was questioned as early as 1925, when the historical topographer Muhammad Ramzi, appointed to a newly created street-naming committee, submitted to the minister of public works a *Memorandum Setting Out the Mistakes Made by the Planning Authority in the Naming of Streets and Roads in the City of Cairo and Its Suburbs Presented to His Excellency the Minister of Public Works*, in which he presents ten examples of what he believed was bad naming practice, ranging from giving streets the names of historical sites to which they had no connection to naming important streets after unimportant people and vice versa. One striking example of the seemingly random planting of historical names in places their eponyms probably never knew is the naming of no fewer than four streets (Share' 'Abd el-Rehim el-Bisani, Share' Bustan el-Fadel, Share' Manshiyet el-Fadel, and Share' el-Qadi el-Fadel) after the same thirteenth-century man of letters, even though, according to Ramzi, none of their locations was associated with him. However, we regard Ramzi's criticism as misplaced: the intention presumably was to evoke and glorify Cairo's past in a general fashion rather than to document it—even if four streets for one man does seem excessive.

Streets and their signs are, or should be, inseparable. Mention of street signs was first made in 1847 in an order of the Tanzim Council that simultaneously both officially pronounced (or perhaps ratified) the names of fifty streets and ordered that the approved names be painted on boards, to be nailed to buildings at the streets' corners, according to a color scheme graded, apparently, according to the street's size and importance (white background with black border and lettering for the most important, then yellow background with red border and lettering, and so on).[16] It is not known when the distinctive blue enamel plates with their elegant white Arabic lettering (as well, sometimes, as Latin-character transliterations following a bewildering variety of conventions) first appeared in Cairo but that the authorities once regarded them as crucial is proved by the fact that in 1924 the Ministry of Public Works employed four men whose sole job was the installation of new street signs and the cleaning of old ones.[17] Today, signage is sporadic. Street signs are missing, or damaged, or concealed behind store fronts. More remarkably, signs bearing different names sometimes appear on the same street. This may be due partly to the fact that responsibility for the erection of signage does not lie with the committee charged with naming streets and partly to the fact that signs can be ordered by private citizens from specialized hardware stores. This may explain too why signs bearing names that have been officially superseded sometimes appear to be newer than those bearing officially current names. In any case, a plethora of signs is preferable, in our opinion, to their absence.

As noted, the transliteration of Arabic into Latin characters that is used on street signs is not standardized. For the letter *qaf*, for example, we have seen *q*, *k*, and even *c*. In this book (exception made for bibliographical references in the list of sources), we have used a consistent system that avoids the academic (emphasis is not marked and neither is vowel length, with the exception of *–aa'*, where this literary pronunciation is retained in speech, e.g., el-Galaa') and favors Cairene pronunciation (for example, *g* for the letter *jim*, elision of short vowels in closed syllables; thus Shawarbi not Shawarebi, Fatma not Fatema) while following some of the commoner conventions of the signs (such as *e* for the short vowel *kasra*); the letter *'ayn* is represented by ', the letter *hamza* by ' (not used initially). This system has been adopted in the hope that though Arabists may wince they will understand, while non-Arabists will find a general similarity to what they see on the streets.

Many street names referring to persons include a title, either before the personal name (el-Sheikh So-and-so, el-Duktur So-and-so) or between two of its elements (Hesein Basha el-Daramalli, Ebrahim Beih el-Nabarawi) or at the end ('Ali Galal Basha, Kulut Beih). The first kind is sometimes dropped in referring to the streets bearing such names, while the second and third are usually dropped. We have therefore retained initial titles in the entry headings, with cross-references, but in most cases have dropped medial and final titles; these titles are, however, given in the body of the entry when their owner's name is given in full. The choice between medial and final seems in most cases to be free; one hears and reads "X Basha/Beih Y" as often as one does "XY Basha/Beih"; we have presented names with such titles as we found them with no attempt at consistency.

Given the ambiguities and gaps referred to above, this book must be seen as a work in progress. Readers who can improve its accuracy and completeness by providing documented evidence of the dates at which street names changed or of the identity of the persons or things after which streets are named are invited to do so by contacting the authors at <cairostreets@aucegypt.edu>.

This work is an accumulation of debts that a short note of thanks can hardly repay. Our greatest debt is to the driver, Aymen Salah, who took ownership of this project from start to finish, relentlessly searching through the alleys and lanes to identify obscure names, always with a sense of humor. We were fortunate to have access to the records of Cairo Governorate's Street Naming Committee and the maps of the General Authority for the Survey of Egypt. Others who gave of their time, knowledge, and contacts were Abbas Helmi, Adam Mestyan, Ahdaf Soueif, Ahmed Seddik, Ahmed Shawket, Alia Nassar, Benito Cruciani, Carl Petry, Chris Mikaelian, Emad el-Din Abou Ghazi, Eman Morgan, Hala Halim, Hala Salah el-Din Talaat, Heba Handoussa, Hesham el-Arabi, Iman Abdulfattah, Ingrid Wassmann, Karim Sayyed ʿAbd el-ʿAziz, Khalid Abdul Rahman, Lisa Kaaki, Mahmoud Abdallah, Mahmoud Sabit, Mekkawi Saʿid, Michael Mitchell, Mike Mikaelian, Mohamed Salah, Mona Abd el-Tawwab Abd el-Fattah, Mona Anis, Mona Zaki, Muhammad Ashur, Muhammad Shahbur, Nabil Shawkat, Nagi Gad, Nairy Avedissian, Nazli Sherine, Nicholas Warner, Riham Arram, Raphael Cormack, Ryder Kouba, Shaimaa Ashour, Sherif Hefni, Vittoria Capresi, Yahia Shawkat, Yasmine el Dorghamy, and Ziad el-Tawil. We are also grateful to the editorial staff of the American University in Cairo Press, and especially Neil Hewison, whose extensive knowledge of Cairo's urban development made him an ideal editor. Certain individuals are owed a special acknowledgment because of their already established contributions to the study of Cairo's historical topography: Amr Talaat, Ayman Fu'ad Sayyid, Hamdi Abu Golayyel, Khaled Fahmy, Mohamed Abou el-Amayem, Omar el-Nagati and CLUSTER, Samir Raafat, Tareq Atia and *Mantiqti*, Wael Abed, and Yasser Thabet have all written in this field and all were unstintingly generous with their expertise. Above all, we wish to underline our debt to Fathi Hafez el-Hadidi, whose studies of Cairo's urban development at the level of both its built fabric and the nomenclature of its streets are foundational. And finally, we extend our thanks to every Cairene resident, shopkeeper, and bystander who guided us, answered our questions, and shared memories and knowledge about the streets on which they live and work.

Notes
1   As a category, the passageway (*mamarr*), which in Cairo ranges from a space barely wide enough to allow one person to pass (for example, Mamarr el-Duktur ʿAbd el-Hamid Saʿid) to a

substantial street (former Mamarr Behlar), has an ambiguous status. While some passageways are officially recognized, others are regarded as "setbacks," that is, mere spaces between buildings. This has not prevented many of the latter from acquiring names, which must, however, remain forever unofficial and which are sometimes ephemeral. We have tried to include all official passageways, as well as a selection of the others, based on how well they are known and on their historical or other interest.

2   The words are those of Edmé-François Jomard, a *savant* who accompanied the French expeditionary force, quoted by Abu Lughod (*Cairo*, p.65).

3   Fahmy, "Modernizing Cairo," pp.191–94.

4   Abu Lughod *Cairo*, p.83.

5   Abu Lughod, *Cairo*, pp.110–11.

6   Mubarak, *al-Khiṭaṭ*, 3: 404–405.

7   F. Barham Zincke, quoted in Abu Lughod, *Cairo*, p.106.

8   Mubarak, *al-Khiṭaṭ*, 3: 404.

9   See Mestyan and Volait, "Affairisme."

10 Lane, *Description*, p.76.

11 Specifically, Amin, *Cairo A–Z*, 2000; and El Kolaly, *Cairo City Key*, 2008.

12 McPherson, *Moulids*, p.239.

13 Cairo Governorate, Decree 9050 of 2013.

14 *Journal Officiel* 4/1913 p.306.

15 *El-Waqa'i' el-Misriya*, 1933, Issue 5 (9 January), p.4.

16 The order is reproduced in Sāmī, *Taqwīm*, 2: 547–52.

17 Ministry of Public Works Annual Report 1924–25, Street Sign Cleaning Budget.

GLOSSARY OF ARABIC TERMS

ard	large yard or open area
'atfa (before a name, *'atfet*)	alley; *'atfa*s were the small component streets of the *hara*s, or quarters; to this day, *'atfa*s are usually found in association with *hara*s
bab	gate, especially one in the city's walls
Basha	title assumed by Egypt's nineteenth-century rulers; later awarded to upper-level bureaucrats and office-holders; abolished after the 1952 revolution
Beih	title awarded to mid-level bureaucrats and office-holders under the monarchy (earlier used more generally); abolished after the 1952 revolution; elsewhere often spelled *Bey*
berka (before a name, *berket*)	lake; both the older part of the city and the area of the Esma'iliya project contained several of these bodies of water ranging in size from veritable lakes, such as Birket el-Azbakiya, to mere ponds; *see* Introduction, page 4
bustan	plantation; an area devoted to agricultural production, in the form of either fruit or vegetables
darb	side street; the term originally meant a street leading off a major thoroughfare, from which *hara*s in turn branched; it occurs today only in the names of older streets that once had that function and is often preceded by *share'* ('street')

geneina (before a name, *geneinet*)	garden
hadiqa (before a name, *hadiqet*)	large or formal garden
hara (before a name, *haret*)	lane; until the change in urban patterns in the second half of the nineteenth century, a *hara* was a 'quarter,' meaning a complex of small streets to which access was through a gate, closed at night; though modern naming practice has tried to apply the principle of one street, one name, thoroughfares called Haret ———— today sometimes consist of two or more small but distinct linked streets, reflecting the older pattern
hekr	originally, starting in the late thirteenth century, an area of land granted to an individual on a long-term lease; such areas were used at first for commercial agriculture but often became residential quarters reserved for the rich; with time, they often deteriorated into slums, and in today's Arabic the term means a pocket of low-grade housing
hosh	literally, 'enclosure' or 'courtyard' but referring in nineteenth-century Cairo to a space providing cheap accommodation; *hosh*es were much condemned for overcrowding and squalor
khalig	canal; Cairo had two canals: the ancient el-Khalig el-Masri, within the older city, and the thirteenth-century el-Khalig el-Naseri, which crossed the area now occupied by Downtown and parts of which had their own names (for example, Khalig el-Maghrabi); *see* Introduction, pages 2–3; in modern usage, el-Khalig may refer to the Arab Gulf
kubri	bridge over the Nile (compare *qantara*); also flyover and elevated highway
mamarr	passage; a way, usually pedestrian, between buildings; such passages range in width from no more than a meter to that of a typical street

manshiya or *munshah* (before a name, *manshiyet* or *munshat*)	a settlement or housing compound for the elite built on previously empty land
midan	square (including spaces that are round or irregular in shape)
qantara (before a name, *qantaret*)	bridge, over one of Cairo's now vanished canals; compare *kubri*
qasr	palace, or mansion; the term is used of palaces belonging to the royal family and of any other large house standing in its own grounds
saray	royal palace
sekka (before a name, *sekket*)	connecting street; a short street joining two larger streets
share'	street; this is now the only term used when new streets are named, with the exception of the recently introduced *tariq*, meaning highway, of which there are no examples in our area
zuqaq	cul-de-sac

MAPS

Downtown and Surrounding Districts

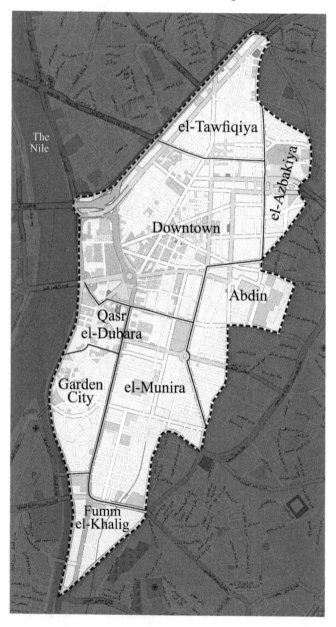

el-Gezira and el-Zamalek

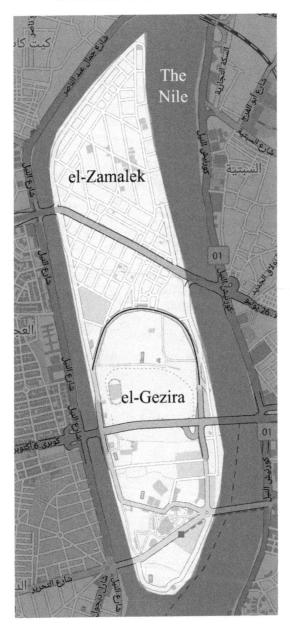

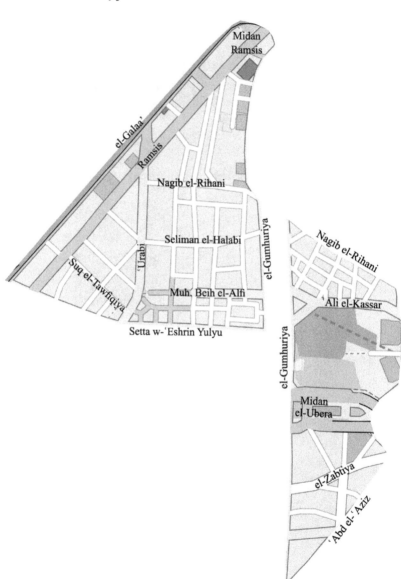

el-Tawfiqiya

Midan
Ramsis

el-Galaa'

Ramsis

Nagib el-Rihani

Seliman el-Halabi

'Urabi

Suq el-Tawfiqiya

Muh. Beih el-Alfi

Setta w-'Eshrin Yulyu

el-Gumhuriya

Nagib el-Rihani

'Ali el-Kassar

el-Gumhuriya

Midan
el-Ubera

el-Zabtiya

'Abd el-'Aziz

el-Azbakiya

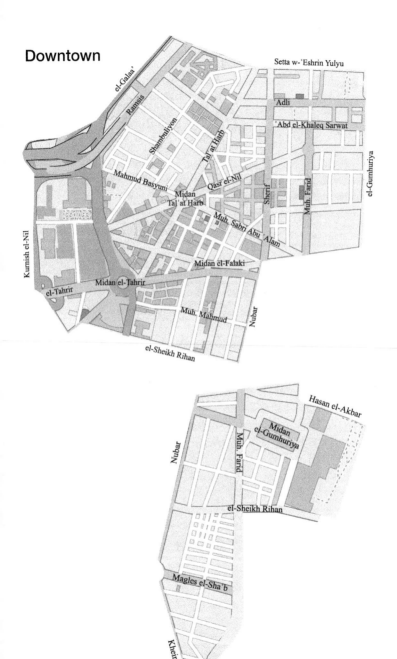

Downtown

el-Galaa'

Ramsis

Shambuliyon

Tal'at Harb

Setta w-'Eshrin Yulyu

Adli

'Abd el-Khaleq Sarwat

el-Gumhuriya

Mahmud Basyuni

Qasr el-Nil

Midan
Tal'at Harb

Sherif

Muh. Farid

Kumish el-Nil

Muh. Sabri Abu 'Alam

Midan el-Falaki

Midan el-Tahrir

el-Tahrir

Muh. Mahmud

Nubar

el-Sheikh Rihan

Nubar

Muh. Farid

Midan
el-Gumhuriya

Hasan el-Akbar

el-Sheikh Rihan

Magles el-Sha'b

Kheirat

'Abdin

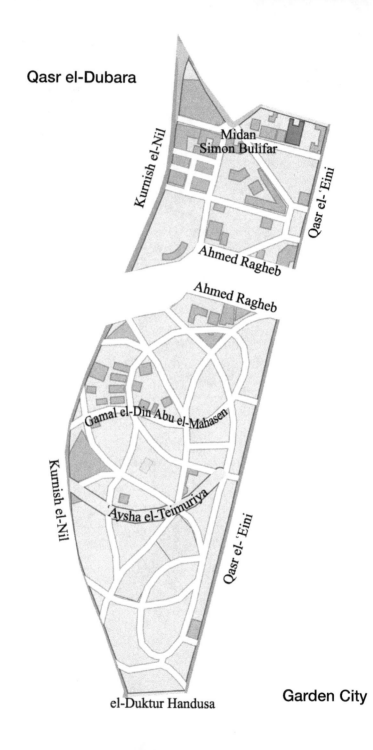

Qasr el-Dubara

Kurnish el-Nil

Midan
Simon Bulifar

Qasr el-'Eini

Ahmed Ragheb

Ahmed Ragheb

Gamal el-Din Abu el-Mahasen

'Aysha el-Teimuriya

Kurnish el-Nil

Qasr el-'Eini

el-Duktur Handusa

Garden City

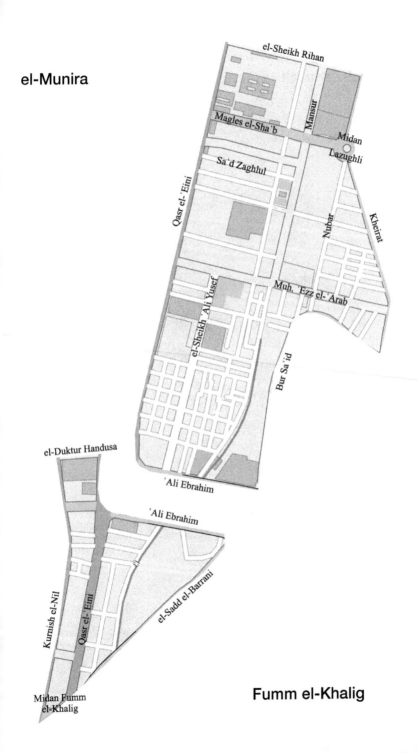

el-Munira

el-Sheikh Rihan

Mansur

Magles el-Sha'b

Midan
Lazughli

Sa'd Zaghlul

Qasr el-'Eini

Nubar

Kheirat

Muh. 'Ezz el-'Arab

el-Sheikh 'Ali Yusef

Bur Sa'id

el-Duktur Handusa

'Ali Ebrahim

'Ali Ebrahim

Kurnish el-Nil

Qasr el-'Eini

el-Sadd el-Barrani

Midan Fumm
el-Khalig

Fumm el-Khalig

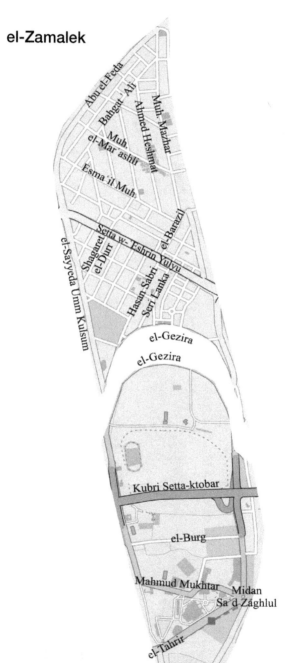

el-Zamalek

Abu el-Feda
Bahgat 'Ali
Muh. Mazhar
Ahmed Heshmat
Muh.
el-Mar'ashli
Esma'il Muh.
el-Barazil
Setta w- Eshrin Yulyu
Shagaret el-Durr
el-Sayyeda Umm Kulsum
Hasan Sabri
Seri Lanka
el-Gezira
el-Gezira
Kubri Setta-ktobar
el-Burg
Mahmud Mukhtar
Midan Sa'd Zaghlul
el-Tahrir

el-Gezira

Cairo's Ancient Canals and Lakes and the Course of the Nile in 800CE and Today

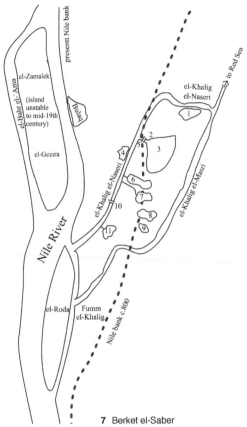

1 Berket el-Ratli

2 Khalig el-Dakar (*see* Haret Qantaret el-Dekka)

3 Berket el-Azbakiya formerly Berket Batn el-Baqara (*see* Share' Saray el-Azbakiya)

4 Berket Qarmut (*see* Share' Manshiyet el-Kataba)

5 Qantaret el-Dekka (*see* Haret Qantaret el-Dekka, Share' el-Gumhuriya, Share' Nagib el-Rihani)

6 Berket el-Fawwala (*see* Share' el-Sayyed Muhammad Taher)

7 Berket el-Saber

8 Berket el-Farayin (or Berket el-Yaraqan or Berket el Shuqaf; *see* Midan el-Gumhuriya, Haret Berket el-Shuqaf)

9 Berket el-Damalsha (*see* Haret el-Damarsha)

10 Qantaret Qadadar (or Qantaret el-Madabegh; *see* Share' el-Amir Qadadar)

11 Berket el-Nasriya (or Berket Setti Nasra or Berket el-Saqqayin; *see* 'Atfet Nasra, Share' el-Saqqayin, Share' Berket el-Nasriya)

(Sources: Abu-Lughod, 1971, 8, 34; Behrens-Abouseif, 1985, 3, 5; Cooper, 2015, 189)

THE GUIDE

A

ʿAbd el-ʿAl Seliman, ʿAtfet (Downtown)
Probably since 1914; unidentified. The name is that of a man, perhaps an early resident.

ʿAbd el-ʿAziz, Shareʿ (el-Azbakiya)
Since 1870, after Ottoman Sultan ʿAbd el-ʿAziz (r.1861–76), who visited Egypt in 1863, the first Ottoman sultan to do so since Selim the Magnificent when he conquered the country in 1517. The name—no doubt a gesture of gratitude for the sultan's 1866 recognition of Esmaʿil's male children's right to succeed him by primogeniture and his 1867 recognition of Egypt's rulers' right to the title of khedive—has never changed. As host to one of the city's first streetcar lines and the headquarters of the streetcar workers' union, Shareʿ ʿAbd el-ʿAziz was informally known in its early years as **Shareʿ el-Turulli** (Trolley Str.).

ʿAbd el-ʿAziz Al Saʿud, Kubri *see* el-Funduq, Kubri

ʿAbd el-Aziz Gawish, Shareʿ *see* el-Sheikh ʿAbd el-Gawish, Shareʿ

ʿAbd el-Dayem, ʿAtfet (ʿAbdin)
By 1848, after the mosque of Sheikh ʿAbd el-Dayem, an otherwise unknown Sufi saint, along whose north side it runs. The mosque, though much rebuilt, dates to c.1766, before which only the tomb existed.

'Abd el-Dayem, Haret ('Abdin)
By 1888; after the mosque of Sheikh 'Abd el-Dayem (*see* 'Atfet 'Abd el-Dayem), along whose east side it runs.

'Abd el-Halim Hafez, Share' *see* el-Fannan 'Abd el-Halim Hafez, Share'

'Abd el-Hamid Sa'id, Share' *see* el-Duktur 'Abd el-Hamid Sa'id, Share'

'Abd el-Hamid el-Shawarbi, Haret (Downtown)
Probably by 1934; 'Abd el-Hamid Basha el-Shawarbi (1906–?) was the son of Muhammad Basha el-Shawarbi (*see* Share' el-Shawarbi). A millionaire businessman, el-Shawarbi was briefly (1956) president of the el-Zamalek Club.

'Abd el-Khaleq Sarwat, Share' (Downtown)
Since 1949, after 'Abd el-Khaleq Sarwat (Tharwat) Basha (1873–1928), lawyer, judge, public servant, and politician, hailed by some as a nationalist and condemned by others as a pawn of the British. Twice prime minister (1922–23 and 1927–28), Sarwat helped to negotiate conditional independence in 1922 and to draft the post-independence constitution of 1923. After 1923, he joined the Liberal Constitutionalist Party, the main rival to the Wafd Party.

> 1938–49: **Share' el-Maleka Farida** (Queen Farida Str.), after the first wife of King Faruq (whom he divorced in 1948). This name absorbed those of three aligned earlier streets:
>
>> From Share' Ramsis east to Share' Tal'at Harb:
>> From at least 1887 to 1938: **Share' Deir el-Banat** (Maidens' Monastery Str.), after a convent belonging to the Comboni Fathers (*see* Share' Kumbuni).
>>
>> From Share' Tal'at Harb east to Share' el-Gumhuriya:
>> From at least 1888 to 1938: **Share' el-Manakh** (Camel Ground Str.), after an area for the loading and unloading of camels next to the Kekhya Mosque at the corner of Share' Qasr el-Nil and Share' el-Gumhuriya

that was created by Ebrahim Basha during the reign of
Muhammad ʿAli Basha.

From east of Midan el-Ubera to Midan el-ʿAtaba:
From at least 1905 to 1938: **Shareʿ Taher Basha**, after
Taher Basha el-Kebir (*see* Shareʿ Taher).

ʿAbd el-Latif el-Sufani, Shareʿ (Downtown)
Since 1949, after nationalist politician ʿAbd el-Latif el-Sufani
(d.1925), National Party colleague of Mustafa Kamel, and long-
time parliamentarian. This street, and cross-street Shareʿ el-Batal
Ahmad ʿAbd el-ʿAziz, were created in the 4000m² area made available for development in 1936 by the demolition of the Ebrahimiya
Secondary School for Boys (formerly the Lycée Français and before
that the Mazlum family mansion, *see* Shareʿ Muhammad Mazlum).

ʿAbd el-Megid el-Remali, Shareʿ (Downtown)
Since 1972, after a rich miller from the Sayyeda Zeinab district who
became a socialite, member of parliament, and head of the Chamber
of Commerce during the reign of King Faruq. In 1954, as a member of
Cairo Municipality's Administrative Commission, he chaired a meet-
ing that changed the names of fifteen Cairo streets and three squares
from those of members of the former ruling family to others deemed
less ideologically offensive. His mills were nationalized in 1960.

From at least 1904 to 1972: **Shareʿ Fahmi**, after ʿAli
Fahmi Basha (died c.1908), a successful irrigation engineer
(he worked under Willcocks on the first Aswan dam) and
self-made millionaire whose fortune was based on land spec-
ulation in Upper Egypt. His son, ʿAli-Kamel Beih Fahmi,
dubbed "the Prince of Youth" by the popular press, grew up
in the family home on this street and inherited his father's
great wealth while still a child. Known for his lavish spend-
ing (he built himself a palace in el-Zamalek in imitation of
Versailles), he was shot dead in London's Savoy Hotel on
10 July 1923 by his wife, French femme fatale Marguerite
(Maggie) Miller. Miller's trial, the subject of intense interest
in the Egyptian and European press, resulted in her acquittal
on the grounds that her husband's sense of inferiority as an

Oriental male had driven him to make intolerable demands upon her. The case inspired many movies and plays.

'Abd el-Men'em, 'Atfet ('Abdin)
Probably by 1908; unidentified. *See* Share' 'Abd el-Men'em.

'Abd el-Men'em, Share' ('Abdin)
Since at least 1908; unidentified. 'Abd el-Men'em is a male given name, probably that of an early resident.

'Abd el-Men'em Reyad, Midan *see* el-Fariq Awwal 'Abd el-Men'em Reyad, Midan

'Abd el-Qader Hamza, Share' (Qasr el-Dubara)
Since 1947, after 'Abd el-Qader Hamza Basha (1880–1941), journalist and historian. Hamza received a law degree from the Khedivial Law School but soon started work as a journalist in the nationalist camp (*el-Garida, el-Ahali, el-Balagh*). Eventually a member of the senate and of the Arabic Language Academy, he translated several books on Egypt's modern history from English into Arabic.

> From at least 1912 to 1947: **Share' el-Sheikh el-Arbe'in** (Fortieth Sheikh Str.), after the mosque–tomb of Sheikh Muhammad el-Arbe'in, a little-known saint. It is said that any sheikh whose full name is unknown is referred to as el-Sheikh el-Arbe'in ('the Fortieth Sheikh') in the belief that, at any given time, forty persons on whom God has bestowed special grace, and who are known as his wards (*awliyaa'*), exist in the world. As a result many saints, and many Cairo streets, have this name. Some maps give this saint's name as Teibars el-Arbe'in. The mosque was demolished to make way for the rebuilt Hotel Semiramis (completed 1988).

'Abd el-Qader el-Mazni, Share' *see* Ebrahim 'Abd el-Qader el-Mazni, Share'

'Abd el-Rahman Fahmi, Share' (Garden City)
From after 1946, after 'Abd el-Rahman Fahmi (1870–1946), a pioneering labor organizer and first president (1924) of the

General Federation of Labor Unions of the Nile Valley. Fahmi was elected to the Chamber of Deputies in 1924 as a Wafdist and in 1938 as a Sa'dist.

> From at least 1925 to after 1946: **Share' el-Salamlek** ('Public Reception Palace Str.'), after the *salamlek* of the el-Qasr el-'Ali palace complex on whose grounds today's Garden City is built. The *salamlek* was built by Ebrahim Basha (1789–1848) in 1835, ceded by newly installed Esma'il Basha (later Khedive Esma'il) to his mother Khushyar (Hoshiar) Kadinafandi in 1863, and rebuilt for her, after which it became known as the Palace of the Khedive's Mother (*see* former Share' Walda Basha, *under* Share' 'Aysha el-Teimuriya). It was demolished, along with the other palace buildings, in 1903. One historical topographer, writing in 1925, claims that the street is not in the same place as the historical building.

'Abd el-Rehim el-Bisani, Share' (el-Munira)

By 1918, after Muhy el-Din Abu 'Ali 'Abd el-Rehim ebn 'Ali el-Bisani el-'Asqalani el-Masri (1135–1200), commonly referred to as el-Qadi el-Fadil ('the Learned Judge'), statesman, model of elegant epistolary style, poet, and head of chancery to Salah el-Din (Saladin) and his two immediate successors. As his name shows, the judge's father was from Bisan, in Palestine, while he himself was born in Asqalan, also in Palestine, but moved to Cairo, where he assisted in the transition from the Shiite Fatimid caliphate to the rule of the Sunni Ayyubids. The assignment of the name of el-Qadi el-Fadel to this location is not historically accurate: the plantation and settlement established by el-Qadi el-Fadel were located farther north, in the area between Share' Muhammad 'Ezz el-'Arab on the north and Share' Esma'il Serri on the south, and Share' Qasr el-'Eini on the west and Share' Bur Sa'id and Share' Nubar on the east. The street is one of four, in various parts of the city, whose names allude to el-Qadi el-Fadel (*see* Introduction, page 16).

'Abd el-Salam Aref, Share' *see* el-Ra'is 'Abd el-Salam Aref, Share'

'Abd Rabbuh, 'Atfet ('Abdin)
Probably from after 1935; unidentified. 'Abd Rabbuh is a man's given name, perhaps that of an early resident.

Abu el-'Azm, Share' (el-Zamalek)
Probably since the 1980s, after Engineer 'Ali Mahmud Abu el-'Azm, current owner of the building at #3 on this street, and his family.

Abu Bakr Kheirat, Share' (Downtown)
Probably from the late 1960s, after architect and musician Abu Bakr Kheirat (1910–63), first dean of the National Institute of Music (the Conservatoire); since 1993, an annual music prize has been awarded in his name. Not to be confused with Share' Kheirat in el-Munira (named after Abu Bakr Kheirat's great-grandfather). This and surrounding streets were pedestrianized in the early 1990s.

> From at least 1946 probably to the late 1960s: **Share' Musa Qattawi Basha** or **Share' Qattawi Basha**, after Musa Basha Ya'qub Qattawi (Moses Cattaoui) (1850–1924), a prominent businessman from whose family the head of Egypt's Sephardic Jewish community traditionally was drawn. Qattawi bought the triangular plot now formed by Share' Qasr el-Nil (north), Share' Muhammad Sabri Abu 'Alam (south), and Share' el-Sherifein (east) from Muhammad Sherif Basha (*see* Share' Sherif) in 1884, and built a palace overlooking Midan Tal'at Harb. Sherif, whose palace was on the site of the old Broadcasting Building on Share' el-Sherifein, had bought the plot in 1872 from Yusef Beih Hakakiyan (Hekekian, d.1875), director of the Engineering School, who had acquired it in 1869. Qattawi's heirs initiated subdivision of the property in 1907; creation of internal streets (Share' el-Qadi el-Fadel, Share' Ebn Ta'lab, and Share' el-Mahrani) had begun by 1921 and was complete by 1934. Not to be confused with Share' Qattawi Beih, former name of nearby Share' Ebrahim el-Qabbani.

Abu el-Feda, Sekket (el-Zamalek)
By 1910: a short connecting street linking Share' Abu el-Feda (*see* next entry) to Share' el-Gezira el-Wusta.

Abu el-Feda, Shareʿ (el-Zamalek)
By 1910, after el-Malik el-Muʾayyad ('the [God-]Assisted King')
Abu el-Feda Esmaʿil ebn ʿAli (1273–1331), a descendent of the
Ayyubid dynasty who made a name for himself fighting the Cru-
saders in Syria and was made ruler of Hama by the Mamluks. The
prince was a historian, from whom Europe derived much of its
early knowledge of the Arabs, and also a geographer; the moon's
Abulfeda crater is named for him.

Abu Gabal, ʿAtfet (Downtown)
Probably after 1914; unidentified. Abu Gabal is a family name, perhaps that of early residents.

Abu Quta, ʿAtfet (Downtown)
By 1801, after a certain Muhammad Abu Quta, whose tomb was
originally attached to the minaret of the mosque of ʿUsman Kekhya
(d.1736). The tomb was demolished in 1933 and its occupant's
remains moved to the cemetery of Bab el-Wazir.

Abu el-Sebaʿ, Haret (Downtown)
By 1887, after the mosque and tomb of ʿAbd el-Rahman Abu
el-Sebaʿ, located opposite the end of this very short thoroughfare on Haret Bab el-Luq. Until 1913, this name also applied to
the part of Haret Bab el-Luq containing the tomb (*see also* former
Shareʿ el-Sheikh Abu el-Sebaʿ, *under* Shareʿ el-Shahid Gawad
Husni).

Abu Seif, Haret (el-Azbakiya)
By 1887; unidentified. Abu Seif may be a family name, perhaps that
of early residents.

el-ʿAdel, Midan (el-Zamalek)
By 1913: *see* Shareʿ el-ʿAdel Abu Bakr, which runs into this square.

el-ʿAdel Abu Bakr, Shareʿ (el-Zamalek)
By 1913, after el-Malek el-ʿAdel ('the Just King') Sayf el-Din Abu
Bakr Ahmad (or Muhammad) ebn Najm el-Din Ayyub, brother
of Salah el-Din (Saladin) and fourth Ayyubid ruler of Egypt
(1200–18).

'Adli, Share' (Downtown)

Since 1933, after 'Adli Basha Yakan (1864–1933), a descendent of
Muhammad 'Ali Basha, politician, foreign minister, interior min-
ister, minister of public education, and three times prime minister
(1921, 1926–27, 1929–30). An ally, then a rival, of Sa'd Zaghlul (*see*
Share' Sa'd Zaghlul) in seeking to end British occupation, Yakan
founded the Constitutional Liberals party (1922) in opposition to
Zaghlul's Wafd party. From 1934, the street was home to the Turf
Club, symbol of British domination, burned by a mob on 26 January 1952, the site of which is now a gas station (opposite the Omar
Effendi department store, east of Share' Tal'at Harb; originally, the
club was at No. 32 on the other side of the street, west of the syn-
agogue). It is also the home of Cairo's central synagogue (Sha'ar
Ha-Shamim, or the Gates of Heaven), built in 1902.

> From 1888 to 1933: **Share' el-Maghrabi**, after Qantaret
> el-Maghrabi, a bridge over the el-Khalig el-Naseri canal, this
> stretch of which, at right angles to the street, was known as
> Khalig el-Maghrabi. The canal took its name in turn from
> Sheikh Salah el-Din Yusef el-Maghrabi (d.1355), a physician
> whose prominent tomb was demolished in 1953, the sheikh
> moving to smaller and less elegant quarters inside the lobby
> of the apartment block built on its site at #30.

el-Ahkar, Zuqaq ('Abdin)

Probably by 1904: 'Land Grants Cul-de-sac.' Why this three-
meter-deep cul-de-sac is so named is not known, but the plural noun
calls attention to the presence of *hekr*s, or long-term grants of land,
whose ground rent went to the beneficiaries of the *waqf*, or religious
endowment, to which the land belonged. In the area on which
el-Esma'iliya would later be built, such grants were usually made,
starting in the late thirteenth century, to Mamluks or others (including women) associated with the ruler. These *hekr*s, of which medieval
Cairo topographer el-Maqrizi (1364–1442) mentions at least twenty,
could be farmed (note the large number of street names in this area
that contain the word *bustan* or 'plantation') but often turned over
time into residential settlements, some of which eventually disappeared while others were neglected. Thus, in common speech today,
the term denotes a pocket of slum housing in the middle of the city.

Ahmad 'Abd el-'Aziz, Share' *see* el-Batal Ahmad 'Abd el-'Aziz, Share'

Ahmad Abu el-'Ela, Share' *see* el-Duktur Ahmad Abu el-'Ela, Share'

Ahmad Basha, Share' (Garden City)

By 1935, after Ahmad Basha Ref'at (1825–58), son of Ebrahim Basha and older brother of Khedive Esma'il, who was heir presumptive to Muhammad Sa'id Basha (r.1854–63) until he drowned when his train car fell off a float while crossing the Nile at Kafr el-Zayyat in the Delta. Ref'at inherited the building on nearby Share' el-Saray el-Kubra that had initially housed the *haramlek* (private family quarters) of the el-Qasr el-'Ali palace complex (*see* former Share' el-Qasr el-'Ali, *under* Share' Qasr el-'Eini) on the death of his father in 1848. The name was apparently overlooked in the wholesale replacement of street names commemorating members of the former ruling dynasty that was decreed in September 1954.

Ahmad Heshmat, Share' (el-Zamalek)

By 1937, after Ahmad Heshmat Basha (1858–1926), Egyptian administrator and politician. Heshmat trained as a lawyer, including in France, then worked in government, rising to become governor of several governorates and subsequently minister of finance, education, religious endowments, and, finally, foreign affairs; in the latter capacity, he headed the committee that wrote the 1923 constitution. As minister of education, he introduced kindergartens and reformed the administration of the National Library; he also wrote on education. His house (now a school) was built on this street in 1923.

Ahmad 'Isa, Share' *see* el-Duktur Ahmad 'Isa, Share'

Ahmad el-Kashef, Share' (el-Zamalek)

Since 1954, after Ahmad el-Kashef (1878–1958), an Egyptian poet of aristocratic background known for his patriotic verse.

> From 1913 to 1954: **Share' el-Amir Mahmud**, after
> Mahmud Hamdi Esma'il (1863–1921), sixth son of Khedive
> Esma'il, who pursued a career in the Ottoman army. This area

of el-Zamalek—immediately north of Khedive Esma'il's palace
of Saray el-Gezira and extending to Share' Setta w-'Eshrin
Yulyu—is home to twelve streets named after princes of the
ruling family. Of these, six were the sons of Khedive Esma'il
(not represented were two who died young, plus his second
son, Muhammad Tawfiq, later to become khedive and have
the whole district of el-Tawfiqiya named after him), the others his cousins or grandsons.

Ahmad Nabil, Share' *see* el-Shahid Ahmad Nabil, Share'

Ahmad Ragheb, Share' (Garden City)
Since at least 1948, after Ahmad Basha Ragheb Badr, a counselor at
the Native Appeals Court, who received his title in 1920, though little else is known of his career. In all likelihood, he lived on this street.

From at least 1925 to at least 1948: **Share' Warshet el-Tun-
bak** ('Pewter Workshop Str.' or 'Narghile Tobacco Workshop
Str.'), after a facility devoted to the production of either
(depending on the authority) of the two listed items to serve
the needs of the el-Qasr el-'Ali palace complex, on whose
grounds today's Garden City is built. At least one historical
topographer, however, writing in 1925, claims that the street
is not in the same place as the historical building.

Ahmad Sabri, Share' (el-Zamalek)
Since no earlier than 1937, after Ahmad Sabri Pasha (1889–1955),
a leading member of the first generation of Egyptian painters.
Sabri, born in the Darb el-Ahmar district of medieval Cairo, studied at the Prince Yusef Kamal School of Fine Arts, presented his
first exhibition in 1925, and received a scholarship to study painting in Paris in 1929. In the same year, he became one of the first
Egyptians to teach at the Higher School of Fine Arts. Later he
became head of its painting department, a position he kept until
his retirement in 1951.

From no earlier than 1926 to at least 1937: **Share' Munsinyur
Sugaru,** after Monsignor Francesco Sogaro (c.1840–1912),
first successor to the founder of the Comboni Congregation,

Roman Catholic missionaries whose primary vocation lay in sub-Saharan Africa. In 1884, Sogaro created a farm on land sold to the missionaries on favorable terms by the government and originally including as much as two thirds of the island north of this street, to be worked by Christian refugees fleeing the Mahdist uprising in Sudan. The area between this street and Shareʿ Hasan ʿAsem continues to be occupied by the Comboni School and St. Joseph's Roman Catholic Church.

Ahmad Shukri, Shareʿ (Downtown)
Since c.1979, after, according to residents, an officer who gave his life for his country in the 1973 war with Israel.

> From at least 1946 to c.1979: **Shareʿ Naws**, after Henri Naus Beih (1875–1938), a Belgian, who rose from being manager of a sugar plantation in Upper Egypt to become director-general of the semi-monopolist French-owned sugar company la Société Générale des Sucreries et de la Raffinerie d'Egypte, also known as the Egyptian Sugar Company. In 1922, Naus founded the Egyptian Federation of Industries, of which he remained president until his death.

Ahmad Talʿat, Shareʿ (el-Munira)
Since after 1935, possibly after either Ahmad Talʿat Basha (d.1927), head of chancellery at the court of Khedive ʿAbbas Helmi II (r.1892–1914) and a noted book collector, who bequeathed collections to the National Library and the National Archives, or Ahmad Talʿat Basha, president, in 1928, of the Court of Appeal at the Native Courts. Not to be confused with nearby Shareʿ Talʿat.

Ahmad ʿUrabi, Midan *see* ʿUrabi, Midan

Ahmad ʿUrabi, Shareʿ *see* ʿUrabi, Shareʿ

ʿAlam el-Din, ʿAtfet (Downtown)
By 1888, after Sidi ʿAlam el-Din el-Ansari, a Sufi saint. A mosque bearing his name is located on this street, though it no longer holds his tomb.

el-Alfi, Share' *see* Muhammad Beih el-Alfi, Share'

'Ali 'Abd el-Latif, Share' ('Abdin)
Since 1950, after 'Ali 'Abd el-Latif Ahmad (1896–1948), a Sudanese of mixed Nuba Mountain and Dinka parentage and a junior
officer in the army of the Anglo-Egyptian Condominium who
founded the anti-British White Flag Society. On trial in 1925
for sedition, membership of a banned organization, and instiga-
tion of demonstrations, 'Abd el-Latif asserted the insoluble bond
between Sudan and Egypt, condemned the British presence in
the country, and received a ten-year sentence. Released only in
1938, he was allowed to travel from his place of exile in Waw,
southern Sudan, to Egypt, where he died and is now buried in the
Martyrs' Cemetery.

> From at least 1888 to 1950: **Share' Nasra**, after a female
> saint, Setti Nasra, and her tomb (no longer to be found),
> which gave their name to Berket Setti Nasra (My Lady
> Nasra's Lake, or el-Berka el-Nasriya (*see* Share' el-Nasriya),
> or Berket el-Saqqayin (Water Sellers' Lake)), a large nearby
> depression that filled with water during the Nile flood.

'Ali Ebrahim, Share' (el-Munira, Fumm el-Khalig)
By 1948, after 'Ali Basha Ebrahim (1880–1947), one of the first
Egyptian surgeons, first Egyptian dean of the College of Medicine at Qasr el-'Eini (1929), minister of health (1940–41), and
president of Fu'ad I (now Cairo) University. Of peasant background, Ebrahim was adopted by a wealthy family, went to school
in Cairo, and graduated from the Qasr el-'Eini medical school
in 1901. Later, as dean, he modernized the school and opened
its doors to women. In 1940, he founded the first doctors' union.
At some point, probably in the 1950s, this street, which formerly
ended at Share' Qasr el-'Eini, was driven through to link with
Kubri el-Manyal, dividing the campus of the Faculty of Medicine,
Cairo University, in two.

The name **Share' Nafezet Sheyam el-Shaf'i** ('Sheyam
el-Shaf'i Pedestrian Overpass Str.') appears attached to this street
on some maps, as it also does to Kubri el-Manyal, the bridge to
which it leads. Sheyam el-Shaf'i was a gifted medical student whose

parents both taught at the faculty. Sheyam, who had just graduated, was killed in a car accident on this street in the mid-1960s. At some point before 1984, an overpass that allowed pedestrians to cross the street in safety apparently was erected in her memory, and it is probably to this that the name more properly belonged. The overpass no longer exists, but a mosque dedicated to Sheyam el-Shafʿi was inaugurated inside the faculty in the mid-1980s.

> From at least 1907 to no later than 1948: **Shareʿ Madraset el-Tebb** (School of Medicine Str.), after the Qasr el-ʿEini medical school, in this location since 1837 and incorporated into Cairo University as its Faculty of Medicine in 1925.

ʿAli Hasan, Shareʿ (el-Munira)
Since 1954, possibly after ʿAli Hasan Ebrahim el-ʿAnkuri (1796–1853), known as el-Darwish ('the Dervish'), man of letters and poet laureate of ʿAbbas Helmi I Basha.

> By 1935 to 1954: **Shareʿ el-Amira Fatma Hanim**, after Princess Fatma (1853–1920), second daughter of Khedive Esmaʿil, known for her interest in the arts and her charitable activities, most notably her donation of her palace at Bulaq el-Dakrur, along with four hundred faddans of land, as the site of the Egyptian University (now Cairo University), which opened its doors in 1908.

ʿAli el-Kassar, Haret (el-Tawfiqiya)
Probably from after 1957: after the comedian of this name (*see* Shareʿ el-Fannan ʿAli el-Kassar). The street was home to Yusef Wahbi's Ramsis Theater from 1923 to 1935 and, from the early years of the twentieth century, to the offices of the Société Orientale, which published such English- and French-language journals as *The Egyptian Gazette* and *Le Progrès Egyptien*; the Société Orientale was nationalized (as Dar el-Tahrir) in 1952.

> From after 1946 to probably after 1957: **Haret el-Sheikh Sayyed Darwish**, after the musician Sayyed Darwish (1892–1923), who likely performed in the theater here (*see further* Shareʿ el-Sheikh Sayyed Darwish).

From at least 1887 to at least 1946: **Haret Galal**, after 'Ali
Galal Basha (*see* Share' Galal).

'Ali el-Kassar, Share' *see* el-Fannan 'Ali el-Kassar, Share'

'Ali Labib Gabr, Share' *see* el-Muhandes 'Ali Labib Gabr, Share'

'Ali Yusef, Share' *see* el-Sheikh 'Ali Yusef, Share'

'Ali Zu el-Fiqar, Share' ('Abdin)
Since 1927, after 'Ali Basha Zu el-Fiqar (1866–1952), uncle of
Queen Farida (first wife of King Faruq) and government servant
(governor of Cairo in 1913); his large villa on this street was demolished when the street was widened.

From at least 1863 to 1927: **Share' el-Sanafiri**, after Sufi
sheikh Esma'il el-Sanafiri, whose tomb and small mosque
there almost blocked access to Midan Muhammad Farid to
their west before they were demolished during the widening
of the street in 1927, the sheikh's remains being moved to
the Sayyeda Nafisa cemetery. The name **Haret el-Sanafiri**
appears also to have been used, but was quashed in 1913.

At the same time as the above: **Share' Bab el-Luq** ('Silt Gate
Str.'), after the original Bab el-Luq that stood close to the
mosque of el-Tabbakh in today's Midan Muhammad Farid (*see*
Haret Bab el-Luq). The name applied originally to the entire
length of the thoroughfare leading to Midan Muhammad
Farid from Midan Bab el-Khalq (out of area) via Share' Sami
el-Barudi (out of area), Share' Hasan el-Akbar, and this street.

el-'Alma, 'Atfet ('Abdin)
'Singing Woman's Alley.' By 1888; the *alma*s of Egypt directed
troupes of singers and dancers who performed at weddings, in the
houses of grandees, and so on.

Amin Sami, Share' (el-Munira)
By 1962, after (Muhammad) Amin Basha Sami (1857–1941), engineer, educationalist, and historian, who for twenty-five years was

principal of the venerable Nasriya School, located between this street and Share' Muhammad 'Ezz el-Arab and now named for him; he was also a member of the upper house of parliament. His best-known work is the six-volume 'Nile Almanac' (*Taqwim el-Nil*), an account of Egyptian history from the advent of Islam to 1915.

> From at least 1908 to no later than 1961: **Share' el-Madrasa** ('School Str.'), after the Nasriya school (*see* above), which occupied the premises of the older school known as Madraset el-Mubtadayan (*see* Share' Muhammad Ezz el-Arab).

el-Amir Qadadar, Share' (Downtown)
By 1911, after a governor of Cairo under Mamluk ruler el-Malek el-Naser Muhammad ebn Qalawun (late thirteenth and early four-teenth centuries). Between c.1926 and 1938, this small street was the only means of entry from this point on the east to Midan el-Tahrir (via Share' el-Tahrir). In the first half of the twentieth century, it contained the offices of such well-known journals as *Roz el-Yusef* (1929–31), *el-Gumhuriya* (1925), and others, as well as the Dar el-Hilal publishing house (1923–46). The name evokes the presence in this area of sometime Qantaret Qadadar, a bridge over the now vanished el-Khalig el-Naseri canal, alternatively known, according to some, as Qantaret el-Madabegh. However, Qantaret el-Madabegh seems to have been northeast of this point, at about where Midan Tal'at Harb is located today, and the identification is not certain. The name Qadadar is misspelled on the street's only sign.

el-Ansari, 'Atfet ('Abdin)
By 1887, after Muhammed el-Ansari, a Sufi saint, said to hail from Iraq, whose mosque and tomb are on nearby Share' Mushtuhur.

'Arafa, 'Atfet ('Abdin)
Probably by 1904; unidentified. 'Arafa is a proper name, perhaps that of an early resident.

el-'Arbakhana, Haret (el-Azbakiya)
'Coach House Lane' (or **Haret el-'Arbakhanat**, 'Coach Houses Lane'). By 1888, after the livery stables for donkeys and horses and coach houses that dominated the area and provided transport for

goods and people in this popular commercial and residential district. From at least 1904, the name **Share' el-'Arbakhanat** ('Coach Houses Str.') was also in use but was officially discontinued in 1916. Originally, the lane ran only between Share' Shalabi and Share' el-Bab el-Bahari. By 1921, it had been extended west of Share' Shalabi to Share' el-Madrastein and east of it to Haret el-Hesein.

el-'Ashmawi, Share' (el-Azbakiya)

Since 1913, after Darwish el-'Ashmawi (d.1831), a Sufi saint, descended from the Prophet Muhammad, who is said to have been driven insane by the death of his elder brother in their home village of 'Ashma in el-Menufiya. After three years in a lunatic asylum, el-'Ashmawi emerged with spiritual powers, and moved to nearby Haret el-Haddara (out of area), where he was visited and venerated by commoner and elite alike. He moved to this street in 1819, and was buried here; the mosque erected over the tomb in 1850 by the future ruler 'Abbas Helmi I during his tenure as deputy viceroy still stands, though damaged by the earthquake of 1992.

> From after 1831 to 1913: **Share' Sidi el-'Ashmawi** ('My Master el-'Ashmawi Str.'), the gazetted change of 1913 simply removing the title by which saints are commonly addressed.

> In the early nineteenth century, and popularly until the mid-twentieth century, the names **Share' el-Bakri** and **Share' Suq el-Bakri** ('el-Bakri Market Str.') were used of the chain of streets running between Share' Mushtuhur on the southwest, through the el-Fawwala neighborhood, to today's Midan el-'Ataba el-Khadra on the northeast (former Share' Rahabet el-Tebn [*see under* Share' el-Sharekat], plus Share' el-'Ashmawi and Share' el-Zabtiya), in reference to the sometime presence on 'Atfet 'Abd el-Haqq el-Sunbati, to the north of this street, of a house belonging to the influential el-Bakri family of *sayyed*s, or descendants of the Prophet Muhammad and of the first caliph, Abu Bakr el-Seddiq. During the French occupation, Khalil el-Bakri, head from 1799 of the guild of the Prophet's descendants, was accused of collaboration with the occupier and driven from this house, which was sacked.

el-'Ashsh, Haret (el-Azbakiya)

From before 1888 to 1931 and again after 1954. Writing in 1888,
'Ali Mubarak gives the name of the street as **Haret el-'Ashshi**,
after a certain Usta (master craftsman) Ebrahim el-'Ashshi, whose
house was here, and the name continues to be found on maps in
this form until at least 1926. In 1931, the name of the street was
changed (*see below*), only to revert following the revolution of
1952. Today's residents and modern maps give the name as Haret
el-'Ashsh, implying that the old name was misremembered in 1954
in favor of another, more common family name.

> From 1931 to 1954: **Haret el-Amira Dawlat Fadel** ('Prin-
> cess Dawlat Fadel Lane'). Fatma Dawlat Fadel (1863–1911)
> was the wife Prince Ebrahim Rashed Fadel, a grandson of
> Ebrahim Basha. It is thought that the princess owned land in
> the area.

el-'Ashshi, Haret *see* el-'Ashsh, Haret

el-'Assal, Share' (el-Zamalek)

Probably from the mid-1970s, after 'Abd el-'Azim and Mahmud
el-'Assal, brick factory owners and builders of the apartment block
on the southeast corner of the street.

el-'Ataba (el-Khadra), Midan (el-Azbakiya)

'(Green) Threshold Sq.' From at least 1888 to 1938 and from 1953
to the present; until 1936, however, the name applied only to what
is now the southeast side of the square (*see below*). Today, the square
is generally referred to simply as Midan el-'Ataba.

The name, 'the Green Threshold'—a name intended to evoke
good fortune—was that of a palace built for his mother in 1850
by Abbas Helmi I (r.1848–54) on the site of an earlier mansion
built in 1747 by the Mamluk emir Radwan Katkhuda el-Julfi on
the eastern bank of the el-Azbakiya lake, which itself replaced the
house of a certain Hagg Muhammad el-Dada el-Sharaybi, then (or
perhaps only later) popularly known as 'the House of the Father of
the Three Wards of God.' El-Julfi had called his mansion el-'Ataba
el-Zarqa ('the Blue Threshold')—a name intended to ward off envy;
later, it was briefly occupied by Ahmad Taher Basha el-Kebir (*see*

Share' Taher). From 1873, the el-'Ataba el-Khadra palace served as the ministry of the interior. In 1878, it was demolished and replaced by the Mixed Courts Tribunal, Egypt's first purpose-built courthouse; parts of the building also served other purposes, such as providing a home for the Council of Deputies (1878–81) and a headquarters for the Geographical Society (1881–95). This building was demolished in 1934, when the tribunal (which would be abolished in 1935) moved to the site of the present High Court on Share' Setta w-'Eshrin Yulyu.

A small square, **Midan Azbak** (from at least 1905), after Azbak men Tutukh (*see* Share' Saray el-Azbakiya), occupied the space between the north side of the Mixed Courts Tribunal and the el-Azbakiya Gardens; the square was home to the Matatya Café, a renowned gathering place of artists and intellectuals, named for its owner since 1872, Mattatias Nahman, a Greek Jewish merchant. The removal of the tribunal in 1934 meant that Midan Azbak became a part of the enlarged Midan el-'Ataba el-Khadra, and the name ceased to exist. However, in the period immediately following the draining of Berket el-Azbakiya ('el-Azbakiya Lake') in 1848, the same name had applied to the entirety of today's Midan el-Khazendar, Midan el-'Ataba, and Midan el-Ubera. Similarly, a **Share' Azbak** occupied (from at least 1888 until at least 1934) what is now the northeast side of Midan el-'Ataba el-Khadra.

The removal of the courthouse allowed the creation of the square as it exists today. Until then, on available maps, the name Midan el-'Ataba el-Khadra is applied to the space to the southeast of the old palace created by the demolition in 1874 of the mosque of Azbak (built in 1477) which stood at the entrance to Share' el-Azhar (out of area), and another building. This space was wide enough to accommodate Egypt's first streetcar terminus (1896), contributing immeasurably to its importance. Against this, some authorities claim that the official name (present from at least 1863) for this same space was *Share'* el-Ataba el-Khadra (a name that applies today to a street that exits the square to the northeast in alignment with the former, smaller, square) and that it was only the breadth of the street at this point that led to its being referred to, informally and incorrectly, as a square. According to this second account, the name Midan el-'Ataba el-Khadra did not come into formal existence until 1936, after the demolition of the Mixed Courts Tribunal building.

1949 to 1953: **Midan Muhammad ʿAli**, or **Midan Muhammad ʿAli el-Kebir**, after the founder of Egypt's modern monarchy (r.1805–48).

1938 to 1949: **Midan el-Maleka Farida** ('Queen Farida Sq.'), after King Faruq's first wife, Queen Farida, who was divorced by the king in 1948. The square figures under this name in Naguib Mahfouz's *Midaq Alley* as the symbolic watershed between ancient and modern Cairo.

el-ʿAwayed, Haret (Downtown)
'Property Tax Lane.' Since 1887, after the offices administering the property taxes (*ʿawayed*) collected by the Municipality against the provision of services; these occupied #43 Shareʿ Qasr el-Nil, on the corner of this street, from 1881 to 1887.

Awlad ʿEnan, Haret (el-Tawfiqiya)
'Sons of Enan Lane.' By 1946, after a large mosque, Gameʿ el-Sada Awlad ʿEnan ('Mosque of the Masters, Sons of ʿEnan'), built in 1368 on the site of a Fatimad-period mosque, itself originally a church. The mosque was adopted by Sufi sheikh Muhammad ebn ʿEnan (d.1516) and his descendants and later demolished and rebuilt at twice its original size by Khedive Abbas Helmi II (1894). This last iteration of the mosque was itself demolished (1969), along with the ʿEnan house, to make way for the large mosque known as Gameʿ el-Fath (inaugurated 1990), which has Egypt's tallest minaret (130 meters) and the only one equipped with an elevator. The stones from the older mosque were used to rebuild the then derelict mosque over the tomb of el-Sayyeda ʿAysha (reopened 1979). Cairo's original port of el-Maqs lay immediately to the west of the mosque before the westward recession of the Nile (*see* Introduction page 2).

ʿAysha el-Teimuriya, Shareʿ (Garden City)
Since 1954, after ʿAysha el-Teimuriya (1840–1902), poet and feminist. El-Teimuriya was the daughter of Esmaʿil Pasha Teimur, head of the foreign affairs department at the court of Khedive Esmaʿil and head of the royal court under Khedive ʿAbbas Helmi II. She was also the older sister of Ahmad Teimur Pasha, a prominent man of letters, and the aunt of Muhammad and Mahmud Teimur, both writers. She

wrote in Arabic, Persian, Turkish, and French; her booklet *Mir'at el-Ta'ammul fi-l-Umur* ('The Mirror of Contemplation') offered a feminist reading of the Qur'an. A crater on Venus is named after her.

> From at least 1933 to 1954: **Share' Walda Basha** ('Dowager Str.'), in honor of Khushyar (Hoshiar) Kadinafandi (c.1813–86), concubine of Ebrahim Pasha and mother of Khedive Esma'il, who in 1863 restored and ceded to her the old *salamlek* (public reception building) of the el-Qasr el-'Ali palace complex, on whose grounds today's Garden City is built. Despite her position, Khushyar supported Ahmad 'Urabi's revolt against foreign influence over the country's finances. She had a small mosque near the citadel that held the tombs of two little-known saints (Sheikh 'Ali Abu Shubbak el-Refa'i, from whom the mosque takes its name, and Sheikh 'Abdallah el-Ansari) rebuilt and turned into a royal mausoleum for herself and many of her descendants. Walda Basha (literally, 'Mother-Basha') was a Turkish title borne by mothers of rulers of the Muhammad 'Ali dynasty. Not to be confused with nearby former Share' el-Walda (*see* Share' Tawfiq Deyab), farther north, in the Qasr el-Dubara district, named after another khedivial dowager.

'Azab, 'Atfet (Downtown)
By 1913; unidentified: 'Azab is a family name, derived from that of an Ottoman regiment of irregular light infantry (the Azap, literally 'the Bachelors'), membership in which was opened to Egyptians in the late sixteenth century.

'Azab, Haret (el-Munira)
Date unknown; unidentified: *see* preceding entry.

el-Azbakiya, Share' *see* Saray el-Azbakiya, Share'

'Aziz Abaza, Share' *see* el-Sha'er 'Aziz Abaza, Share'

el-'Aziz 'Usman, Sekket (el-Zamalek)
By 1910, after el-Malik el-'Aziz ('the Mighty King') I 'Usman ebn Salah el-Din Yusef (*see* next entry). Oddly, this small street connecting

Shareʿ Abu el-Feda to Shareʿ Yusef Kamel is not contiguous with or even close to the larger street named after the same person.

el-ʿAziz Usman, Shareʿ (el-Zamalek)
By 1913, after el-Malik el-ʿAziz ('Mighty King') I ʿUsman ebn Salah el-Din Yusef, a son of Salah el-Din (Saladin) and second Ayyubid sultan of Egypt (r.1193–98). He ordered the demolition of the Great Pyramids of Giza, starting with Menkaure's Pyramid, in one side of which his workers made a large gash before giving up.

B

el-Bab el-Bahari, Shareʿ (el-Azbakiya)
'North Gate Str.' (or **Shareʿ el-Geneina el-Bahari**, or 'North Garden Str.'). From 1913, after the northern gate into the el-Azbakiya Gardens.

> From 1904 to 1913: **Shareʿ Bab el-Geneina el-Bahari** ('North Garden Gate Str.').

Bab el-Luq, Haret (ʿAbdin)
'Silt Gate Lane.' From before the Esmaʿiliya project, after the district of Bab el-Luq, which lay between the medieval city to the east and the gate (*bab*) formerly located on today's Midan Muhammad Farid, close to the mosque of el-Tabbakh, on the west. The latter opened onto a large enclosure laid out for equestrian exercises by el-Malek el-Saleh Negm el-Din Ayyub (r.1240–49) that stretched to Qantaret Qadadar just east of Midan el-Tahrir (*see* Shareʿ el-Amir Qadadar) and was known as el-Midan el-Salehi; later, as the Nile receded farther, another enclosure was built by Mamluk sultan el-Zaher Beibars (r.1260–77), and this was known as el-Midan el-Zaheri. These enclosures were situated in an area known as Ard el-Luq, meaning 'the Land of the Soft Earth,' referring to the expanse of alluvial silt left behind as the Nile receded to the west during the twelfth and thirteenth centuries that eventually covered the area from Shareʿ Nagib el-Rihani in the north to Shareʿ Qasr el-ʿEini and Shareʿ el-Sheikh Rihan in the south, and from the Nile in the

west to the city's western walls in the east; it was on this Land of the Soft Earth that the new quarter of el-Esmaʿiliya would be constructed. Building in the area of Bab el-Luq began as early as the reign of Sultan Beibars, who settled Mongol soldiers there. The more detailed map of Cairo prepared for the *Description de l'Égypte*, compiled no later than 1801, shows the district protruding westward from the older city into the Land of the Soft Earth like a tongue, its tip (at which stood the gate) touching the el-Khalig el-Naseri canal. Home in medieval times to criminals and thieves, the district of Bab el-Luq was estimated by Leo Africanus in the sixteenth century to have a population of three thousand persons. In the late seventeenth century, the city's tanneries were moved there (*see* former Shareʿ el-Madabegh, *under* Shareʿ Sherif), only to be moved again in 1866 to el-Fustat (out of area). Despite the district's prominent status in the history and imagination of the city, the name of this small lane is the only one that officially alludes to it.

> From at least 1904 to 1913: the name **Haret Abu el-Sebaʿ** covered the part of this lane where the tomb of the Sufi saint ʿAbd el-Rahman Abu el-Sebaʿ stands.

Baba Sharu, Shareʿ (el-Zamalek)
Probably early 2000s, after Muhammad Mahmud Shaʿban (1912–99), aka Baba Sharu, children's entertainer, radio and TV news anchor, and (from 1971) head of the Egyptian Broadcasting Service.

> After 1948 probably to the early 2000s: **Shareʿ el-Shahid Hesein Masʿud,** after a member of the armed forces who gave his life for his country but on whom no further information has been found.

el-Babli, Haret (el-Munira)
By 1914; unidentified, but presumably after the owner of the Ard el-Babli ('el-Babli's Yard') that was subdivided to create the surrounding streets (Shareʿ el-Malek el-Naser, Shareʿ el-Qasr el-Kebir, etc.).

Bahaa' el-Din Qaraqosh, Shareʿ (el-Zamalek)
By 1913, after Abu Saʿid Qaraqosh ebn ʿAbd Allah el-Asadi, known as Bahaa' el-Din (d. c.1200), a freedman of the Ayyubid family who

served Salah el-Din (Saladin) and his descendants in many roles, including that of Salah el-Din's deputy during the latter's absences and supervisor of the construction of the Citadel and the city's northern walls. Despite his achievements, his name is associated in the popular imagination with arbitrary and despotic rule.

Bahgat 'Ali, Share' (el-Zamalek)
By 1937, after ('Ali) Bahgat 'Ali Basha (1858–1924), Egypt's first archaeologist and the first Egyptian to enter a field of scholarship previously reserved for Europeans. 'Ali was educated at Madraset el-Alsun (*see* Share' Madraset el-Alsun) and later taught history there. He developed the Museum of Islamic Art, excavated el-Fustat (Egypt's first Arab capital), and was Egypt's representative at the 1899 Conference of Orientalists in Rome.

> By 1919: **Share' el-Duktur Fathi Bayyumi el-Shawarbi** ('Dr. Fathi Bayyumi el-Shawarbi Str.'), reportedly after a physician, married to an Englishwoman, whose house was on this street and who is described as being among the first Egyptian residents of el-Zamalek.

el-Balaqsa, Haret ('Abdin)
'People of Belqas Lane.' By 1913; *see* Share' el-Balaqsa. Earlier, this lane was treated as part of Haret el-Sheikh Rihan, the change being attributable to the creation of Share' el-Qased (today's Share' Muhammad Mahmud), which severed the lane close to its northern end.

el-Balaqsa, Share' ('Abdin)
'People of Belqas Str.' Since 1847, presumably after Belqas, a town in the Delta (governorate of el-Gharbiya), people from which (in Arabic, *Balaqsa*) perhaps settled here.

el-Bank el-Ahli el-Masri, Share' (Downtown)
'Egyptian National Bank Str.' Since 1960, after the National Bank of Egypt, whose headquarters are on the corner of this small pedestrianized street with Share' Muhammad Farid. The bank is the successor to another, called el-Bank el-Watani (*see below*), the use of *ahli* (literally, 'native') underlining the change.

From at least 1906 to 1960: **Share͑ el-Bank el-Watani**
('National Bank Str.'), after a private bank founded by a
British–Egyptian consortium in 1898. From 1951 to 1961, it
acted as Egypt's central bank, issuing currency. In 1960, it was
nationalized as el-Bank el-Ahli el-Masri (*see above*).

Bank Misr, Share͑ (Downtown)

'Bank of Egypt Str.' From at least 1934, after the first Egyp-
tian-owned bank, founded in 1920 by entrepreneur Muhammad
Tal͑at Harb (*see* Share͑ Tal͑at Harb) to provide capital for the coun-
try's economic development; the bank was nationalized in 1960.
The bank's headquarters moved to adjacent Share͑ Muhammad
Farid in 1927.

From at least 1888 to at least 1934: **Share͑ el-Kenisa
el-Gedida** ('New Church Str.'), after St. Joseph's Church
(Latin Catholic) on the corner with Share͑ Muhammad
Farid. The church was demolished and rebuilt in 1907.

el-Banna, Darb (͑Abdin)

Probably by 1888; unidentified. El-Banna (literally, 'Builder') is a
family name, perhaps that of early residents.

el-Barazil, Share͑ (el-Zamalek)

'Brazil Str.' From at least 1973 to present, after the Embassy of
Brazil, formerly located on the street.

From 1940 to before 1973: **Share͑ Hasan Sabri.** This
name, which formerly applied to the entire street, both
northeast and southwest of Share͑ Setta w-͑Eshrin Yulyu,
still applies to its western stretch, as did its predecessor,
Share͑ el-Gabalaya (*see* main entry on Share͑ Hasan
Sabri).

Barlin, Share͑ (el-Zamalek)

'Berlin Str.' Since the mid-1970s, in honor of the German
Embassy, located at #2 on the street. Construction of the current
building began in the mid-1970s, and it was inaugurated in 1982.
Construction required the demolition of the École de Zamalek,

formerly known as Cours Morin, a privately-run French-language
school favored by the district's elite from the 1930s until the mid-
1950s, when it was nationalized.

> From at least 1910 to the mid-1970s: **Share' Ebn
> el-Mashtub**, in historical evocation of Emad el-Din
> ebn el-Mashtub (c.1179–c.1222), a Kurdish vassal of the
> Ayyubids in Syria who eventually ran afoul of their interne-
> cine struggles and died in prison in Harran.

Barukh, 'Atfet (el-Munira)
By 1935, after an unidentified Jewish family that presumably lived
on this small alley.

el-Batal Ahmad 'Abd el-'Aziz, Share' (Downtown)
'Hero Ahmad 'Abd el-'Aziz Str.' Since 1949, after Ahmad 'Abd
el-'Aziz (1907–48), maverick officer with the Egyptian contingent
of the Arab League forces that entered Palestine in 1948 who was
killed by friendly fire at the siege of Faluja. This street, and cross
street Share' 'Abd el-Latif el-Sufani, were created in the 4000m²
area made available for development in 1936 by the demolition of
the Ebrahimiya Secondary School for Boys (formerly the Lycée
Français and before that the mansion of Ahmad Basha Mazlum).
A major thoroughfare in the el-Muhandesin district (out of area)
bears the same name.

el-Baz, Haret (Downtown)
By 1888, after a certain Salama Beih el-Baz, whose house was on
this street at the date given.

Behlar, Mamarr *see* el-Muhandes 'Ali Labib Gabr, Share'

el-Beidaq, Share' (el-Azbakiya)
Since 1847, after the still standing tomb and mosque of Sufi saint
Sheikh Muhammad el-Beidaq. Until 1932, the street was discontinuous, being blocked by buildings between Share' el-'Ashmawi
and Share' el-Zabtiya. After 1950, the portion of the street that
formerly defined the eastern side of the Opera House was assigned
the name Share' el-Fariq Ahmad Hamdi Seif el-Nasr.

el-Beiraqdar, Haret ('Abdin)
'Standard Bearer's Lane.' By 1913; earlier, the lane was treated as part of Haret el-Sheikh 'Abdallah.

el-Bekbashi, Haret ('Abdin)
'Lieutenant-Colonel's Lane.' By 1904; the street name is pronounced locally as given, though the more usual pronunciation of this word is *bembashi*.

el-Berka el-Nasriya, Share' (el-Munira)
'El-Malek el-Naser's Lake Str.' By 1914, after a large depression that filled with Nile water during the annual flood. The name of this 'lake' may be taken as referring either specifically to the Mamluk ruler el-Malek el-Naser Muhammad ebn Qalawun, who dug it to provide building material for the new quarter that he created west of el-Khalig el-Masri in the first half of the fourteenth century, or more generally to the district to which he lent his name (*see* Share' el-Malek el-Naser). In a map included in the *Description de l'Égypte* and dating to about 1800, the same body of water is named Berket Setti Nasra ('My Lady Nasra's Lake'), suggesting an alternative connection to the female saint commemorated in the names of Share' Nasra and 'Atfet Nasra at its northern end; the nature of this dynamic—Nasra/Nasriya—remains unclear. The lake was also known as Berket el-Saqqayin ('Water Sellers' Lake'); *see* Share' el-Saqqayin.

Berket el-Shuqaf, Haret (Downtown)
'Pottery Lake Lane.' By 1925, in historical evocation of a lake presumably associated with the potters of nearby Haret el-Shuqafatiya. However, the assignment of the name to this street appears to be an error: Berket el-Shuqaf was an alternative name for Berket el-Farayin, which, until drained in the 1870s, covered today's Midan el-Gumhuriya, some distance to the east. The fact that the lane is located on a rise strengthens this supposition.

Beshara, 'Atfet ('Abdin)
By 1913; unidentified. Beshara is a male given name, perhaps that of an early resident.

Beshara, Zuqaq (ʿAbdin)
Probably by 1913; *see* ʿAtfet Beshara, from which this cul-de-sac branches.

Bur Saʿid, Midan (Fumm el-Khalig)
'Port Said Sq.' By 2000, after Shareʿ Bur Saʿid, to whose southern end it is close. The square, previously the intersection of the canal with Shareʿ ʿAli Ebrahim, Shareʿ el-Sadd el-Barrani, and Shareʿ el-Madbah (out of area), was created by slum clearances during the 1940s but does not appear on maps until later.

> From the 1940s to no later than 2000: **Midan el-Khalig el-Masri** ('Cairo Canal Sq.'; *see* former Shareʿ el-Khalig el-Masri, *under* Shareʿ Bur Saʿid). During the same period, the square appears also to have been referred to as **Midan Abu el-Rish**, after the saint whose tomb is located there (*see* former Shareʿ Abu el-Rish, *under* Shareʿ Bur Saʿid).

Bur Saʿid, Shareʿ (Fumm el Khalig, Munira)
'Port Said Str.' Since 1957, to commemorate the resistance of the city of Bur Saʿid (Port Said), at the northern end of the Suez Canal, to the 1956 attack by British, French, and Israeli forces seeking to occupy the canal following its nationalization in that year, known as the Tripartite Aggression.

> From 1897 to 1957: **Shareʿ el-Khalig el-Masri** ('Cairo Canal Str.'), after a former waterway dug to provide a navigable channel between the Nile and the Red Sea, whose origins go back at least to the Romans and probably to the pharaohs; by the nineteenth century, however, it no longer extended beyond el-Daher, a suburb to the north of the city (*see* Introduction page 2). Before the creation of a piped water system (*see* former Shareʿ Wabur el-Miyah, *under* Shareʿ Shambuliyon), the canal provided Cairo with much of its drinking water. However, it was filled only seasonally, with great celebration, at the height of the Nile flood, and later in the year turned into a stagnant ditch that came to be regarded as a public nuisance. Eventually, el-Khalig el-Masri was filled in and turned into a street, in stages, starting in

the el-Ghamra district in the north in 1897 and finishing at
Midan Fumm el-Khalig in 1899, after which it provided the
route for Cairo's first streetcar line. Originally of the same
width as the canal (which, based on the evidence of photo-
graphs, was less than ten meters), the street was progressively
widened between 1927 and 1957, a process that entailed the
demolition of the once affluent and elegant houses and other
buildings with which it was lined. It now measures forty
meters in width along much of its length, making it the wid-
est, as it is perhaps also the longest, street in central Cairo.

The street was reduced in length at its southern end due
to the widening of the south end of Share‘ Qasr el-‘Eini and
the construction of the Helwan light rail line in 1904, since
when the street has begun at a point east of the new railroad,
opposite Share‘ el-Muwaffaq; this stretch of the canal had also
borne the name of Khalig el-Mawardi (*see* Share‘ el-Mawardi).

From at least 1918 to an unclear date in the twenty-first
century, the southern section of this street, from Midan Bur
Sa‘id to the site of today's Sayyeda Zeinab metro station, was
known as **Share‘ Abu el-Rish**, after a saint, Sidi Muhammad el-Saddi, known by that name (which means literally
'the Feathered One'), whose tomb is located in Midan Bur
Sa‘id, to which the street leads. The Cairo Pediatric Surgery
Department, in a building donated in 1983 by the Japanese
government and located on nearby Share‘ el-Duktur ‘Ali
Ebrahim, is popularly known as Mustashfa Abu el-Rish ('the
Abu el-Rish Hospital').

el-Burg, Share‘ (el-Gezira)

'Tower Str.' Since 1960, after the Cairo Tower, a structure topped
by a revolving restaurant, officially opened on 11 April 1961 and
restored in 2009. The tower was built using $600,000 presented to
President ‘Abd el-Naser by the United States as a personal gift and
transferred by the president to the Egyptian Government for use in
this project, as a public rebuke for this attempt at bribery.

From 1868 to 1960: **Share‘ Hadayeq** (or **Hadiqet**)
el-Zuhriya ('Flower Pot Garden(s) Str.') or **Share‘ el-Zuhriya**
('Flower Pot Str.'), after the Villa Zuhriya ('Flower Pot Villa'),

a small (forty-room) palace surrounded by two acres of gardens built by Khedive Esma'il and inhabited until the 1952 revolution by members of the royal family; today, it is used by the Sports and Youth Authority. The Ministry of Agriculture took responsibility for the gardens, a part of which still exists, in 1917. This narrow street is distinguished by a very large Bengal fig tree in its middle, around which it is forced to part.

(el-)Bursa, Share' (el-Tawfiqiya)
Since 1887. The name normally appears as Share' Bursa on maps and in official records. On the single sign on the street, however, the name is given as Share' *el*-Bursa. If the former is correct, the name may refer to Bursa in Turkey, known for its verdancy, though it is difficult to say for sure why this particular street was named after that city. If the name is taken to be Share' el-Bursa, a greater puzzle is posed, since Cairo's original stock exchange was located not here but on Midan el-Khazendar, some distance to the east of this street. It is also possible that the word *bursa* was used here in another, now obsolete, sense, namely 'large café.'

el-Bursa el-Gedida, Share' (Downtown)
'New Stock Exchange Str.' Since 1909, when the Cairo Stock Exchange moved from its first, temporary, home at the Ottoman Bank (now Groppi's) on Share' 'Adli, to purpose-built headquarters on this street. The 'new' in the name alludes indirectly to Cairo's first stock exchange, situated on Midan el-Khazendar. In 1928 it would move again, to its current location on Share' el-Sherifein. Today's café el-Bursa el-Gedida bears sole witness to the exchange's earlier presence on this street.

el-Busta, Share' (el-Azbakiya)
'Post Office Str.' Since at least 1888, after Cairo's first, and central, post office, on Midan el-'Ataba.

> From at least 1888 to no later than 1923 the section of this street running along the southeastern corner of the el-Azbakiya Gardens and connecting Midan Azbak to Share' el-Busta was known as **Share' Midan Azbak**, after the square that once occupied the northeast corner of today's Midan el-'Ataba

el-Khadra. Starting in 1924, maps show that the name Share'
el-Busta had been extended to include this section.

el-Bustan, Share' *see* el-Ra'is 'Abd el-Salam 'Aref, Share'

Bustan el-Dekka, Share' (el-Tawfiqiya)
'Bench Plantation Str.' Since between 1933 and 1946, after a
plantation, originally laid out in the fourteenth century, to which
Mamluk high official Radwan Katkhuda el-Julfi added a 'bench,'
meaning a kiosk or garden pleasure-dome, in the eighteenth century. This street follows the southern stretch of the old Khalig
el-Khor canal, which brought water from the el-Khalig el-Naseri
canal to a depression farther north and which is aligned with Share'
Khalig el-Khor, which follows the former canal's northern stretch.

> From at least 1912 to 1935: **Share' Hammam el-'Om**
> ('Swimming Bath Str.') or **Share' Hammam el-'Umum**
> or **Share' el-Hammam el-'Umumi** (both meaning 'Pub-
> lic Baths Str.')—all these forms appear in various maps and
> official records of the time. These baths may have been on the
> site of today's Windsor Hotel.

> From at least 1896 to no later than 1912: **Share' Hammam
> Shenaydar** ('Schneider's Baths Str.'). These are mentioned in
> Murray's 1896 Handbook to Egypt as being "close to Shep-
> heard's Hotel" and "recommended for use by Europeans." In
> the same year, Schneider's Baths provided the venue for the
> first cinematograph showings in Cairo.

Bustan Ebn Qureish, Share' (Downtown)
'Ebn Qureish Plantation Str.' By 1911; unidentified. Presumably
in historical evocation of one of the plantations that from Ayyubid
times provided Cairo with fruit and produce.

> From 1887 to no later than 1911: **Haret el-Daramalli** (*see*
> 'Atfet el-Daramalli). Originally, this name applied not only
> to today's Share' Bustan Ebn Qureish but also to Share'
> Mustafa Abu Heif (from north of Share' el-Tahrir to Share'
> Huda Sha'rawi).

Bustan el-Fadel, Share' (el-Munira)

'El-Fadel's Plantation Str.' By 1908, in historical evocation of a plantation belonging to Muhy el-Din Abu 'Ali 'Abd el-Rahim ebn 'Ali el-Bisani el-'Asqalani el-Masri (1135–1200), commonly referred to as el-Qadi el-Fadel ('the Learned Judge'), statesman, model of elegant epistolary style, poet, and head of chancery to Salah el-Din (Saladin) and his two immediate successors. As his name shows, the judge's father was from Bisan, in Palestine, while he himself was born in Asqalan, also in Palestine, but moved to Cairo, where he assisted in the transition from the Shiite Fatimid caliphate to the rule of the Sunni Ayyubids. The assignment of the name of el-Qadi el-Fadel to this location is not historically accurate: the original plantation, which is said to have been large enough to supply Cairo with fruit, was located farther north, in the area between Share' Muhammad 'Ezz el-'Arab on the north and Share' Esma'il Serri on the south, and Share' Qasr el-'Eini on the west and Share' Bur Sa'id and Share' Nubar on the east. The plantation disappeared in 1252, during a ten-year-long eastward incursion by the Nile. The street is one of four, in this and other parts of the city, whose names allude to el-Qadi el-Fadel (*see* Introduction, page 16).

Bustan el-Khashshab, Share' (Fumm el Khalig)

'Timber Merchant's Plantation Str.' (or **Share' el-Khashshab**, 'Timber Merchant's Str.'). By 1918, after a large cultivated area belonging to a certain el-Khashshab (literally, 'the Timber Merchant'), of whom we know no details, who established a plantation in the location formerly occupied by that of el-Qadi el-Fadel, which had been destroyed by an incursion by the Nile that lasted from 1252 to 1262 (*see* Share' Bustan el-Fadel). The assignment of the name to this location is not historically accurate, as the plantations in question were located farther north, in the area between Share' Muhammad 'Ezz el-'Arab on the north and Share' Esma'il Serri on the south, and Share' Qasr el-'Eini on the west and Share' Bur Sa'id and Share' Nubar on the east. In the later thirteenth century, the latter tract was acquired by Mamluk sultan el-Malek el-Naser, who used it in part as a site for archery training (*see* former Share' Madrab el-Nashshab, *under* Share' Mudiriyet el-Tahrir).

el-Bustan el-Saʿidi, Mamarr   68

el-Bustan el-Saʿidi, Mamarr (Downtown)
'Saʿidian Plantation Passage.' Since 1926, after Shareʿ el-Bustan el-Saʿidi (*see* next entry). This street, originally open to vehicles, had by the 1970s been transformed into a pedestrian passageway through the encroachment of two well-known cafes.

el-Bustan el-Saʿidi, Shareʿ (Downtown)
'Saʿidian Plantation Str.' Since 1926; unidentified. Presumably in historical evocation of a plantation situated here or nearby owned by a man called Saʿid.

el-Busti, Haret (Downtown)
Probably after 1914; unidentified. El-Busti is a family name, perhaps that of early residents.

C

Centrale, Mamarr *see* Senteral, Mamarr

Chaldjian, Shareʿ *see* Shaljiyan, Shareʿ

Champollion, Shareʿ *see* Shambuliyon, Shareʿ

Clot Beih, Shareʿ *see* Kulut Beih, Shareʿ

el-Corniche, Shareʿ *see* Kurnish el-Nil, Shareʿ

D

el-Dabtiya, Shareʿ *see* el-Zabtiya, Shareʿ

el-Damalsha, ʿAtfet and Haret *see* el-Damarsha, ʿAtfet and Haret

el-Damarsha or el-Damalsha, ʿAtfet (ʿAbdin)
By 1887; *see* Haret el-Damarsha.

el-Damarsha or el-Damalsha, Haret (ʿAbdin)

By 1863; *Damalsha* may mean 'people of Demellash,' a village in the district of Belqas (*see* Shareʿ el-Balaqsa) in the Delta, which became depopulated during the Ottoman period. The name appears in documents with both spellings but the current pronunciation is *el-Damarsha*. A map drawn around 1825 shows a Berket el-Damalsha ('el-Damalsha Lake') on this site.

Dar el-ʿUlum, Shareʿ (el-Munira)

'House of Sciences Str.' From between 1924 and 1935, after the higher educational institution of that name located on the street. Dar el-ʿUlum was founded in 1872 by ʿAli Mubarak (who played a major role in the implementation of the Esmaʿiliya project) when minister of education to provide an alternative to the curriculum and pedagogy provided by the mosque–university of el-Azhar (founded c.970); in its early years, Dar el-ʿUlum played a key role in the formation of an intelligentsia educated according to European norms. Since 1946, it has been incorporated into Cairo University as a faculty offering degrees in Arabic Language and Literature and Islamic Studies.

el-Daramalli, ʿAtfet (Downtown)

By 1888, after Hesein Basha el-Daramalli, undersecretary of the interior ministry at the time of the ʿUrabi uprising, whose mansion stood between this street and Shareʿ Talʿat Harb. His name derives from the town of Drama, in Macedonia, and he was a descendent of Defterdar Muhammad Khusru Beih el-Daramalli, general and son-in-law of Muhammad ʿAli Basha. The defterdar was known as the Avenger of Shendi, for his massacre of thousands of Sudanese in reprisal for the burning to death by Makk Nemr, ruler of Shendi, of Muhammad ʿAli's third son Prince Esmaʿil Kamel (1796–1822), commander-in-chief of the Egyptian forces sent to drive the last Mamluks from their refuge in northern Sudan; the makk was responding to the prince's overweening and insulting behavior (versions differ as to its exact nature). The defterdar also conquered Sennar and Kordofan for Egypt. This and Zuqaq el-Daramalli maintain the presence of a name that once applied to the much longer street off which they branch (*see* Shareʿ Mustafa Abu Heif).

el-Daramalli, Zuqaq (Downtown)
By 1888; *see* ʿAtfet el-Daramalli.

Darb el-Bunduq, Haret (ʿAbdin)
'Cannonball Side Street Lane.' From at least 1908 to at least 1935; in 1831, Muhammad ʿAli Basha (r.1805–48) established a factory for the manufacture of cannonballs on Shareʿ Marasina about half a kilometer away, to the east of Midan el-Sayyeda Zeinab (out of area), but it is not known if there is a connection to this street.

el-Darb el-Gedid, ʿAtfet (Downtown)
'New Side Street Alley.' Probably by 1809; the term *darb* indicates that this short cul-de-sac was once a more important street, from which *hara*s, or self-contained alleys, branched. The name **Sekket el-Sawwafa** ('Wool Merchants' Connecting Street') appears to have been used of this and surrounding alleys until 1913, when it was officially quashed.

Darih Saʿd, Shareʿ (el-Munira)
'Saʿd's Tomb Str.' Since 1936, after the tomb of Saʿd Zaghlul (1859–1927), nationalist leader and founder of the Wafd Party (*see* Shareʿ Saʿd Zaghlul). The tomb is not located on the street but in the block defined by Shareʿ Saʿd Zaghlul on the north, Shareʿ el-Falaki on the west, Shareʿ Mansur on the east, and Shareʿ Esmaʿil Abaza on the south. The tomb was paid for by public subscription, and Zaghlul's remains were moved from the Imam el-Shafeʿi cemetery and reinterred there in 1936, though only after his wife had successfully fought off an attempt by Esmaʿil Sedqi's government (1930–33) to turn the monument into one for all great Egyptians, a move that saw the mummies of three pharaohs briefly transferred there from the Egyptian Museum, to which they were returned on the installation of a new government in 1934.

> From no earlier than 1914 to 1936: **Shareʿ Nazer el-Geish** ('Army Minister Str.'), probably in recognition of the War Office, located slightly to the south on Shareʿ el-Falaki. Before Egypt's break with the Ottoman Empire in 1914, the term *nazer* (literally, 'overseer') was used of

ministers of the Egyptian government, today's term *wazir* then applying only to ministers of the Ottoman Empire.

From at least 1906 to at least 1914: **Shareʿ el-Fekar**. Unidentified. As no Arabic-language map of this period that shows this street is at our disposal, even the original spelling remains uncertain.

Debana, ʿAtfet (el-Tawfiqiya)
Perhaps from before the Esmaʿiliya project; *see* Haret Debana, off which this branches.

Debana, Haret (el-Tawfiqiya)
Perhaps from before the Esmaʿiliya project, probably after the Debana family (*see* Shareʿ Debana). A sign at one end of Haret Debana bears the name **Mamarr Delbani**, which appears to be a mistake.

Debana, Shareʿ (el-Tawfiqiya)
Perhaps from before the Esmaʿiliya project, probably after the Debana (Debbane, Debbané) family, Greek Catholics from Sidon, some of whom migrated to Egypt as early as 1783. A Yusef Afandi Sarkis Debana worked as a translator for the government in the Ministry of Public Works' engineering department of the el-Faggala district (next to el-Tawfiqiya) in 1890. One branch of the family prospered in the timber trade, its patriarch acquiring the title of 'count' by virtue of his position as Brazilian consul; **Ard Debana** (Debana's Yard), the name given by locals to the wider, western section of the street, was perhaps one of the family's timber yards.

Delbani, Mamarr *see* Debana, Haret

el-Diwan, Shareʿ (Garden City)
Since at least 1935: after the business offices (Arabic *diwan*) of the el-Qasr el-ʿAli palace complex, on whose grounds today's Garden City is built.

el-Duktur ʿAbd el-Hamid Saʿid, Mamarr (Downtown)
From after 1946, after Shareʿ el-Duktur ʿAbd el-Hamid Saʿid, from which this network of passageways branches.

el-Duktur ʿAbd el-Hamid Saʿid, Shareʿ (Downtown)
From 1946, after nationalist and Muslim activist Dr. ʿAbd el-Hamid Saʿid (1882–1940), a Sorbonne-trained lawyer who was the first president of the Young Men's Muslim Association (founded 1927; *see* Shareʿ el-Shubban el-Muslemin).

> From at least 1887 to at least 1946: **Shareʿ el-Nemr**; unidentified. El-Nemr (literally, 'the Tiger') may be a family name, perhaps that of early residents.

el-Duktur Ahmad Abu el-ʿEla, Shareʿ (el-Zamalek)
Since c.2007, after a mid-twentieth century physician, who, according to residents, was director of the fever hospital at el-ʿAbbasiya and lived on this street.

> From at least 1948 to c.2007: **Shareʿ Habib ʿAyrut**, after Habib ʿAyrut (1876–1956), a Lebanese–Egyptian architect who participated in the planning and construction of Masr el-Gedida (Heliopolis); architects Charles and Max ʿAyrut, who also practiced in Cairo, were his brothers. Habib's son Henri Habib ʿAyrut was a Jesuit priest, educator, and scholar, whose book *Moeurs et coutûmes des fellahs* (1938; translated into English as *The Egyptian Peasant*) was the first modern comprehensive sociological account of rural Egypt.

el-Duktur Ahmad Fuʾad el-Ahwani, Shareʿ (el-Zamalek)
Since 1976, after Ahmad Fuʾad el-Ahwani (1908–70), Egyptian philosopher, head of Cairo University's Department of Philosophy from 1965 until his death. This name is a correction of that which immediately preceded it (*see below*).

> From 1970 to 1976: **Shareʿ el-Duktur Fuʾad el-Ahwani** (*see above*).

> From the 1880s to 1970: **Haret el-Mursalin** ('Missionaries' Lane'), after the priests of the Roman Catholic Comboni Congregation, whose school and other facilities still exist in the surrounding area. Not to be confused with nearby **Shareʿ el-Mursalin**, which still exists.

el-Duktur Ahmad 'Isa, Share' (Fumm el Khalig)
By 1988, after Dr. Ahmad 'Isa Beih (1876–1946), physician, historian, and man of letters. A pioneering gynecologist who wrote some of the first works in Arabic devoted to women's health, 'Isa was a linguist who knew Greek and Latin in addition to several Semitic languages, and a polymath who wrote on such diverse topics as medieval Arab medical instruments and hospitals, lullabies and children's games, urology, plant names, and Arabic (including colloquial Egyptian) grammar. He was a member of the Red Crescent, a trustee of the National Library, a senator (1923–25), and a member of the International Academy of the History of Science (from 1936).

> From at least 1921 to no later than 1988: **Share' Farah el-Nufus** ('Joy of All Souls Str.'), after a plantation called Bustan Farah el-Nufus that formerly covered this location and which may have been named after its owner (who in that case would have been a woman) or because of the charm of its location.

el-Duktur Ebrahim Badran, Share' (Garden City)
Since 2016, after Ebrahim Gamil Badran (1934–2015), professor of surgery at Qasr el-'Eini Medical School (1966), minister of health (1976), president of Cairo University (1978), and president of the Science Research Academy (1980). Badran lived on this street.

> From 1995 to 2016: **Share' 'Abd el-Latif Bultiya**; 'Abd el-Latif Bultiya (1924–93) was head of the Egyptian Labor Union, minister of labor, head of the Popular Committee of the Cairo Governorate, and a member of the political bureau of the National Party. Bultiya lived on this street.

> From at least 1935 to 1995: **Share' Dar el-Shefa** ('House of Healing Str.'); the term Dar el-Shefa was used during the nineteenth century of civilian (public) hospitals (one so named once stood on Share' el-'Ataba el-Khadra). The existence of a hospital on this street has not been established; however, a Jewish hospital stood on Share' el-Nabatat, the northern continuation of this street.

el-Duktur Gamal Hemdan, Share' (el-Zamalek)

Since 2000, after Gamal Hemdan (1928–93), independent geographer and scholar best known for his encyclopedic work *Shakhsiyat Misr* (The Personality of Egypt, 1967).

> From at least 1937 to 2000: **Share' el-Ward** ('Roses Str.'),
> one of a group of small streets connecting Share' Yusef Kamel
> with Share' Bahgat 'Ali that are named after flowers.

el-Duktur Handusa, Share' (Garden City)

Since 1958, after Professor Dr. Ahmad Handusa Beih (1900–58), an eminent ear, nose, and throat surgeon. Handusa graduated from Qasr el-'Eini Faculty of Medicine in 1924 and won a scholarship to study otorhinolaryngology in London (1928–30). In 1938, he chaired the first independent otolaryngology department at Cairo University, where he trained and examined the first generation of ORL specialists to be produced in Egypt, while himself publishing in Britain's *Journal of Laryngology and Otology*. He is cited in textbooks as having published the largest number of cases of extra-ocular proptosis (protrusion of the eyeball due to a tumor in the nose or sinuses) by type. Prof. Handusa also served as dean of the Faculty of Medicine of Cairo University (1954–56). Umm Kulsum (*see* Share' Umm Kulsum) regularly consulted him before her performances.

> From at least 1929 to 1958: **Share' Mustashfa el-Leidi
> Kuromar** ('Lady Cromer Hospital Str.'), *see* Haret Mustashfa
> el-Leidi Kuromar *below*. The upgrade from *hara* ('lane') to
> *share'* ('street') may have been associated with the widening
> of the road, which, from 1908 on, provided access to a new
> bridge (former Kubri el-Amir Muhammad 'Ali, *see* Kubri
> Qasr el-'Eini).

> From at least 1914 to before 1929: **Haret Mustashfa
> el-Leidi Kuromar** (Lady Cromer Hospital Lane), after a
> dispensary on this street for poor women and children, one
> of several hospitals in Cairo founded by Ethel Errington
> (d.1898), first wife of Evelyn Baring (1st Earl of Cromer),
> British controller-general (1879) and later (1883–1907) agent
> and consul-general in Egypt.

el-Duktur Mahmud ʿAzmi, Shareʿ (el-Zamalek)

Since 1954, after Mahmud ʿAzmi (1889–1954), journalist, politician, and academic. ʿAzmi founded the journals *el-Istiqlal* (Independence, 1920), *The Arab World* (in English, 1933), and *el-Shabab* (Youth, 1936); in 1935, he became editor-in-chief of literary and satirical magazine *Roz el-Yusef.* He was head of Egypt's delegation to the United Nations and chaired the United Nations Commission on Human Rights from 1953 until his death in 1954.

> From 1913 to 1954: **Shareʿ el-Amir Ahmad Fu'ad**
> ('Prince Ahmad Fu'ad Str.'), after Khedive Esmaʿil's seventh and youngest son, father of King Faruq. Ahmad Fu'ad became 'Sultan of Egypt and the Sudan and Sovereign of Nubia, Kordofan, and Darfur' in 1917, a title that was changed in 1922 to King Fu'ad I of Egypt. This area of el-Zamalek—immediately northeast of Khedive Esmaʿil's palace of Saray el-Gezira and extending to Shareʿ Setta w-ʿEshrin Yulyu—is home to twelve streets formerly named after princes of the ruling family. Of these, six were the sons of Khedive Esmaʿil (not represented were two who died young, plus his second son, Muhammad Tawfiq, later to become khedive and have the whole district of el-Tawfiqiya named after him), the others his cousins or grandsons.

el-Duktur Mahmud Fawzi (Garden City)

Probably since the late 1980s, after Mahmud Fawzi (1900–81), vice president of Egypt from 1972 to 1974. After taking a law degree in Egypt in 1923, Fawzi obtained a doctorate in international law from Columbia University in the United States and then served as a diplomat, becoming Egypt's representative to the United Nations in 1946 and ambassador to Great Britain in 1952. After the 1952 revolution, Fawzi became Egypt's foreign minister, remaining in that post until 1964. He was appointed prime minister by President el-Sadat in 1970 and vice president in 1972, and he retired in 1974. Many, even recent, maps show Shareʿ el-Haras (*see* what follows), but at least one sign on the street supports this name.

From at least 1935 to probably the late 1980s: **Shareʿ el-Haras** ('Guards' Str.'), presumably after the soldiers assigned to guard the *haramlek* of the el-Qasr el-ʿAli palace complex, on whose grounds today's Garden City is built.

el-Duktur Muhammad ʿAbd el-ʿAzim, Shareʿ (Garden City) Since 1954, after Dr. Muhammad ʿAbd el-ʿAzim el-Zurqani (d.1948), a writer on Islam and teacher at the College of Religious Principles of the University of el-Azhar.

From at least 1935 to 1954: **Shareʿ el-Amir Seif el-Din** ('Prince Seif el-Din Str.'), after Ahmad Seif el-Din (1877–1937), a grandson of Ebrahim Basha who in 1920 was reputedly Egypt's second richest man, owning 119,000 faddans of agricultural land and numerous buildings, including a palace on this street. Seif el-Din was imprisoned and placed in an asylum in England after shooting and wounding Prince Ahmad Fu'ad at the Khedivial Club on Shareʿ el-Manakh (now Shareʿ ʿAbd el-Khaleq) in 1898, accusing the future king of mistreating his sister, to whom the prince was married. On escaping to Turkey, he was pronounced sane and granted citizenship in 1925.

el-Duktur Muhammad Hasan el-Geziri, Shareʿ (el-Zamalek) From after 2000, after Muhammad Hasan el-Geziri (d.2004), a physician and, apparently, a sometime resident of this street.

From c.1928 to 2000: **Shareʿ Murgeil** or **Shareʿ Margeil**, after (Dieudonné) Eugène Mougel Beih (1808–90), a French engineer who worked for the Egyptian government as chief engineer for bridges and roads. Mougel was involved in the initial stages of work on the Qanater barrages north of Cairo and on other barrages on the Rashid branch of the Nile, intended to control water flows to the Delta. He was also general supervisor of the digging of the Suez Canal. As Mougel died some years before el-Zamalek was settled, the choice of his name for the street appears to have been intended to honor his work, and not, as in other similar cases, because his house was there.

el-Duktur Muhammad Khalil, Share' (Fumm el-Khalig)
By 2008, after a leading ophthalmologist, recorded as a member of
the Société d'Ophtalmologie d'Egypte in 1939. In the absence of
both street signs and any businesses or residences with addresses,
the street has become popularly known as **Share' Huda Sha'rawi**,
after the Huda Sha'rawi Club and the headquarters of the Huda
Sha'rawi Association, formerly the Egyptian Feminist Union
(founded 1923), as well as the Huda Sha'rawi School for Girls, all
of which occupy the block between this street and Share' Ahmad
'Isa, the next street to the south (to which, confusingly, the same
name is also, and for the same reason, popularly applied).

> From no earlier than 1935 to no later than 2008: **Share'**
> **Kulliyet el-Saydala** ('Faculty of Pharmacology Str.').
> The street runs south of Cairo University's Faculty of
> Pharmacology, established in its present form in 1881 but
> descended from an older institution founded at Abu Za'bal,
> north of Cairo, in 1824, which moved to its present site
> in 1837.

> Probably from before the Esma'iliya project to at least 1935:
> **Share' el-Murada** ('Beach Str.'), after a beach or slope on
> the Nile's bank originally used, in this case, for the unloading
> of tiles. According to some authorities, however, the historical
> beach in question was farther north, and ran the length of the
> riverbank west of Share' el-Sheikh 'Abd el-Latif Deraz (for-
> mer Share' Hod el-Laban) and Share' el-Duktur Ebrahim
> Badran (former Share' Dar el-Shefa).

el-Duktur Mustafa el-Diwani, Share' (Garden City)
Since 1995, after Dr. Mustafa Khalil el-Diwani (1906–?), a pedia-
trician, who lived on the street.

> From no earlier than 1973 to 1995: **Share' el-Duktur Mah-**
> **mud Ahmad el-Hefni**, after a musicologist (1896–1973)
> who worked for the Ministry of Culture from 1931 to 1954.
> El-Hefni wrote more than forty-five books on music and
> founded the journals *el-Musiqa* (Music, 1935) and *el-Musiqa*
> *we-l-Masrah* (Music and Theater, 1949).

From at least 1925 to at least 1973: **Share' Ma'mal el-Sukkar** ('Sugar Refinery Str.'), after a commercial sugar refinery built by Ebrahim Basha (1789–1848) in the grounds of the el-Qasr el-'Ali palace, on which Garden City would later be built. A large, seven-story building, it was still operating under Muhammad Sa'id Basha (r.1854–69). Before the construction of such refineries during Muhammad 'Ali Basha's reign (1805–48), Egyptian sugar had been sent to Marseilles for refining. A historical topographer, writing in 1925, claims that the street is not in the same place as the historical building.

el-Duktur Mustafa Khalil, Share' (el-Zamalek)
Since 2013; Mustafa Khalil (1920–2008) served as minister of foreign affairs (1979–80) and prime minister (1978–80).

From no earlier than 1962 to 2013: **Share' el-Ferdos** ('Paradise Str.'), one of several unofficial street names in the area chosen presumably for their pleasing associations (*see also* Share' el-Safa, Share' el-Ward, etc.).

el-Duktur Selim Hasan, Share' (Downtown)
Since 1954, when the street was created on land in front of the Egyptian Museum that previously had been part of the British army's Qasr el-Nil barracks complex; after the Egyptologist (1886–1961) who led the movement to save the ancient sites of Nubia before they were flooded by Lake Naser. Hasan was also the first Egyptian to be admitted to the International Academy of Sciences.

el-Duktur Taha Hesein, Share' (el-Zamalek)
Since 1974, after Taha Hesein (1889–1973), novelist, short-story writer, journalist, translator, critic, editor, and minister of education (1950–52). Though blind from early childhood, Hesein became one of Egypt's most revered literary figures, in later life often referred to as the Dean of Arabic Literature. Hesein studied the traditional curriculum at el-Azhar University, of which he would later write critically in his celebrated autobiography *el-Ayyam (The Days)*, and then moved to the Egyptian University (now Cairo University), where he was the first graduate to earn a doctoral degree; he received

a second doctorate from the Sorbonne in 1918. As a scholar, he was known for his adamant and controversial championing of western critical methodology, while as minister of education he worked tirelessly for universal free education.

> From at least 1928 to 1974: **Share' el-Ser Welyam Welkuks**, after Sir William Willcocks (1852–1932), who lived on this street. Willcocks was an irrigation and hydraulic engineer who started his career in India. He designed the first Aswan Dam (the largest of its kind at the time) and the Asyut barrages (both completed in 1902). He later became chairman of the Cairo Water Works Company and was president of the Anglo-Egyptian Land Allotments Company, which played a major role in the urbanization of Zamalek. Subsequently, he designed and implemented major irrigation projects in Iraq, Romania, and Bengal before returning to Egypt, where he died. Willcocks believed that colloquial Arabic should replace formal Arabic in all uses and supervised, or perhaps himself undertook, a translation of the New Testament into colloquial; conceivably, this influenced the choice of Taha Hesein, a promoter of classical Arabic purism, to provide the street's new name.

E

Ebn Meisar, Share' *see* Ebn Meyassar, Share'

Ebn Meyassar (or **Muyassar**), **Share'** (el-Zamalek)
Since 1954, after Muhammad ebn 'Ali ebn Muyassar (1230–78), author of a chronicle of Fatimid Egypt that exists in a unique and incomplete manuscript copied by Cairo's most famous medieval historian and topographer el-Maqrizi (1364–1441). The huge Bengal fig tree that divides the narrow street in two must be a survivor of Saray el-Gezira, Khedive Esma'il's palace, whose gardens formerly covered the area. The name appears on some European-language maps in garbled forms such as Ebn Meisar and Ebn Maysara.

From 1913 to 1954: **Share' el-Amir Gamil** ('Prince Gamil
Str.'), after Prince Muhammad Gamil Tusun (1874–1932),
son of Prince Muhammad Tusun, a son of Muhammad Sa'id
Basha and grandson of Khedive Esma'il. This area of
el-Zamalek—immediately northeast of Khedive Esma'il's
palace of Saray el-Gezira and extending to Share' Setta
w-'Eshrin Yulyu—is home to twelve streets formerly named
after princes of the ruling family. Of these, six were the sons
of Khedive Esma'il (not represented were two who died
young, plus his second son, Muhammad Tawfiq, later to
become khedive and have the whole district of el-Tawfiqiya
named after him), the others his cousins or grandsons.

Ebn el-Nabih, Share' (el-Zamalek)
By 1913, after Abu el-Hasan 'Ali ebn Muhammad ebn el-Nabih
(c.1164–1222), a poet of the Ayyubid period who wrote panegyrics
to Ayyubid princes and, on moving to Mesopotamia, odes express-
ing nostalgia for Egypt.

Ebn Sa'lab, Share' *see* Ebn Ta'lab, Share'

Ebn Ta'lab, Share' (Downtown)
Also Ebn Sa'lab, Ebn Tha'lab. By 1926, a historical reference, no
doubt based on the report of the historian and topographer of Cairo
el-Maqrizi (1364–1441) that the area of today's Share' Mushtuhur,
Share' el-Sawwafa, and Haret el-Kafarwa north of Midan Muhammad Farid was covered during the Ayyubid period by a residiential
development called Munshat Ebn Tha'lab, after the early Ayyubid
army commander Fakhr el-Din Esma'il ebn Tha'lab (d.1216 or 1217),
a descendent of the Prophet Muhammad who also owned Bustan
Ebn Tha'lab, a vast plantation and market garden that stretched from
Bab el-Luq north almost to Midan Ramsis. Today's Share' Ebn Ta'lab
lies somewhat to the west of the historical sites it commemorates.

Ebn Tha'lab *see* Ebn Ta'lab

Ebn Zanki, Share' (el-Zamalek)
Also Ebn Zenki. By 1913, after el-Malek el-Adel ('the Just King')
Nur el-Din Abu el-Qasem Mahmud ebn Zanki (1118–74), ruler

of Syria of the Turkic Zengid dynasty whose lieutenant, the Kurd Sherkuh, conquered Egypt in 1169 (*see* Share' Sherkuh). When Ebn Zanki died, Sherkuh's nephew Salah el-Din (Saladin) married his widow, established the Ayyubid dynasty, and realized Ebn Zanki's dream of uniting Egypt and the Muslim lands of Syria in a single kingdom. The house at #22 was built by 'Ali Labib Gabr (*see* Share' el-Muhandes 'Ali Labib Gabr) on the site of the house of Thomas Russell Basha, Cairo's chief of police from 1913 to 1946.

Ebn Zenki, Share' *see* Ebn Zanki, Share'

Ebrahim 'Abd el-Qader el-Mazni, Share' (el-Tawfiqiya)
From no earlier than 1947, after the writer, critic, translator, poet, and philosopher (1889–1949), among whose best-known works are the short-story collection *Sunduq el-Dunya* (Peep Show, 1929) and the novel *Ebrahim el-Katib* (Ebrahim the Writer, 1931); el-Mazni was one of the three poets who made up the Diwan Group.

> From no earlier than 1929 to at least 1947: part of **Midan Halim** (*see* Share' Halim)

Ebrahim Badran, Share' *see* el-Duktur Ebrahim Badran, Share'

Ebrahim Gawish, Haret (el-Munira)
Probably by 1935, unidentified. Perhaps the name of an early resident.

Ebrahim Nagib, Share' (Garden City)
By 1934, after Ebrahim Basha Nagib (1856 or 1857 to after 1913). Nagib studied law at Aix-en-Provence, was appointed an assistant prosecutor at the Mixed Courts on his return, and was a member of the commission established in 1882 to look into the crimes committed in Alexandria on 11 June of that year and that were attributed to Ahmad 'Urabi's followers. Thereafter he continued his career with the judiciary, becoming president of the Native Courts of First Instance in 1889. He also served as governor of Cairo (c.1910–13) and director-general of religious endowments (from 1913).

Ebrahim el-Qabbani, Share' (Downtown)
From no earlier than 1947, after Ebrahim el-Qabbani (1852–1927), a composer and a teacher of Umm Kulsum (*see* Share' Umm Kulsum).

From no earlier than 1926 to at least 1947: **Share' Qattawi Beih**, after Ya'qub Menashsha (Menasche) Qattawi Beih (1800–83), founder of a prominent dynasty of Egyptian Sephardic Jews. Qattawi rose to prominence during the reign of Abbas Helmi I Basha (r.1848–54), under whom he held the post of master of the mint, and eventually became the personal banker of Khedive Esma'il. By 1897, the Qattawi family had come to reside in the area at the apex of Share' Qasr el-Nil and Share' Muhammad Sabri Abu 'Alam. Subdivision of the Qattawi property, with its mansions and gardens, and the creation of streets, had begun by 1921 and was complete by 1934. Not to be confused with Share' Musa Qattawi Basha, the name by which nearby Share' Abu Bakr Kheirat was known from at least 1934 to some time in the late 1960s. A second Share' Qattawi Beih was located out of area, to the east of Midan el-Khazendar.

From at least 1910 to 1927: **Share' (Funduq) Safuy** ('(Hotel) Savoy Str.'), so named because it led to the hotel of that name (opened 1898), located at the apex of Share' Qasr el-Nil and Share' Tal'at Harb. The hotel, considered in its day the best in Cairo, operated for only sixteen years before being taken over by the British as their military headquarters during the First World War (T.E. Lawrence had an office there). In 1924, it was demolished by Charles Baehler, to make way for the still-standing Baehler Building.

el-Ebrahimi, Share' (Qasr el-Dubara)
'Ebrahim's [Palace] Str.' By 1912, after the more northerly of the two palaces (the *haramlek*) that constituted the el-Qasr el-'Ali palace complex, on the site of which today's Garden City is built (*see* Share' el-Qasr el-'Ali, *under* Share' Qasr el-'Eini). Ebrahim Basha (1789–1848) was the eldest son of Muhammad 'Ali Basha and the first member of his family to move his residence from the Citadel to the Nile; he succeeded his father on the latter's abdication but died before him.

el-ʿElwa, Haret (Downtown)

'Rise Lane.' By 1913, after the rise on which the alley is located. The name **Sekket el-Sawwafa** ('Wool Merchants' Connecting Street') appears also to have been used of this and surrounding alleys until 1913, when it was quashed.

ʿElwi, Shareʿ (Downtown)

Since 1912, after Muhammad ʿElwi Basha (d.1918), father of modern ophthalmology in Egypt, who lived on parallel Shareʿ el-Sherifein. Ophthalmologist to the khedivial family, he was instrumental in persuading Princess Fatma, second daughter of Khedive Esmaʿil, to donate land and money for the creation of what is today Cairo University. He was also a member of the committee, first convened in 1909, that called for the erection of a statue to the memory of nationalist leader Mustafa Kamel, a goal achieved only in 1940, after ʿElwi's death (*see* Midan Mustafa Kamel).

> From at least 1906 to 1912, **Shareʿ Zerfudakki**, after an Alexandrian Greek merchant family (Zervudachi/Zervudaki), who owned a house on this street. The family was involved in banking, a member being on the founding board of the National Bank.

ʿEmad el-Din, Shareʿ (el-Tawfiqiya)

After a Sufi saint—said by some to have been a late fourteenth-century cameleer, by others a page boy belonging to the late-thirteenth-century Salah el-Din el-Ayyubi (Saladin)—whose tomb stands behind the mosque at the intersection of Shareʿ Muhammad Farid and Shareʿ el-Sheikh Rihan. The name has had two applications:

> Present-day **Shareʿ ʿEmad el-Din** has been so called since at least 1906, following the extension of original Shareʿ ʿEmad el-Din (*see below*) north from Shareʿ Sitta w-ʿEshrin Yulyu to Shareʿ Ramsis. From the last decades of the nineteenth century to the late 1960s, this street was the heart of Cairo's entertainment district, being lined with cinemas, theaters, and night-clubs, some of which remain, and frequented by the country's stars of stage and screen and its best-known

musicians. As such, it gained the nickname of **Shareʿ el-Fann** ('the Street of Art').

Original **Shareʿ ʿEmad el-Din** was so called from at least 1888 and ran for approximately two and a half kilometers from Shareʿ Gameʿ el-Esmaʿili in the south to Shareʿ Setta w-ʿEshrin Yulyu in the north. This section was renamed Shareʿ Muhammad Farid in 1941, leaving the tomb of Sheikh ʿEmad el-Din stranded far from the street that bears his name.

el-ʿEmad el-Kateb, Shareʿ (el-Zamalek)

'el-ʿEmad the Scribe Str.' Since c.1910, after ʿEmad el-Din el-Esfahani (1125–1201), a writer in Arabic of Persian origin. El-Esfahani worked as a scribe for both Nur el-Din ebn Zanki (*see* Shareʿ Ebn Zanki) and Salah el-Din (Saladin; *see* Shareʿ Salah el-Din) and wrote, among many other works, an account of Salah el-Din's conquest of Jerusalem.

ʿEmaret el-Yamani, Shareʿ *see* ʿUmara el-Yamani, Shareʿ

Eshaq Yaʿqub, Shareʿ *see* el-Shahid Eshaq Yaʿqub, Shareʿ

Esmaʿil Abaza, Shareʿ (el-Munira)

By 1942, after Esmaʿil Basha Abaza (1854–1927), lawyer, politician, and newspaper editor and owner, who hailed from a Mamluk family of Abkhazian origin. In 1894, Abaza founded the influential nationalist newspaper *el-Ahali* (The People). In 1907, he was among the founders of the nationalist Umma (Nation) Party of ʿAdli Yakan (*see* Shareʿ Adli), under whom he served subsequently as a minister in five governments. In 1908, he was a member of a delegation to London that sought increased prerogatives for the Egyptian government under British occupation.

From at least 1906 to no later than 1942: **Shareʿ el-Turqa el-Gharbi** ('Western Corridor Str.') and **Shareʿ el-Turqa el-Sharqi** ('Eastern Corridor Str.'). The relationship of the two streets is complex: maps from 1874 to before 1906 show one continuous (unnamed) street from Shareʿ Qasr el-ʿEini to

Share' Kheirat. In 1906, this continuous street is divided into
a western and an eastern part by the light rail line from Bab
el-Luq to Helwan, the two parts being rendered discontinuous
and separated by a wide strip of empty land west of the railway
line. Share' el-Turqa el-Gharbi now ran from Share' Qasr
el-'Eini to Share' el-Falaki, while Share' el-Turqa el-Sharqi
ran from Share' Mansur to Share' Kheirat. By 1929, however,
the western street had been extended east across the strip from
Share' el-Falaki to Share' Mansur, thus making the two streets
continuous once again. The names appear simultaneously with
the railway line and probably refer to some feature associated
with the latter, though exactly what has not been discovered.

Esma'il Muhammad, Share' (el-Zamalek)
By 1937, after Esma'il Basha Muhammad, an irrigation engineer
and member of parliament. Esma'il Muhammad worked as chief
irrigation engineer for the Ebrahimiya Canal, served as president
of the Consultative Council (Maglis el-Shura) from 1899 to 1902,
and in 1923 built his palace (since 1958, the Faculty of Music of
Helwan University) on the corner of this street with Share' Shagaret el-Durr.

> From at least 1919 to no later than 1937: **Share' Meltun**,
> after Frank Milton, a professor of clinical surgery at the Qasr
> el-'Eini government hospital between approximately 1890
> and 1915, who is believed to have lived on the street. Not
> to be confused with former Share' Meltun in el-Munira (*see*
> Share' Esma'il Serri).

Esma'il Sabri, Share' (Fumm el-Khalig)
By 1918, probably after Esma'il Basha Sabri (1835– after 1905),
known as el-Tubgi ('the Gunner'), who trained at the School of
Artillery, rose fast through the ranks, and was appointed aide-de-
camp to Khedive Esma'il in 1869. Sabri served with distinction
as commander-in-chief of artillery in Ethiopia, where he was
badly wounded, and in the Crimea, where he was decorated. On
retirement, he received the honorary rank of mirmiran (provincial
governor) and assumed the post of Commander of the Pilgrimage,
responsible for the safety of pilgrims to the Hejaz.

Esma'il Serri, Share' (el-Munira)
From after 1935, after Esma'il Serri Basha (1861–1937). Serri trained as an irrigation engineer in Egypt and France and practised in England. On his return to Egypt, he proved his talent when, in 1899, following the building of the first Aswan Dam, he successfully converted some 312,000 faddans of agricultural land in Upper Egypt from annual to perennial irrigation. Thereafter, Serri served five times as minister of public works and of war in the years between 1904 and 1926. Serri wrote and translated in the field of engineering.

> From at least 1918 to at least 1935: **Share' 'Umar ebn 'Abd el-'Aziz**, after the eighth caliph of the Umayyad dynasty (r.717–20), noted for his piety.

> By 1908 to before 1918: **Share' Meltun**, after either Frank Milton, a professor of clinical surgery at the Qasr el-'Eini government hospital from approximately 1890 to 1915, or his brother Herbert, also a professor at the hospital. Share' Esma'il Muhammad in el-Zamalek also once bore this name.

el-Esma'ili, Haret ('Abdin)
Probably from before the Esma'iliya project, after Mamluk commander Arghun Shah el-Esma'ili el-Kameli (d.1357; *see* Share' Game' el-Esma'ili).

Esturil, Mamarr *see* el-Sharq, Mamarr

el-'Etri, Haret ('Abdin)
By 1913; according to residents, the el-'Etri family were the first to build a house here.

Ettehad el-Muhamin el-'Arab, Share' (Garden City)
'Union of Arab Lawyers Str.' Since 1977, after the non-governmental organization of that name, founded in 1944 and constituted from elected lawyers' associations and syndicates of the Arab World. The Union's permanent headquarters are located on this street.

> From at least 1925 to 1977: **Share' el-Tulumbat** ('Pumps Str.'), after the pumps installed to irrigate the gardens of

el-Qasr el-ʿAli palace complex (*see* Shareʿ el-Qasr el-ʿAli, *under* Shareʿ Qasr el-ʿEini), on whose grounds today's Garden City is built. A historical topographer, writing in 1925, claims that the street is not in the same place as the historical pumps.

F

Fadda, ʿAtfet (ʿAbdin)
By 1904, according to residents, after a woman named Fadda ('Silver'), an early resident of the street. Earlier, this alley was regarded as part of Haret Selim.

el-Fadl, Shareʿ (Downtown)
By 1934; unidentified. El-Fadl may be a male or female given name or, though less likely, used in its common sense of 'grace, amiability, erudition.'

Fakturya, Mamarr (el-Tawfiqiya)
'Victoria Passage.' Also **Mamarr Funduq Fakturya** ('Victoria Hotel Passage'), or **Mamarr el-Funduq** ('Hotel Passage'). Probably by 1934, after the Victoria Hotel, which dates to the reign of Khedive Esmaʿil (r.1863–79) and is still open.

el-Falaki, Midan (Downtown)
'Astronomer's Sq.' Since 1930, after Mahmud Ahmad Hamdi (1815–85), known as Mahmud Basha el-Falaki ('Mahmud Basha the Astronomer'; *see* Shareʿ el-Falaki), whose villa (demolished 1970) was located at the western end of the street between Shareʿ el-Tahrir and Shareʿ el-Raʾis ʿAbd el-Salam ʿAref. Because of its position as the district's hub and despite the changes of name, this square has been popularly known throughout its history as **Midan Bab el-Luq** and is therefore sometimes referred to in older European-language maps as *Place* de Bab el-Luq to distinguish it from the *Rondpoint* de Bab el-Luq farther to the east (now Midan Muhammad Farid).

From 1913 to 1930, **Midan el-Azhar** ('Square of the Flowers'), after a garden created there by a French horticulturalist in 1875; Baedeker's guide for 1885 notes that, in that year, the square was "beautifully planted with flowers of the Turkish national colors."

From c.1867 to 1913: **Midan Bab el-Luq** ('Silt Gate Sq.'), after the district in which it is located. This name continues to be used (*see* main entry).

Anciently to c.1867: a larger area that covered both the present square and today's Midan Muhammad Farid was known as **Rahabet Bab el-Luq** ('Silt Gate Field'). This was the successor to Ayyubid- and early Mamluk-era equestrian training grounds known respectively as el-Midan el-Salehi and el-Midan el-Zaheri (*see* Haret Bab el-Luq). The square's present layout dates to the initiation of the Esma῾iliya project.

el-Falaki, Share῾ (Downtown)
'Astronomer's Str.' By 1904, after engineer, mathematician, astronomer, and scientist Mahmud Ahmad Hamdi (1815–85), known as el-Falaki, 'the Astronomer,' who lived on the street. An early graduate of the Engineering School founded by Muhammad ῾Ali, el-Falaki studied in France, published widely, taught ῾Ali Mubarak (implementer of the Esma῾iliya project), was director of the Engineering School (el-Muhandiskhana) and of the observatory (el-Rasdakhana, then in el-῾Abbasiya), and served briefly as minister of public works (1882) and of education (1884). He is credited with creating the science of comparative calendrometrics, which permits conversion among dates from the Hegri (Islamic), Coptic, and Gregorian calendars, and of drawing the first map to show both Upper and Lower Egypt.

el-Fannan ῾Abd el-Halim Hafez, Share῾ (el-Tawfiqiya)
'Artist ῾Abd el-Halim Hafez Str.' Since 1977, after heart-throb singer, songwriter, producer, and actor ῾Abd el-Halim Hafez (1929–77), known as el-῾Andalib el-Asmar ('the Dusky Nightingale'). Hafez is believed to have been the best-selling Arab artist of his time and his name is often coupled with those of Umm Kulsum, Muhammad ῾Abd el-Wahhab, and Farid el-Atrash, the other giants of modern Egyptian song. He died of schistosomiasis, a disease contracted while playing in village canals as a child. Four

women are alleged to have thrown themselves from their balconies as his funeral cortège passed.

> From after 1947 to 1977: **Share' Nadi el-Musiqa el-'Arabiya** ('Arabic Music Club Str.'), after the music club established in 1914 by Mustafa Reda from which, by 1921, emerged the Higher Arabic Music Insitute. The latter, which contains museums and an exquisite concert hall, is located nearby at #22 Share' Ramsis.

el-Fannan 'Ali el-Kassar, Share' (el-Azbakiya)

'Artist 'Ali el-Kassar Str.' From 1990, after stage name of comedian 'Ali Khalil Salim (1887–1957), creator of 'Usman 'Abd el-Basit, a comic Nubian designed to rival Nagib el-Rihani's Kishkish Beih (*see* Share' Nagib el-Rihani).

> From at least 1887 to 1990, **Share' el-Geneina** ('Garden Str.'), after the el-Azbakiya Gardens (*see* Share' Saray el-Azbakiya). The street appears on maps as early as 1877, though without name, and was probably created following the draining of Berket el-Azbakiya ('el-Azbakiya Lake') in 1848. It continues to appear on some maps.

el-Fariq Ahmad Hamdi Seif el-Nasr, Share' (el-Azbakiya)

'Lieutenant-General Ahmad Hamdi Seif el-Nasr Str.' Since after 1950; Seif el-Nasr (d.1950) was a Wafdist member of parliament and statesman who served as minister of war from 1936 to 1937. The name applies to the streets that trace the north, east, and south sides of the site of the old Opera House, now a multi-story car park. Previously, each side had a different name.

> North side:
> From at least 1905 to after 1950: **Share' el-Teyatru** ('Theater Str.'), after the Opera House (*see* Midan el-Ubera).

> East side:
> From at least 1905 to after 1950: **Share' el-Beidaq**, after Sheikh Muhammad el-Beidaq (*see* Share' el-Beidaq, main entry).

South side:
From 1949 to after 1950: **Share' 'Abd el-Khaleq Sarwat**, after the judge and politician (*see* Share' 'Abd el-Khaleq Sarwat, main entry).

From 1938 to 1949: **Share' el-Maleka Farida** ('Queen Farida Str.'), after the first wife of King Faruq (divorced 1948); this made the street an extension of that immediately to its west.

From at least 1905 to 1938: **Share' Taher**, after Taher Basha (*see* Share' Taher, main entry).

el-Fariq Awwal 'Abd el-Men'em Reyad, Midan (Downtown) Since 1969, after Field Marshal Muhammad 'Abd el-Men'em Muhammad Reyad 'Abdallah (1919–69), whose statue has presided over the square since 2002. Reyad's army career spanned the Second World War, the Palestine War (1948), and the 1956 and 1967 wars with Israel. He became chief of staff in 1967 and was killed by shrapnel on the Suez Canal on 3 March 1969 while directing operations against the Bar Lev Line. The square, which marks the boundary between el-Esma'iliyya and Bulaq, took shape following a series of demolitions of large buildings, including, on the northwest the Sewers Authority headquarters (after 1954), on the northeast the old tram company headquarters (demolished 1956), on the south the former headquarters of the Antiquities Department (within the then larger grounds of the Egyptian Museum; demolished 1976), and on the west All Saints Anglican cathedral (built in 1938 on land formerly occupied by outliers of the Qasr el-Nil Barracks complex and demolished in 1977). The exact chronology of the naming of the square is hard to establish but went approximately as follows:

From 1962 to 1969: **Midan el-Shuhada** ('Martyrs' Square'), in honor of those who gave their lives for their country in its wars with Israel.

From at least 1953 to 1962: **Midan el-Marafeq** ('Public Utilities Sq.'), after the Sewers Authority headquarters that occupied its northeast side until at least 1954.

Previously, the space was defined or crossed by two, or three, streets, depending on the stage of development:

> The north side:
> From 1947 to 1969: **Share' el-Galaa'** ('Evacuation Str.'); *see* main entry.

> From 1902 to 1947: **Share' Fumm el-Ter'a el-Bulaqiya** ('Bulaq Canal Inlet Str.'); *see* Share' el-Galaa', main entry.

> The west side:
> From 1950 to at least 1953: **Share' Mahmud Basyuni** (*see* main entry), running along the north and south sides of the cathedral (*see next below*).

> From 1913 to 1950: **Share' el-Antikkhana el-Masriya** (*see* main entry for Share' Mahmud Basyuni); following construction of the cathedral in 1938 but not before 1948, this street, which formerly ran through the middle of the space taken over by the cathedral, was redefined as running along its north and south sides.

> The south side:
> From 1863 to 1938(?): **Share' Fumm Ter'et el-Esma'iliya** ('Esma'iliya Canal Inlet Str.'); *see* Share' Ter'et el-Esma'iliya.

el-Fatikan, Share' (el-Zamalek)
'Vatican Str.' Since c.1929, after the Apostolic Nunciature (the Vatican embassy), whose entrance is on adjoining Share' Muhammad Mazhar.

Fatma el-Yusef, Share' (el-Munira)
Probably since 1954, after Fatma el-Yusuf (1897 or 1898–1958), pioneering theater actress and journalist, known as Roz (Rose) el-Yusef. El-Yusef, who came to Egypt from Lebanon as a young girl and first made a name for herself on the stage, taking lead roles with the troupes of Georges Abyad (from 1912) and Yusef Wahbi (from 1923) and being hailed by the press as the 'Sarah Bernhardt of the East.' She then turned to journalism and founded a highly

successful and often controversial cultural and political weekly magazine that she named after herself (first issue October 1926) and which continues to appear, though nationalized (1960). She was the mother of novelist Ehsan 'Abd el-Quddus, who from 1945 served as the magazine's editor.

> From at least 1914 probably to 1954: **Share' Afrah el-Angal** ('Nuptials of the Royal Children Str.'), after the combined weddings of three of Khedive Esma'il's sons and one of his daughters, which began on 15 January 1873 and were cele-brated in the el-Qasr el-'Ali palace on the other side of Share' Qasr el-'Eini; the three brides and one groom were all, likewise, descendants of Muhammad 'Ali. The eldest son was Prince Muhammad Tawfiq (1852–92), who would succeed Khedive Esma'il (*see* former Share' Tawfiq, *under* Share' Muhammad Beih el-Alfi and Share' 'Urabi); he married Princess Amina Elhami (1858–1931), daughter of Khedive Abbas Helmi I (*see* former Share' el-Walda, *under* Share' Tawfiq Deyab). The next oldest was Prince Hesein Kamel (1853–1917), who would succeed Khedive 'Abbas Helmi II (*see* former Share' el-Sultan Hesein Kamel, *under* Share' el-Sheikh Rihan); he married Princess 'Ein el-Hayah Ahmad (1858–1910), daughter of Khe-dive Esma'il's elder brother. The third son was Prince Hasan (1854–88); he married Princess Khadiga Muhammad 'Ali (1856–1915), a granddaughter of Muhammad 'Ali Basha. The daughter was Princess Fatma Esma'il (1853–1920) (*see* former Share' el-Amira Fatma Hanim, *under* Share' 'Ali Hasan); she married Prince Muhammad Tusun (1853–76), a son of Muhammad Sa'id Basha, Khedive Esma'il's predecessor. The celebrations lasted forty days and nights and the illuminations decorating the palace and its surroundings were so brilliant that, according to some authorities, they gave the adjacent district of el-Munira ('the Radiant') its name. They are also said to have contributed to the country's bankruptcy, which led to foreign control of its budget.

el-Fawwala, Share' (Downtown)

'Bean Sellers' Str.' Since 1957, after the old neighborhood of el-Fawwala (Ard el-Fawwala, or 'Bean Sellers' Yard), whose narrow lanes were destroyed, starting as early as 1911, by the running through of this and other broad, straight streets and the construction on them of buildings belonging to Bank Misr and the companies created by it (*see* Share' el-Sharekat). The former streets that most closely corresponded to today's Share' el-Fawwala were Share' el-Mashhadi (which ran east from Share' Muhammad Farid before turning north) and Haret el-Mashhadi (which continued Share' el-Mashhadi's eastward course but stopped approximately in the middle of the block). Some maps still label this street Share' el-Mashhadi.

Fayed, Haret (el-Azbakiya)
By 1887, after a certain Fayed Beih, whose house was on this street at the date given.

Fayruz, Haret (el-Munira)
Probably by 1914; unidentified. Fayruz ('Turquoise') is a female given name, perhaps that of an early resident.

Filibs, Mamarr (Downtown)
'Philips Passage.' Since c.1971, after the Netherlands-based Philips Company, which formed a joint-stock enterprise with the Egyptian state in 1957 for the production of lighting and other electrical appliances. The company occupied two floors of the building on the northwest corner of the passageway at the Share' 'Adli end, with administration on the upper floor, showrooms on the lower; the factory was in Alexandria. The joint-stock company was sold to private Egyptian companies in 2002. The passageway has probably existed since construction of the apartment block at #33 Share' Sherif, which backs onto it, between 1913 and 1928; the building, in the French Neo-Baroque Style, is listed as being of historical interest.

Fu'ad Serag el-Din, Share' (Garden City)
Since 2001, after Muhammad Fu'ad Serag el-Din Basha (1911–2000), politician and elder statesman. Serag el-Din, member of a family long involved with the Wafd Party, became its secretary-general in 1936, held numerous ministerial posts between 1942 and 1950, and was imprisoned several times following the

banning of political parties in 1962. In 1977, following the relaxation of restrictions on formal party politics, he founded the New Wafd Party. Serag el-Din's family mansion stands on this street at #10, at the intersection with Share' Kamel el-Shennawi.

> From at least 1925 to 2001: **Share' el-Saray el-Kubra** ('Great Palace Str.'), after the *haramlek* (private family quarters) of the el-Qasr el-'Ali palace complex on whose grounds Garden City is built. The *haramlek* was built by Ebrahim Basha (1789–1848) and demolished, along with the rest of el-Qasr el-'Ali, in 1903. A historical topographer, however, writing in 1925, claims that the street is not in the same place as the historical building.

Fumm el-Khalig, Midan (Fumm el-Khalig)
'Canal Mouth Str.' By 1909, after the inlet on the Nile that, from 1241, fed the el-Khalig el-Masri canal; it was here that annual festivities celebrating the cutting of an earth dam to admit fresh water into the canal took place at the height of the Nile flood, in August. Share' el-Khalig el-Masri, which follows the course of the old canal, no longer connects to the square, its southernmost stretch having disappeared under buildings and the widening of Share' Qasr el-'Eini and Share' Helwan.

Funduq Fakturya, Mamarr *see* Fakturya, Mamarr

el-Funduq, Kubri (Garden City)
'Hotel Bridge.' Since 1965, built to serve the then Meridien (later Grand Hyatt, now Grand Nile Tower) Hotel and the Higher Institute for Tourism and Hotels on Roda Island. On some maps, the bridge is called **Kubri 'Abd el-'Aziz Al Sa'ud**, after Share' 'Abd el-'Aziz Al Sa'ud, one of the main arteries on el-Manyal Island, toward which the bridge leads; the street is named after 'Abd el-'Aziz ebn 'Abd el-Rahman ebn Feisal ebn Turki ebn 'Abdallah ebn Muhammad Al Sa'ud (b.1875), founder of the Third Saudi State and King of Saudi Arabia from 1932 until his death in 1953.

el-Funduq, Mamarr *see* Fakturya, Mamarr

G

Gaber Salah (Jika), Share' *see* el-Shahid Gaber Salah (Jika), Share'

Gad Shahin, Haret (Downtown)
Probably since c.1914; unidentified. Gad Shahin is a man's name, perhaps that of an early resident.

el-Galaa', Kubri (el-Gezira)
'Evacuation Bridge.' Since 1947, in celebration of the evacuation (Arabic *galaa*) in March of that year of British forces from their barracks at Qasr el-Nil (army) and Bab el-Hadid (military police) and the dismantling of the railroad connecting the two. The choice of name was no doubt prompted by the fact that the bridge had previously been known popularly as Kubri el-Engeliz ('the Bridge of the British,' *see below*).

> From 1871 to 1947: **Kubri el-Bahr el-A'ma** ('Blind River Bridge'); the name refers to the channel that separates el-Gezira from el-Duqqi, el-'Aguza, and Embaba, which originally held water only during the annual flood. The channel was deepened in the 1870s to allow a year-round flow of water, permanently separating el-Gezira, for the first time, from the Nile's western bank. The original bridge (built 1872, widened 1914) opened using a swing mechanism to allow boat traffic to pass. In pre-1954 European-language maps, the bridge is usually referred to as "the English Bridge" or "le Pont des Anglais," and in official documents as **Kubri el-Engeliz** ('the Bridge of the British'). In popular parlance, the bridge is still sometimes referred to as **Kubri Badi'a**, after Badi'a Masabni (1892–1974), Turco-Lebanese dancer, actress, troupe-leader, and sometime wife of actor Nagib el-Rihani (*see* Share' Nagib el-Rihani), who built and managed a well-known open-air venue, the Casino Badea, to the south of the bridge on the Giza shore, where the Cairo Sheraton now stands.

el-Galaa', Share' (Downtown, el-Tawfiqiya)
'Evacuation Str.' By 1949, in commemoration of the evacuation (Arabic *galaa*) of British forces from their barracks at Bab

el-Hadid and Qasr el-Nil in March 1947. The choice of this street
to mark this event was probably due to the street's strong British associations: Qasr el-Nil barracks, the British army's largest in
Egypt, were located at its southern end, the British military police
barracks overlooked Midan Ramsis, and the British had built a
railroad parallel to the street to connect these. Previously the street,
which until the filling in of the Esma'iliya Canal in 1893 was a
simple field path running along the west side of the canal, was conceived of as consisting of two sections, as follows:

From its western end to a point opposite Share' Suq
el-Tawfiqiya:

From 1902 to 1947: **Share' Fumm el-Ter'a
el-Bulaqiya** ('Bulaq Canal Inlet Str.'), after an agricultural canal dug during the reign of Muhammad
'Ali Basha. Its inlet was originally just north of that of
the Esma'iliya Canal (inaugurated 1863; later, Share'
Ramsis) but later (after 1908) was moved to a point
near the mosque of Abu el-'Ela (taking its water from
the Esma'iliya Canal). The original inlet channel, which
this street represents, was filled in in 1902, following a
cholera outbreak, and the rest of the canal was filled in in
1912. Opposite Share' Suq el-Tawfiqiya the canal veers
to the north, away from the street.

From the same point to Midan Ramsis:

From c.1893 to 1947: **Share' Sidi el-Madbuli** (or
el-Matbuli), after the tomb of Sufi saint Ebrahim
(or Esma'il) el-Madbuli (or el-Matbuli), buried at an
unknown date in the late-thirteenth-century mosque of
'Usman el-Zaheri, located on the east side of the canal
on the northwest side of Midan Ramsis, under a huge
sycamore fig. This mosque was demolished in 1912
to make way for the British barracks, and the saint's
remains were moved to another resting place farther
south and on the west side of the street, which was visible until the 1970s; it has since been destroyed.

Galal Basha, Share' (el-Tawfiqiya)

By 1904, after 'Ali Galal Basha (d.1892) owner of the palace and grounds that were cleared to make way for the extension of Share' 'Emad el-Din north of Share' Setta w-'Eshrin Yulyu. Galal was the only son of Ahmad el-Manikali (or el-Manakli, and other variants) Basha (d.1862), prominent companion-in-arms of Ebrahim Basha, sometime (1843–45) governor-general of the Sudan and minister of war, and model for the dyspeptic pasha who returns from the dead to inveigh against the changes taking place in Egypt in Muhammad el-Muwelhi's novel *What 'Isa ebn Hesham Told Us* (first published as a series, from 1898 to 1902). From him, Galal inherited land stretching from el-Azbakia to the Esma'iliya Canal in what would become the district of el-Tawfiqiya, whence the plethora and wide distribution there of thoroughfares (two *share's* and a *hara*) that have at times borne his name. 'Ali Galal's eldest son, Muhammad 'Ali Galal (1873–1922), Vienna-educated and a notable dandy, inherited further holdings from his mother, Princess Zubeida (1854–1940), a granddaughter of Muhammad 'Ali Basha. This did not prevent him from achieving penury, a state he attempted, unsuccessfully, to escape by founding in 1897, in a building erected on the site of his father's palace (farther south, at the corner of Share' Nagib el-Rihani and Share' Emad el-Din) the private gaming club for the aristocracy, and (in an annex) theater, known as the Club des Princes ('Princes' Club'), or Club des Quarante ('Club of Forty'). The art nouveau building, designed by Antonio Lasciac, still stands, though disfigured. The theater, which later would be taken over by Yusef Wahbi and (after division) shared with his rival Nagib el-Rihani, was probably the first to appear in what would become Cairo's 'Broadway,' which flourished along and around Share' 'Emad el-Din from the end of the nineteenth century to the revolution of 1952. On the role of the Galal family in the creation of the el-Tawfiqiya district, *see* Introduction page 7. Not to be confused with former Share' Galal (without the title 'Basha,' though this distinction is occasionally overlooked by mapmakers), now Share' Ahmad Zakariya, farther south.

Gamal el-Din Abu el-Mahasen, Midan (Garden City)

Since 1954; *see* Share' Gamal el-Din Abu el-Mahasen.

From at least 1935 to 1954: **Midan Esma'il Basha** (*see* former Share' Esma'il Basha, *under* next entry).

Gamal el-Din Abu el-Mahasen, Share' (Garden City)
Since 1954, probably in honor of the historian Gamal el-Din Abu el-Mahasen Yusef ebn Taghriberdi (c.1409–70), whose *Radiant Stars concerning the Kings of Egypt and Cairo* is the most important biographical chronicle of the Mamluk era.

From at least 1925 to 1954: **Share' Esma'il Basha**, after either (1) Khedive Esma'il (r.1863–79; *see* former Share' el-Khedeiwi Esma'il, *under* Share' el-Tahrir), in which case the name may have been chosen because the street runs in the direction of the three palaces built by the khedive for three of his daughters, Fa'iqa (adopted), Gamila, and Tawhida, on the opposite (east) side of Share' Qasr el-'Eini, or (2) Esma'il Basha Seddiq (1830–76), Khedive Esma'il's milk-brother, who rose, through his skill as a financial administrator and because of his efforts to promote Khedive Esma'il's image among his subjects, to the post of general supervisor (*mufattesh*) of both Lower and Upper Egypt, a position of such influence and power that he was known as 'the Little Khedive'; his palace still stands, on nearby Midan Lazughli, east of Share' Qasr el-'Eini, and that too may be claimed as a reason for the choice of name. Esma'il el-Mufattesh eventually lost the favor of Khedive Esma'il, allegedly for insisting that the country's financial difficulties could be solved without resort to European moneylenders. In 1879, it is said, he was visited by Khedive Esma'il, who took him back with him to his palace on el-Gezira, after which he disappeared. Officially, he left for a new posting in Dongola, became sick there, and died. Unofficially, he was brutally murdered and thrown into the Nile. When asked about the ambiguity of the street's name, the official responsible is said to have claimed that it was deliberate: should anyone object to the absence (at that time) of a street named after the Khedive, he could point to this, and if anyone objected to the Khedive being honored with such a small street, he could say that Esma'il el-Mufattesh was intended. This street appears to have been the first in Garden City to have its name recorded on a map (1929).

el-Gamasa, Darb ('Abdin)

By 1809; unidentified. The name means 'buffalo-herders' but is also the name (changed in 1930, at their request, to Bani Taleb) of a clan of Upper Egyptian Bedouin, and of a town on Egypt's north coast, people from either of which may have come to settle here.

el-Game', Share' *see* Game' 'Abdin, Share'

Game' 'Abdin, Share' ('Abdin)

'Abdin's Mosque Str.,' or **Share' el-Game'** ('Mosque Str.'). By 1907, after the mosque (also known as Game' el-Fath) that is incorporated into the 'Abdin Palace's eastern wall. The mosque was renovated in 1631 by el-Lewaa' el-Sultani 'Abdin Beih, an Ottoman army commander, whose house was located to its east, and who thus provided its alternative name of Game' 'Abdin (but *see also* former Midan 'Abdin, *under* Midan el-Gumhuriya); it was enlarged by King Fu'ad (r.1917–36). The mosque acts as a second home for the remains of notables and holy men whose tombs were demolished, along with many houses, when Khedive Esma'il widened and lengthened this street, which originally stopped short of Share' Hasan el-Akbar, to allow construction of the eastern wall of 'Abdin Palace.

> From 1885 to before 1907: **Share' 'Abdin**, after either the 'Abdin Palace, along whose eastern wall the street runs, or the district in general (*see above*). The name appeared in this location when an older Share' 'Abdin was renamed Share' Kawala (*see under* Share' el-Gumhuriya), and disappeared when that street reverted to its original name.

> By 1885: **Share' Ragheb** (or **Ragab**?) **Agha**, after an individual whose house was located at the southern end of the street. Ragheb and Ragab are two distinct names; curiously, both spellings occur in the Arabic sources with reference to the same street.

Game' el-Esma'ili, Share' ('Abdin)

'Mosque of el-Esma'ili Str.' By 1888, after the mosque built in 1347 by Arghun Shah el-Esma'ili el-Kameli (d.1357), a Mamluk

commander who rose to be governor of Gaza, Aleppo, and finally
Damascus. 'El-Esma'ili' indicates that Arghun was acquired as a
slave during the reign of el-Malik el-Saleh Esma'il ebn Muhammad Naser el-Din (1342–45).

Game' Muhebb, Share' (el-Zamalek)

'Muhebb Mosque Str.' Since 1969, in which year the Muhebb
Mosque, named after Muhammad Muhebb Pasha (1874–1935)
and built by his two daughters "to realize their late father's wishes"
(commemorative plaque), was opened. According to French sociol-
ogist Jacques Berque in *Egypt: Imperialism and Revolution*, Muhebb
was a "wealthy bourgeois" and the first father of high social status
to allow his daughters to go unveiled. The mosque itself is on Share'
Hasan Sabri, opposite the western end of this street.

> From 1954 to 1969: **Share' el-Amir el-Musabbahi**, in
> historical evocation of 'Ezz el-Mulk Muhammad ebn Abi
> el-Qasem el-Musabbahi (977–1029), a high official of
> Fatimid Egypt and boon companion of the Fatimid caliph
> el-Hakim bi-Amr Ellah who wrote some thirty books,
> including a history of the latter's reign and works on astron-
> omy. These survive only in the form of excerpts quoted by
> other medieval historians.

> From 1913 to 1954: **Share' el-Amir Hasan** ('Prince Hasan
> Str.'), after Prince Hasan Esma'il Basha (1854–88), third
> son of Khedive Esma'il, commander-in-chief of the Egyp-
> tian army during the Egyptian–Ethiopian War (1876), war
> minister (1876), commander of the Egyptian contingent in
> the Russo–Turkish War (1877–78), and high commissioner
> for the Sudan (1884–85). This area of el-Zamalek—imme-
> diately north of Khedive Esma'il's palace of Saray el-Gezira
> and extending to Share' Setta w-'Eshrin Yulyu—is home
> to twelve streets formerly named after princes of the ruling
> family. Of these, six were the sons of Khedive Esma'il (not
> represented were two who died young plus his second son,
> Muhammad Tawfiq, later to become khedive and have the
> whole district of el-Tawfiqiya named after him), the others
> his cousins or grandsons.

Gameʿ Nash'at, Shareʿ (el-Zamalek)

'Nash'at Mosque Str.', or **Shareʿ Hasan Nash'at**. Since c.1942, after the nearby Nash'at Mosque built by Hasan Nash'at Basha (1895–1964), King Fu'ad's chef de cabinet (1924) who established the pro-king Union (Ettehad) Party in an attempt to break the power of the Wafd Party at the 1925 parliamentary elections, only to meet with humiliating defeat. During the Second World War, Nash'at served as ambassador to Britain. He is buried in the mosque with his wife.

> From c.1930 to c.1942: **Shareʿ el-Duktur Serubeyan**, unidentified. Dr. Seropian, apparently an Armenian Egyptian, was perhaps an early resident of the street.

Gameʿ el-Rammah, Zuqaq (ʿAbdin)

'El-Rammah Mosque Cul-de-sac.' Before the Esmaʿiliya project to the present, after the mosque of Qani Bay el-Rammah (*see* Haret el-Rammah).

el-Gamʿiya el-Sharʿiya, Shareʿ (Downtown)

'Islamic Law Association Str.' From after 1947, after the Islamic Law Association mosque on this street.

Gamʿiyet el-Shubban el-Muslemin, Shareʿ (Downtown)

'Young Men's Muslim Association Str.' Since 1935, when the head-quarters of the association (founded 1927) moved to this street from earlier premises on Shareʿ Qasr el-ʿEini. The association, founded by Dr. ʿAbd el-Hamid Saʿid (*see* Shareʿ el-Duktur ʿAbd el-Hamid Saʿid), aims to develop Muslim youth intellectually, culturally, and physically through seminars and camps and is represented in all the country's governorates.

el-Ganayni, Haret (Downtown)

'Gardener's Lane.' Probably by 1914.

Ghandi, Shareʿ *see* el-Zaʿim el-Hendi Ghandi, Shareʿ

Garidet el-Seyasa, Haret (el-Munira)

'*El-Seyasa* Newspaper Lane.' Since 1962, after a daily newspaper ('Politics') founded in 1922 as the voice of the newly created Constitutional

Liberals Party, and joined in 1926 by *Magallat el-Seyasa al-Usbuʿiya* (Weekly Politics Magazine), a journal of criticism. Prominent contributors were Taha Hesein (*see* Shareʿ Taha Hesein), who contributed a weekly column of criticism entitled "Hadith el-Arbeʿaa'" (Wednesday Talk), Muhammad Hesein Heikal, and Mahmud ʿAzmi (*see* Shareʿ Mahmud ʿAzmi). The building housing its offices was on this street until demolished (probably before 1970). Some maps already show this name before 1962, which is the date of the decree ratifying this name and quashing the one that follows.

> By 1935 to 1962: **Haret el-Seyasa** ('*el-Seyasa* Lane'), after the above-mentioned journal, the change presumably being considered necessary to allay fears as to the nature of the activity for which the street was named.

Gatenyu, Mamarr (Downtown)
After 1920, after the Gattegno department store (formerly Le Bon Marché), housed in the Gattegno Building (1920) on Shareʿ Muhammad Farid, a notable example of the neo-Venetian style. The store closed recently, its premises taken over by a clothing retailer. Caleb Gattegno (1911–88), the innovative educator in the teaching of mathematics, languages, and reading, belonged to the family that owned the store, being born in Alexandria and living in Egypt until 1935. The passageway is also sometimes called **Mamarr Benseyon Roma** ('Pension Roma Passage'), after a well-known small hotel located there.

Gawad Husni, Shareʿ *see* el-Shahid Gawad Husni, Shareʿ

el-Gawali, ʿAtfet
By 1935; *see* Shareʿ el-Gawali, which this street crosses.

el-Gawali, Shareʿ (el-Munira)
By 1935; *gawali* (literally, 'those in exile') was an Egyptian term for the poll tax paid by non-Muslims before the modernization of the Egyptian state; its relevance to this street is unclear.

el-Gazzar, ʿAtfet (Downtown)
By 1863; literally, 'Butcher's Alley,' though el-Gazzar may also be a family name, perhaps that of early residents.

el-Gehadiya, Share' (Garden City)
'Army Str.' By 1935, probably after the troops quartered at the el-Qasr el-'Ali palace complex, on whose grounds Garden City is built.

Gemei'a, Darb ('Abdin)
'Little Gum'a's Side Street.' By 1913; Gum'a is a male given name, perhaps that of an early resident.

Gemei'i, Share' (Garden City)
Since after the Second World War; unidentified. The street does not appear in the original 1906 layout of Garden City; it may be named after a sometime resident.

Genan el-Zuhri, Share' (el-Munira)
'El-Zuhri's Gardens Str.' By 1914, in historical evocation of market gardens whose original owner was Abu el-'Abbas 'Abd el-Wahhab ebn Musa ebn 'Abd el-'Aziz el-Zuhri, an early Abbasid-era chief of police. El-Zuhri's extensive gardens once included the el-Nasriya neighborhood (in which today's street is located) and parts of 'Abdin.

el-Gendi, Haret (el-Munira)
Date unknown; unidentified. El-Gendi (literally, 'cavalry trooper') may be a male given name or a family name, perhaps that of an early resident or residents.

el-Geneina, 'Atfet ('Abdin)
'Garden Alley.' Since c.1908, probably after the public garden that occupied the surrounding area before the subdivision and development of former Midan el-Mabduli (*see under* Midan el-Gumhuriya).

Geneinet el-Tawashi, Haret (el-Azbakiya)
'Eunuch's Garden Lane.' By 1887, after a large commercial veg-etable-growing enterprise known as 'the Eunuch's Field' (Gheit el-Tawashi), which existed in the area until the laying out of streets for the Esma'iliya project.

el-Gerand, Mamarr (el-Tawfiqiya)
'Grand (Hotel) Passage.' Since 1941, when the hotel from which it
takes its name was built, along with the two other buildings in the
Streamline Moderne style that define the passageway.

el-Gezira, Share (el-Zamalek/el-Gezira)
'Island Str.' Since at least 1897, after the island on which
el-Zamalek stands, formerly known as Geziret Bulaq ('Bulaq
Island') after the settlement closest to it on the Nile's eastern bank.
The street was the first on the island to be named and defines the
eastern and northern sides of the Gezira Sporting Club, created
between 1882 and 1883 (as the Khedivial Sporting Club) from a
portion of the grounds of Esma'il's palace (Saray el-Gezira). Until
sometime before 1937, this name also covered what is now Share
el-Sayyeda Umm Kulsum on el-Gezira's western bank from
its intersection with today's Share el-Gezira south to the end of
the island.

el-Gezira el-Gedida, Share ('Abdin)
'New Island Str.' By 1904, after the district of el-Munira, formerly
known as el-Gezira ('the Island') because originally defined on two
sides by water (the Nile on the west and el-Khalig el-Masri on the
east; *see* Share Bur Sa'id). Not to be confused with Share el-Gezira
in el-Zamalek.

Gheit Abu el-Shamat, 'Atfet (el-Munira)
'Abu el-Shamat's Field Alley.' Date unknown; Abu el-Shamat (literally, 'the man with the birthmarks') may be a family name. A
"Field of Abu Shamat" and a "Lake of Abu Shamat" are recorded
in a map dating to no later than 1801.

Gheyas el-Din, Sekket or **Share** (el-Zamalek)
By 1910, probably to honor Gheyas el-Din Abu el-Fath 'Umar
ebn Ebrahim el-Nishaburi el-Khayyami, better known as Omar
Khayyam (1048–1131), Persian scientist and poet. The choice of
name may have been inspired by Share Abu el-Feda, named after
another medieval scientist, into which this street runs.

Ghubashi, Share᷑ (el-Munira)
Probably c.1935; unidentified. Ghubashi is a family name, perhaps
that of early residents. The area, immediately to the south of shunt-
ing yards belonging to the Helwan Light Railway, appears not to
have been built up before the date given.

el-Gumhuriya, Midan (᷑Abdin)
'Republic Sq.' Since 1954, in honor of the proclamation of a republic in 1953. Some signs (including one put up in 2017) bear this
name; others, however, bear the square's best known former name,
Midan ᷑Abdin. Even an official map published in 2009 refers to the
square as Midan ᷑Abdin, underscoring both the tenacity of older,
popularly adopted names and the fragility of 'official' names. In the
end, it is up to the reader to decide which name s/he prefers.

> From 1952 or 1953 to 1954: **Midan ᷑Urabi**, after Ahmad
> Basha ᷑Urabi. On 9 September 1881, the square had wit-
> nessed a confrontation between ᷑Urabi and the Egyptian
> army on one side and Khedive Tawfiq on the other at which
> the khedive gave in to the army's demands. With the renam-
> ing of the square as Midan el-Gumhuriya, this name was
> transferred to a square in el-Tawfiqiya (*see* Midan ᷑Urabi).

> From 1874 to 1952 or 1953: **Midan ᷑Abdin,** after the district
> of ᷑Abdin, which is closely associated with the Qasr ᷑Abdin
> palace, official seat of the Egyptian monarch from the time of
> Khedive Esma᷑il (r.1863–79). The district takes its name from
> ᷑Abdin Beih, an Ottoman officer with the title of Commander
> of the Sultanic Brigade, who is said to have lived to the east
> of the palace in the seventeenth century. ᷑Abdin Beih built the
> ᷑Abdin mosque that is incorporated into the palace's eastern
> wall (*see* Share᷑ Game᷑ ᷑Abdin) and turned the surrounding
> land into a religious endowment, which Esma᷑il was able to
> acquire by exchanging for it endowed lands elsewhere. Esma᷑il
> appears to have created his first palace on the site at some point
> between 1854 and 1860, before his accession, by remodeling
> and combining two mansions, one belonging to Khurshid
> Basha el-Sennari (perhaps the same Khurshid Basha who
> governed Egyptian Sudan from 1826 to 1838), the other to a

certain Ebrahim Beih el-Khogahdar. Starting in 1863, the year
of his accession, he began the conversion of the palace into a
building fit to serve as Egypt's new center of power, a process
not completed until 1878, shortly before his dethronement.
The creation of the square in front of the palace was facilitated
by the presence of a large pond, later drained, known as Berket
el-Farayin ('Larvae Lake') or Berket el-Yaraqan ('Tadpole
Lake'). In April 1952, a statue of King Fu'ad I (r.1917–36) was
erected at the west end of the square but remained unveiled at
the outbreak of revolution in July of that year; the statue was
removed in 1953, the plinth in 1958.

From 1885 to no later than 1946, the name **Midan el-Mabduli** applied to the space at the southeast corner of the square,
after the mosque of Muhammad Beih el-Mabduli to its south
(*see also* Share῾ el Sheikh Rihan). By 1946, this space had been
given the same name as the larger part of the square, giving
the latter its present-day 'L' shape.

el-Gumhuriya, Share῾
(῾Abdin, el-Azbakiya, Downtown, el-Tawfiqiya)
'Republic Str.' Since 1954, in celebration of Egypt's declaration of
a republic in 1953; the choice of this street to affirm the ideological
shift was probably due to its role as the main artery connecting the
royal palace to the rest of Egypt. As such, the street often witnessed
royal pageantry.

From 1933 to 1954: **Share῾ Ebrahim**, after Ebrahim Basha,
Muhammad Ali's eldest son and heir, thus unifying what had
earlier been four separate, aligned streets and creating a single
corridor from today's Midan el-Gumhuriya to Midan Ramsis
and easing royal access to the railway station at Bab el-Hadid.
These streets were, from south to north:

From Midan el-Gumhuriya to Midan el-Ubera:
From 1847 to before 1882 and again from at least 1908 to
1933: **Share῾ ῾Abdin**, after the ῾Abdin palace and neighborhood. From before 1882 to before 1908, this name was
switched to the street now known as Share῾ el-Game῾ or

Share' Game' 'Abdin. Plans existed to extend this street
southward until it met Share' Darb el-Gamamiz (out of
area) but were abandoned for lack of funds.

From at least 1882 to before 1908: **Share' Qawala** or
Kawala, after Kavala in north-eastern Greece, birthplace of Muhammad 'Ali Basha, founder of Egypt's
modern royal dynasty. In 1908, this name disappeared
from this thoroughfare, which reverted to its former
name of Share' 'Abdin, while the name Share' Qawala
was reassigned to the street running west from Midan
el-Gumhuriya to Share' 'Abd el-'Aziz Gawish.

The west side of Midan el-Ubera:
From at least 1874 to 1933: **Midan el-Ubera** (*see* main
entry).

From Midan el-Ubera to the intersection of Share'
el-Gumhuriya and Share' Nagib el-Rihani (formerly
Midan Qantaret el-Dekka):
From 1885 to 1933: **Share' Kamel**, after Yusuf Basha
Kamel, Ottoman statesman, who built a palace on part
of the site of the former palace of Alfi Beih, which had
been gifted to his wife, Princess Zeinab, a daughter of
Muhammad 'Ali Basha, by his father-in-law (the rest of
the building was sold by her to Samuel Shepheard, who
turned it into Shepheard's Hotel, whose terrace overlooked
this street). Kamel Basha's marriage to Zeinab in 1845 was
one of a number of alliances between the Egyptian royal
family and the Ottoman elite at this time; strife within the
royal family would, however, require the couple to divorce
under Muhammad 'Ali's successor, and send Kamel Basha
into exile in Aswan, from where he escaped to Istanbul;
the couple remarried there in 1851. Many older maps
show the name of this street as **Share' Kiamel**, reflecting
the Turkish pronunciation of the name.

From Midan Qantaret el-Dekka to Midan Ramsis:
From 1905 to 1933: **Share' Nubar**, after Nubar Basha

Nubarian (1825–99), who had his residence on the street; later this name was reassigned (*see* Share' Nubar, main entry). Before 1905, this street was called interchangeably either:

From 1847 to 1905: **Share' Qantaret el-Dekka** ('Bench Bridge Str.'; *see* Haret Qantaret el-Dekka). In 1905, this name was reassigned to the street now called Share' Nagib el-Rihani.

or:

From at least 1863 to 1905: **Share' Bab el-Hadid** ('Iron Gate Str.'), after the westernmost bastion of the northern city wall built by Salah el-Din (Saladin), demolished in 1847, to which it led, or **Share' Midan Bab el-Hadid**, after the square to which it led. These names were durable: their abolition in favor of Share' Nubar had to be officially repeated in 1913.

H

Hadiqet el-Nasr, Haret (el-Tawfiqiya)
'Victory Garden Lane.' After 1952, after the open-air Cinema Nasr ('Cinema Victory'), now closed, on this street. The street runs down the east side of the Victoria Hotel (*see* Mamarr Fakturya), and the post-1952 name transforms the 'Victoria' of the colonial period into the 'Victory' of the revolutionary era.

Haggag, 'Atfet (el-Munira)
Probably by 1935; unidentified. Haggag may be a family name, perhaps that of early residents.

el-Hakim, Share' (el-Munira)
Probably by 1935; unidentified, though in some sources the name is given as Share' Reda el-Hakim. Reda is a given name and el-Hakim may be either a description ('the physician') or a family name.

el-Halawani, ʿAtfet (el-Munira)
'Confectioner's Alley.' Date unknown.

Halim, Shareʿ (el-Tawfiqiya)
Since no earlier than 1947, after Prince Muhammad ʿAbd el-Halim Basha (1830–94), seventeenth son of Muhammad ʿAli Basha, who had a mansion here, created from two older houses. Prince ʿAbd el-Halim held high position, serving as governor of the Sudan in 1856 and president of the privy council (1863–68) but contested Esmaʿil's right to the governorship of Egypt and was exiled to Istanbul in 1868, where he was integrated into the imperial elite; his son Saʿid Halim (1865–1921) became grand vizier of the Ottoman Empire and built a palace, still standing, on Shareʿ Shambuliyon; Saʿid Halim would also be accused of treason (against the Ottoman sultan) and sent into exile, though subsequently acquitted. This name formerly applied to Shareʿ Muhammad Beih el-Alfi.

> From no earlier than 1929 to no later than 1947: part of **Midan Halim**, after Muhammad ʿAbd el-Halim Basha (*see above*), whose palace (replaced by buildings, including baths and cinemas) occupied the center of the quadrant formed today by Shareʿ Madraset el-Alsun on the north, Shareʿ Ebrahim ʿAbd el-Qader el-Mazni on the west, and Shareʿ Halim on the east and south. Despite the changes, signs for Midan Halim abound, and the name is more widely used than any of those that have, officially, replaced it.

Hamada, Haret (Fumm el-Khalig)
Date unknown; unidentified. Hamada is a male given name, perhaps that of an early resident.

Hamdi Seif el-Nasr, Shareʿ *see* el-Fariq Ahmad Hamdi Seif el-Nasr, Shareʿ

Hanna Mikha'il, ʿAtfet (el-Munira)
Since perhaps 1935; unidentified. Hanna Mikha'il is a man's name, perhaps that of an early resident.

Hasan el-Akbar, Share' ('Abdin)

Since 1890, the name supposedly being a distortion of Hasan el-Anwar, a great-grandson (d.784) of 'Ali ebn Abi Taleb, cousin and son-in-law of the Prophet Muhammad: though Hasan el-Anwar is buried in the Hejaz, popular opinion claimed a grave unearthed during road work at the entrance to this street as his. A mausoleum was built over the tomb in 1883, but is now, following further reconfiguration of the area, behind the 'Abdin Palace wall. The same person reportedly has occupied, under his original name, a second tomb, in Old Cairo, since the sixteenth century and lends his name to a street there. The name **Share' Bab el-Khalq** appears in some sources from 1912 to 1928, no doubt reflecting popular usage, since the street leads to the Bab el-Khalq district (out of area).

> From 1847 to 1890: **Share' Bab el-Luq**, after the original Bab el-Luq ('Silt Gate'), in the city's western wall, that stood on the site occupied today by Midan Muhammad Farid, the name applying originally to the entire length of the thoroughfare leading from Midan Bab el-Khalq (out of area) via Share' Sami el-Barudi (out of area) and this street to the square.

> Anciently to 1847: **Share' Gemmeiza**, after the mosque of Gemmeiza (also called el-Sayyed Hashem) formerly on this street.

Hasan 'Asem, Share' (el-Zamalek)

Since 1954, after Hasan Basha 'Asem, public prosecutor (1894–95) and grand chamberlain to Khedive 'Abbas Helmi II. 'Asem's refusal to allow malfeasance by the khedive in the management of lands held as religious endowments led to his dismissal. Thereafter, he devoted his time, gratis, to supervising the educational work of the Islamic Charitable Society. 'Asem's integrity was unshakeable—it is said that he refused admission to one of the society's schools to the son of the donor who had paid for its construction because the boy was one month too old. Previously, the street consisted of three parts, each with a name of its own, the names changing at different times:

From Shareʿ ʿAbd el-ʿAziz Abaza to Shareʿ el-Barazil:

From 1913 to 1954: **Shareʿ el-Amir ʿUmar,** after Prince
Muhammad Umar Tusun (1872–1944), a grandson of
Muhammad Saʿid Basha known both for his own achievements in agriculture, entomology, and archaeology (he
pioneered the rediscovery of abandoned Christian monaster-
ies) and for his patronage in these areas (he became president
of the Royal Agricultural Society in 1932, sponsored the
introduction of improved cereal strains, and offered a prize
for the eradication of the boll weevil). He was particularly
active in Alexandria, where he was born, and was sometimes
referred to in the press as 'the Prince of Alexandria.' This area
of el-Zamalek—immediately north of Khedive Esmaʿil's
palace of Saray el-Gezira and extending to Shareʿ Setta
w-ʿEshrin Yulyu—is home to twelve streets named after
princes of the ruling family. Of these, six are the sons of Khedive Esmaʿil (not represented were two who died young and
his second son, Muhammad Tawfiq, later to become khedive
and have the whole district of el-Tawfiqiya named after him)
and the others his grandsons or cousins.

From Shareʿ el-Barazil to Shareʿ Shagaret el-Durr:
From no earlier than 1926 to 1954: **Shareʿ Kumbuni,** after St.
Daniel Comboni (1831–81), founder of the Comboni Fathers,
a congregation of Roman Catholic missionaries whose primary
vocation originally lay in sub-Saharan Africa. In 1884, Comboni's successor created a farm on land sold to the missionaries
on favorable terms by the government and covering the greater
part of the island north of this street, to be worked by Christian refugees fleeing the Mahdist uprising in Sudan (the size
of the concession may be judged by the fact that a boys' school
was established on this street, a girls' school at a distance on
Shareʿ Muhammad Anis). Most of the land has since been sold
by the Church, but the immediate area still holds the Comboni
School and St. Joseph's Church.

From Shareʿ Shagaret el-Durr to Shareʿ el-Mansur
Muhammad:

From no earlier than 1926 to 1954: **Share' el-Qeddis Yusef** ('St. Joseph Str.'), after the church located nearby between today's Share' Hasan 'Asem and Share' Ahmad Sabri. This name continues to appear on some maps.

Hasan Murad, Share' (Garden City)

Since after 1973, after Hasan Murad (1903–70), a news cameraman who pioneered the Egyptian news reel through his work on *Garidet Masr el-Sinema'iya* (Egypt Cinema Journal), irregularly produced from 1939. Murad, who died in a car accident while filming President Gamal 'Abd el-Naser visiting the Suez Canal front during the War of Attrition (1967–70), lived on the street.

From at least 1935 to at least 1973: **Share' el-Fasqiya** ('Fountain Str.'), after a feature of the el-Qasr el-'Ali palace complex, on whose grounds today's Garden City is built; this may have been the two-tiered, marble fountain that once stood in Midan el-Esma'iliya (today's Midan el-Tahrir), moved there following the demolition of the palace in 1903 and replaced by a larger fountain in 1955.

Hasan Nash'at, Share' *see* Game' Nash'at, Share'

Hasan Sabri, Share' (Zamalek)

Since late 1940 or soon after, after Hasan Sabri Basha (1875–1940), teacher, parliamentarian, cabinet minister, and briefly prime minister. After a career in education, Sabri was elected to parliament in 1926 as a deputy and in 1931 as a senator. In 1933, he served as finance minister and in 1934 became Egypt's last minister to London before the country's legation there was raised to the status of an embassy. In 1936, he served as commerce and communications minister, and, for less than a year—as a compromise candidate considered capable of working with all sides—as prime minister. He died suddenly on the floor of parliament on 14 November 1940 while delivering a speech. Hasan Sabri lived on Share' el-Gabalaya (*see below*).

From at least 1906 to at least 1940: **Share' el-Gabalaya** ('Little Mountain Str.'), after the artificial hill, or grotto, built by Khedive Esma'il in 1867, along whose eastern side the street ran until its renaming as Share' Hasan Sabri (at which point the name Share' el-Gabalaya was assigned to the street west of the grotto, now Share' el-Sayyeda Umm Kulsum; the street to the south of this point already bore this name). The grotto contained an aquarium and both grotto and aquarium were rehabilitated by the government and opened to the public in 1902 as Geneinet el-Asmak ('the Fish Garden').

Hawwash, 'Atfet (Downtown)
Probably by 1887; unidentified. Hawwash may be a family name, perhaps that of early residents.

el-Hekr, Haret ('Abdin)
'Land Grant Lane.' By 1848; the specific *hekr* to which this refers has not been identified (*see further* Zuqaq el-Ahkar).

el-Helal el-Ahmar, Share' (el-Tawfiqiya)
'Red Crescent Str.' Since c.1936, after the trauma hospital on this street, founded in that year by the Red Crescent Society and incorporated in 1964 into the Egyptian government's care system.

el-Helaliya, Haret (el-Munira)
'Lane of the Helalis.' Date unknown; the Helalis were professional café storytellers who sang epic poems exalting the feats of leaders of the Banu Helal tribe, which entered Egypt from the Arabian Peninsula in the second half of the tenth century fleeing famine and wreaked havoc across North Africa, leaving a lasting impression on the popular imagination.

Helwan, Share' (el-Munira, Fumm el-Khalig)
Or **Share' Masr–Helwan** or **Share' Sekket Hadid Helwan** ('Helwan Railway Connecting Str.'). By 1918, after the southern destination, or after the north–south route, of the Masr–Helwan light railway line (opened 1889, now incorporated into the Metro system), which, before it was directed underground, ran parallel to this street on the east, south of Share' Muhammad 'Ezz el-'Arab. Formerly, the name extended to the north, as an alternative name for Share' Mansur.

Heneidi, Haret (Fumm el Khalig)
By 1935; unidentified. Heneidi is a male given name, perhaps that of an early resident.

Hesein Hegazi, Share' (el-Munira)
By 1988, after Hesein Hegazi (1891–1961), a footballer who between 1911 and 1914 played for English clubs Dulwich Hamlet and Fulham, for England against Spain, and, on returning to Egypt, for both the Ahli and Zamalek clubs. Hegazi captained the Egyptian national team at the 1920 and 1924 Olympics and for eighty-eight years held the record for the oldest Olympic goalscorer, at age 37 years and 225 days. Hegazi retired from football in 1931 and in 1942 was appointed Supervisor of Football at the Ministry of Social Affairs.

> From 1940 to before 1988: **Share' Muhammad Sa'id**, after Muhammad Basha Sa'id (1863–1928), lawyer and politician, twice simultaneously prime minister and minister of the interior (1910 to 1914—on the assassination of Butrus Ghali—and 1919), who resigned, nevertheless, in November of the latter year in protest at the imposition on Egypt of the Milner Commission. In 1924, as minister of education in Sa'd Zaghlul's first cabinet, he introduced free education. He was the father of painter Mahmud Sa'id (1897–1964).

> From at least 1908 to 1940: **Share' el-Dakhliya** ('Interior Ministry Str.') after a former interior ministry building on Share' el-Falaki, into which this street runs. The ministry was founded in 1857 and moved into quarters here before the end of the nineteenth century. It moved to Share' el-Sheikh Rihan around 1925 and to a location outside Cairo in 2016.

Hesein el-Me'mar, Share' (Downtown)
'Architect Hesein Str.' By 1918, after Hesein Fahmi Basha (d. c.1885), nephew of Muhammad 'Ali Basha's son-in-law Muharram Beih (sometime governor of Alexandria and naval commander-in-chief). Fahmi was sent to Paris to study architecture and acquired the sobriquet el-Me'mar ('the Architect') on his return. As chief architect for the religious endowments authority

and supervising engineer for the royal palaces, he made the initial design for the el-Refa'i mosque, built by Khedive Esma'il's mother, Khushyar, as a mausoleum for herself and her descendants. He also remodeled the second Qasr el-Nil palace (*see* Share' Qasr el-Nil).

Before 1918 (east of Share' el-Nabarawi to Share' Ma'ruf): **Share' el-Busta** ('Post Office Str.').

el-Heseini, Haret (el-Azbakiya)
By 1888, after a certain el-Sayyed 'Ali el-Heseini el-Nahhas, whose house was on this street in this year.

Hosh Qutb, Haret ('Abdin)
'Qutb's Court Lane.' Since 1913; unidentified. Qutb is a male given name. The name **Haret Hosh el-Gella** ('Dung Court Lane') is used by residents and may be older and more authentic. Before 1913, this lane was part of Haret 'Abd el-Dayem.

Huda Sha'rawi, Share' (Downtown)
Since 1948, after Huda Sha'rawi Sultan (1879–1947), leader of the Egyptian Feminist Union from its foundation in 1923 until her death, and campaigner for women's education and suffrage; atypically, on marriage, she took the name of her husband and cousin, Ali Basha Sha'rawi, who was both a nationalist politician and a social activist. Sha'rawi came to national prominence in 1919 when she led the first protest march by women, against the exiling of Sa'd Zaghlul (*see* Share' Zaghlul). Her dramatic removal of her veil at Cairo's railway station on her return from a feminist conference in Europe in 1923 was another pivotal moment in the history of the Egyptian feminist movement. The choice of this street to commemorate Sha'rawi may have been due to the fact that the grounds of the palace of her father, Muhammad Sultan Basha, lay between this street and Share' Muhammad Sabri Abu 'Alam.

From at least 1887 to 1948: **Share' el-Sheikh Hamza,** after the tomb of Sheikh Hamza ebn Muhammad ebn Hebat Allah ebn 'Abd el-Men'em el-Sahabi, located east of the Felfela restaurant. Local tradition has it that the Sheikh was scheduled for relocation to allow an apartment block to be built on the same plot; all the workers' efforts, however, could not budge him, and the design of the building had to be altered to accommodate his tomb.

Husni Beih, ʿAtfet (el-Munira)
Probably by 1920; *see* Haret Husni Beih, from which it branches.

Husni Beih, Haret (el-Munira)
By 1920; unidentified. Husni is a male given name, perhaps that of an early resident.

I

For names whose first letter is sometimes given as 'I,' *see* under 'E.'

Izis, Shareʿ (Qasr el-Dubara)
'Isis Str.' From after 1947, after the Izis Building, an apartment block on this street, which is one of those built on the site and grounds of the Qasr el-Dubara palace (*see* former Midan Qasr el-Dubara, *under* Midan Simon Bulifar), demolished and subdivided in 1947.

J

el-Jentelman, Mamarr *see* Tawfiq Dos, Mamarr

Jika, Shareʿ *see* Salah Gaber (Jika), Shareʿ

K

el-Kabbara, Haret (el-Tawfiqiya)
By at least 1906; unidentified. In Arabic, *kabbara* may denote a group of people from a single place of origin whose name contains the letters *k–b–r*, such as Tall el-*Kebir*.

(el-)Kabudan, Haret ('Abdin)
'Captain's Lane.' By 1888; unidentified. Though often spelled 'Qabu-dan,' this Turkish title given naval commanders is pronounced as given here.

el-Kafarwa, Haret (Downtown)
By 1801; unidentified. The word *Kafarwa* might mean 'people from a place whose name begins with Kafr (meaning 'hamlet'),' such as Kafr el-Zayyat; several hundred such places exist in Lower Egypt. Alternatively, it may suggest persons linked to Kafur el-Labi (r.961–68), all-powerful regent of the short-lived Ekhshidi dynasty, after whom a nearby planation, el-Bustan el-Kafuri, was named.

> From at least 1801 to 1913: **Sekket el-Kafarwa**; it seems that the *sekka* was incorporated into the pre-existing *hara* in 1913.

Kamal el-Din Salah, Midan *see* el-Shahid Kamal el-Din Salah, Midan

Kamal el-Din Salah, Share' *see* el-Shahid Kamal el-Din Salah, Share'

Kamal Khalil, Share' *see* el-Shahid Kamal Khalil, Share'

Kamal el-Tawil, Share' (el-Zamalek)
Since 2005, after Kamal Mahmud Zaki el-Tawil (1923–2005), a composer who wrote songs for several Egyptian singers, most nota-bly 'Abd el-Halim Hafez and Umm Kulsum.

> From 1936 to 2005: **Share' el-Muntazah** ('Park Str.'), after a public garden created when the street was laid out following the construction of a permanent embankment, made possi-ble by the second raising of the Aswan Low Dam in 1933. Previously, the land had been seasonally farmed. This name still appears on recent maps. Not to be confused with Share' Muntazah el-Gezira at the south end of the island.

el-Kamel Muhammad, Share' (el-Zamalek)
By 1913, after el-Malek el-Kamel ('Perfect King') Muhammad ebn el-'Adel I ebn Naser el-Din, fifth Ayyubid ruler of Egypt

(r.1218–38) and seventh of Syria (r.1238). During the Fifth Cru-
sade, he stopped the Crusaders' advance on Cairo from Damietta
and ultimately defeated them.

Kamel el-Shennawi, Share' (Garden City)
Since 1966, after Mustafa Kamel el-Shennawi (1908–61), journalist, poet, and writer of musicals.

> From at least 1935 to 1966: **Share' el-Nabatat** ('Plants
> Str.'), probably referring to a nursery serving the palaces of
> the el-Qasr el-'Ali complex, on whose grounds Garden City
> is built.

el-Karamani, Share' (el-Munira)
Probably by 1935, after a Sufi saint of that name whose tomb, dating from the eighteenth century, stands on this street.

Karim el-Dawla, Haret (Downtown)
By 1911; unconfirmed reports identify this person as a head of the
Court of Cassation during the British occupation. The street is home
to the headquarters of the Association of Artists and Writers, known
as the Atelier, and of Hezb el-Tagammu' ('the Assembly Party'),
Egypt's first officially recognized leftist political party, founded 1976.

el-Kenisa, Darb *see* el-Kunayyesa, Darb

el-Keridi, 'Atfet (Downtown)
By 1801, after the mosque of Sufi saint Sheikh el-Keridi. The
mosque is ancient, was rebuilt in 1866 or 1867, and has since been
remodeled.

el-Khadrawi, Share' (Downtown)
Since 1970, after an automobile tire dealer of whom little is known.

> From 1940 to 1970: **Share' Afedesyan**, after Ohannes Ave-
> dissian (1890–1965), who came to Egypt from Turkey fleeing
> the massacres of Armenians that started in 1915, set up a
> cobbler's shop on Share' 'Abd el-Khaleq Sarwat, and built the
> apartment block at #3.

Khalifa, Haret (ʿAbdin)
By 1888; unidentified. Khalifa may be a family name, perhaps that
of early residents.

el-Khalig, Share' (el-Gezira)
'Gulf Str.' Probably since the 1970s, in honor of the Arab Gulf and
its nations.

Khalig el-Ghuri, Share' *see* Khalig el-Khor, Share'

Khalig el-Hur *see* Khalig el-Khor, Share'

Khalig el-Kholi, Share' *see* Khalig el-Khor, Share'

Khalig el-Khor, Share' (el-Tawfiqiya)
'Depression Canal Str.' From before the Esmaʿiliya project to c.1890
and from at least 1946 to the present, after an overspill conduit,
in some sources called Khalig Fumm el-Khor ('Depression Inlet
Canal') from el-Khalig el-Naseri leading to a low-lying area (*khor*) to
the north. The street is notable for the number of its aliases, some of
which are plainly mistakes while others may be legitimate alternative
names: thus, in various maps and books, one finds **Share' Khalig
el-Hur**, **Share' Khalig el-Ghuri**, and **Share' Khalig el-Kholi**.

> From c.1890 to no later than 1946: **Share' Tegran Dabru**,
> after Tigrane Basha D'Abro (1846–1904), a scion of the ancient
> Armenian royal family of the Bagratids (latterly accepted into
> the Neapolitan aristocracy) and son-in-law and secretary of
> Nubar Basha (*see* Share' Nubar). D'Abro served as foreign
> minister from 1891 to 1894 and was regarded as supportive of
> the young Khedive ʿAbbas Helmi II and unamenable to British
> pressure. His palace (demolished 1937) was the seat of the
> Société des Amis de l'Art ('Society of the Friends of Art') from
> the 1920s, the site of Cairo's first permanent public exhibition
> of modern art (1927–28) and its first wax museum.

Khalil Agha, Share' (Garden City)
Since 1935, after the chief eunuch (*agha*) of Khedive Esmaʿil's
mother, Khushyar (Hoshiar) Kadinafandi, whose palace, Qasr

el-Dubara, was close to the site of nearby Midan Simon Bulifar. Khalil Agha (d.1880) managed Khushyar's estates and acted as her agent in the political intrigues of the day. He amassed great wealth.

Khamastashar Mayu, Kubri (el-Zamalek, Downtown)

'Fifteenth of May Bridge' Since 2001 (completion of entire length), in commemoration of the day in 1971 on which President Anwar el-Sadat launched the Corrective Revolution, a purge of his enemies that led ultimately to the end of the Free Officers as a political force, as well as to disengagement from the USSR and a more liberal economic policy. The name applies to the entirety of the flyover that starts at Midan Sifinkis ('Sphinx Sq.') in el-Giza on the west, runs above Share' Setta w-'Eshrin Yulyu in el-Zamalek, and ends at Bulaq (Share' Setta w-'Eshrin Yulyu) on the east. The bridge was built in three stages, construction of a flyover above Share' Setta w-'Eshrin Yulyu in el-Zamalek being the last. Stages one and two required the replacement of two earlier bridges, as follows:

> On the west:
> From 1912 to 1982: **Kubri el-Zamalek** (between el-Giza and el-Zamalek), after the district at its eastern end. This bridge—made possible, like many of Cairo's bridges, by the construction of the first Aswan Dam (inaugurated 1902) and the subsequent stabilization of the river's banks—was equipped with a swing mechanism that opened for boats. Its replacement constituted the first stage of the construction of Kubri Khamastashar Mayu.

> On the east (with name changes):
> From 1954 to 1998: **Kubri Abu el-'Ela** (between el-Zamalek and Bulaq), after the mosque containing the tomb of Sufi saint Sheikh el-Saleh Hesein Abu el-'Ela (d.1486) near its eastern end. Following the construction of the first stage of Kubri Setta w-'Eshrin Yulyu, in the 1980s, Kubri Abu el-'Ela continued to be used for vehicular traffic entering el-Zamalek from the east until declared unsafe for vehicles in 1990, after which it was retained for pedestrian use only until finally being dismantled in 1998.

From 1932 to 1954: **Kubri Fu'ad**, after King Fu'ad I
(r.1917–36), simultaneously with the renaming of former
Share' Bulaq as Share' Fu'ad el-Awwal.

From 1912 to 1932: **Kubri Bulaq (el-Gedid)** ('(New)
Bulaq Bridge'), after the district on the eastern bank of
the Nile that the bridge links to el-Zamalek. The qualifier
distinguished this bridge from an earlier Kubri Bulaq (*see
below*). This steel-girder bridge with bascule mechanism
allowing the passage of river traffic was built in 1912 by
William Scherzer, an American, and not, as local legend
would have it, by Alexandre Eiffel, though Eiffel did build
the original Imbaba bridge farther downstream (completed 1892, replaced 1924) and a still-standing bridge in
the grounds of the Zoo; nor did either Eiffel or Scherzer
commit suicide by throwing himself off the bridge, despite,
again, local legend. Another Kubri Bulaq (also popularly
known in its day as Kubri Abu el-'Ela) once crossed the
Esma'iliya Canal at Es'af (intersection of Share' Setta
w-'Eshrin Yulyu and Share' Ramsis) but was demolished in
1911, following the filling in of the canal.

el-Khashshab, Share' *see* Bustan el-Khashshab, Share'

Khatun, 'Atfet ('Abdin)
Since at least 1904; *khatun* means 'lady' and is used as both a title
and a name.

el-Khawaga, Darb (el-Azbakiya)
'Foreigner's Side Street' or 'Coptic Merchant's Side Street.' By
1809; unidentified. *Khawaga* means '(non-Muslim) foreigner' and
was also formerly a title of respect used of Coptic merchants.

el-Khazendar, Midan (el-Azbakiya)
'Treasurer's Sq.' By 1888, after Ahmad Agha el-Khazendar
('Ahmad the Treasurer'; d.1816), a high-ranking Mamluk officer in Muhammad 'Ali's army who was sent by the latter to
accompany his son Prince Tusun on the expedition against
the Wahhabis of the Hejaz in 1815 and nicknamed Bunabarta

(Bonaparte) for his courage in battle. El-Khazendar built a mansion on nearby Share' el-Riwei'i (out of area). During the nineteenth century, the square was at the center of Cairo's hotel district.

This name, mentioned by 'Ali Mubarak (1888) as part of the original Esma'iliya plan, was apparently used interchangeably in its early years with the following:

> From at least 1874 to at least 1908: **Midan el-Bursa** ('Exchange Sq.'); though forgotten now (the official history of today's stock exchange makes no mention of it), a stock exchange must have existed here from at least the early 1870s: a play by Ya'qub Sannu' entitled *A Comedy Called the Cairo Bourse* was produced in 1871, while journalist Ebrahim el-Mewelhi (1844–1906) lost most of his money there, and later inveighed against the institution in his journal *Mesbah el-sharq* (The Lamp of the Orient).

> Over the same period, the name **Midan el-Bawaki** ('Arcade Sq.') was also used, perhaps informally.

Kheirat, Share' ('Abdin, el-Munira)
By 1888, after Kheirat Afandi, a calligrapher and the seal bearer of Muhammad 'Ali Basha, who penned the latter's decrees and lived on this street. The street was known during the first half of the twentieth century for its newspaper and literary review offices (*Mesbah el-sharq, el-'Alam, el-Mesaa', el-Difa' el-watani*) and for its cafes, frequented by poets and writers such as Hafez Ebrahim, Ebrahim 'Abd el-Qader el-Mazeni, and 'Abbas el-'Aqqad.

Khokhet el-Halawani, 'Atfet ('Abdin)
'Confectioner's Little Gate Alley,' or 'Confectioner's Wicket-gate Alley.' Probably by 1913.

Kilut Beih, Share' *see* Kulut Beih, Share'

el-Komi, Share' (el-Munira)
By 1863, after the small mosque on Share' el-Nasriya dedicated to the Sufi saint Sheikh Ebrahim el-Komi, who is buried there.

From 1908 to at least 1926, the now nameless intersection
of the northern end of this street with Share' Kheirat, Share'
Muhammad Mu'ezz el-'Arab, and Share' el-Nasriya was
known as **Midan el-Nasriya**.

Kudak, Mamarr (Downtown)

'Kodak Passage.' Probably since 1940, after the Egypt headquarters of
the Kodak Company, on the corner with Share' Adli. Kodak owned
the building, at first using the basement and first two floors, the upper
floors being rented as apartments, downsizing to only the ground
floor after the 1952 revolution. Kodak closed its offices around 2005.
A dead-end street open to cars until at least the 1970s, the passage
was extended to join Share' 'Abd el-Khaliq Sarwat during the 1990s.
In 2015, the passage was rehabilitated to showcase the potential of
Cairo's passageways to contribute to the city's revitalization.

Kulut (or Kilut) Beih, Share' (el-Azbakiya)

Since 1875, after Antoine Barthélemy Clot (1793–1868), a French
bphysician brought to Egypt by Muhammad 'Ali Basha in 1825,
initially to improve the health of Egypt's recently created modern
army. In 1827, Clot founded Egypt's first School of Medicine at
Abu Za'bal, northeast of Cairo (transferred to Qasr el-'Eini Hospital in 1837), followed by schools of midwifery and nursing; he
was also the first to promote modern sanitation in Cairo. Under
'Abbas Helmi I Basha (r.1848–54), the medical school was dis-
solved and Clot returned to France but he resumed his project
under Muhammad Sa'id Basha (r.1854–63). His books and lec-
ture notes, covering such diverse subjects as dissection, preventive
medicine, and quarantine, were among the first modern works of
science to be translated into Arabic. He also wrote a description
of contemporary Egypt, *Aperçu général sur l'Egypte* (An Overview
of Egypt; 1840). The street was opened around 1873 along with
former Share' Muhammad 'Ali, of which it is the northern extension, to link the Citadel (then the seat of government) with the
railway station at Bab el-Hadid (hence the large number of hotels,
now mostly unstarred). The change of name to Share' Kulut Beih,
which occurs at Midan el-Khazendar, marks a deviation from the
straight route originally planned, made at the request of the Coptic patriarch, to avoid demolition of St. Mark's cathedral, built in

1800. The street shares with Share' Muhammad 'Ali the honor of
being modern Cairo's first officially named street and one of the
few whose name has never changed; the original arcades, of which
some survive, were inspired by those of Rue de Rivoli in Paris.

el-Kunayyesa, Darb ('Abdin)
'Little Church Side Street.' By 1863. There is no church on this
street now. The name is often misspelled 'Darb el-Kenisa' on maps.

Kuntenental, Mamarr (Downtown)
'Continental Passage.' By 1935. These formerly elegant commercial
passageways (originally a single straight street) form part of the
Grand Continental Savoy Hotel, which opened in 1899, replacing
the New Hotel, one of Cairo's earliest. The hotel was gutted in the
26 January riots of 1952 and reopened following rebuilding in 1953
(from which time the present form of the passageway complex
probably dates); it was decommissioned as a hotel in 1990. Though
referred to on some older maps as Galléries Commerciales, it is not
to be confused with el-Mamarr el-Tugari ('Commercial Passage')
immediately to its west.

Kurnish el-Nil, Share'
(Downtown, Garden City, Fumm el Khalig, Qasr el-Dubara)
'Nile Corniche Str.' From the French, *route en corniche* or 'cliff
road.' The Corniche was created piecemeal over decades, starting
in the first half of the twentieth century, by taking land for a variety of pragmatic reasons from buildings whose plots ran down
to the river. For example, in 1910 an esplanade was constructed
from the southern border of the British Embassy's gardens in the
north to Qasr el-'Eini Hospital in the south to serve the residents
of recently laid-out Garden City. Development of the Corniche
climaxed in a burst of activity between 1954 and 1956, by which
time the construction of a single continuous riverside esplanade
had become an explicit aim, credit for this going to 'Abd el-Latif
el-Baghdadi, member of the 1952 Revolutionary Council and later
minister of planning. In 1961, the entire street, from the mouth of
the Esma'iliya Canal at Shubra el-Kheima in the north to Rukn
Helwan in the south, was unified under the name Share' Kurnish
el-Nil. Buildings and gardens in Fumm el-Khalig, Garden City, and

Downtown that were demolished or curtailed include the Palace of
the Queen Mother, demolished 1903 (*see* Share‘ Walda Basha), the
garden of the British Embassy, shortened in 1954, and the Qasr
el-Nil barracks and palace complex, demolished in 1953 to make
way for the Arab League Building and the Nile Hilton (opened
1956, now the Nile Ritz-Carlton; *see* Share‘ Qasr el-Nil).

Streets within our area that were incorporated into Share‘
Kurnish el-Nil are (from north to south):

From at least 1914 to c.1961: **Share‘ Elhami**, after
Princess Emina Elhami (1858–1931), known as Umm
el-Muhsenin ('Mother of the Charitable'), wife of
Khedive Tawfiq and mother of Khedive ‘Abbas Helmi
II. This street ran south from then Midan Elhami (now
Midan el-Shahid Kamal el-Din Salah), north of Hotel
Semiramis, to Share‘ el-Zahraa'.

From at least 1929 to c.1961: **Share‘ el-Qasr el-‘Ali**
('High Palace Str.') after the palace complex on whose
grounds the greater part of today's Garden City was
built. Before the development of Garden City, this name
had applied to an older street defining the eastern border
of the same grounds, now Share‘ Qasr el-‘Eini.

L

el-Labban, Haret (Downtown)
'Milkman's Lane.' Probably after 1887.

Lazughli, Share‘ *see* el-Zahraa', Share‘

Lazughli, Midan (‘Abdin, el-Munira)
By 1908, after Muhammad Beih Lazughli (d.1827). A member of
the Laz ethnic group from the Turkish–Georgian border but born
in Egypt, Lazughli entered Muhammad ‘Ali Basha's service in 1810,
became one of his closest advisors, and was the mastermind behind

the massacre of the Mamluks at the Citadel in 1811. As katkhuda (a post approximately equivalent to deputy viceroy), he organized a spy network to keep an eye on the Turkish-speaking elite and foiled an 1815 plot by Muhammad 'Ali's rival Latif Agha to oust the former during his absence on campaign in Arabia. Lazughli also presided over the first military school founded by Muhammad 'Ali, in Aswan. Lazughli's statue, by Alfred Jacquemart, was erected here in 1872, though it did not acquire a pedestal until 1893. Legend has it that the model for the statue was a poor fruit-seller picked off the street by two of Khedive Esma'il's older courtiers who still remembered what Lazughli looked like.

> From at least 1882 to before 1908: **Midan el-Nasriya**, in historical evocation of the larger area, located between today's Share' Mansur on the west, Share' Game' el-Esma'ili on the north, Share' Kheirat on the east, and Share' Mu'ezz el-Arab on the south, that was developed by the Mamluk-dynasty ruler el-Malek el-Naser ('the Victorious King') Muhammad ebn Qalawun in 1320 as a ground for equestrian exercises and called by him Midan el-Mahari ('Swift Camels Sq.'), where he built a palace (1329). With the renaming of the square in honor of Lazughli, the name Midan el-Nasriya was transferred to another square at the southern end of Share' Kheirat, formed by the now nameless intersection of the latter with Share' el-Komi, Share' Muhammad Mu'ezz el-'Arab, and Share' el-Nasriya (*see* Share' el-Komi).

> The square was also known during this period as **Midan el-Dawawin** ('Government Offices Sq.'), after former Share' el-Dawawin (*see* Share' Nubar), which passes through it on a south–north axis.

M

Madraset el-Alsun, Share' (el-Tawfiqiya)
'School of Languages Str.' From no earlier than 1947, after a translation school founded in 1836 and directed, from 1837, by Rifa'a

Rafi' el-Tahtawi (1801–73), a key figure of the nineteenth-century Egyptian intellectual renaissance; by 1842 it had trained around 142 young translators. Over time, the school widened its scope to include training in many other areas central to Muhammad 'Ali's project to produce Egyptian cadres capable of reforming Egyptian governance along European lines; it thus became, in effect, Egypt's first modern university. The school occupied a building next to el-Alfi's palace (*see* Share' Muhammad Beih el-Alfi), located just to the north of this street. In 1849, when Muhammad 'Ali's successor 'Abbas Helmi I closed the school and exiled el-Tahtawi to Khartoum, the same building became home to Shepheard's Hotel, Cairo's most famous hostelry of the colonial period; the hotel (by then rebuilt) was burned to the ground in the Black Saturday riots of 26 January 1952.

> From no earlier than 1929 to no later than 1947: part of
> **Midan Halim** (*see* Share' Halim, main entry).

Madraset el-Huquq el-Ferensiya, Share' (el-Munira)
'French Law School Str.' By 1935, after the school of law established on half of a plot of land belonging to the Institut Français d'Archéologie Orientale, which moved to this street in 1907 (*see* former Share' el-Madrasa el-Faransawi, *under* Share' Muhammad Helmi Ebrahim); the street divides the plot in two. The school trained lawyers working for the Mixed Courts in French law and thus provided revenue for the institute. When the Mixed Courts were abolished in 1935, the school was no longer needed and it soon closed. The site is now occupied by the French Cultural Institute.

el-Madrastein, Share' (el-Azbakiya)
'Two Schools Str.' By 1888, after the Azbakiya School for Girls and the Azbakiya School for Boys, American protestant missionary schools founded in 1877.

el-Maghrabi, Sekket (Downtown)
By 1918, after former Share' el-Maghrabi, now Share' 'Adli, which it joins to Share' Setta w-'Eshrin Yulyu, running along the east side of the synagogue on the former.

Magles el-Sha'b, Haret (el-Munira)

'People's Assembly Lane.' Probably since 1972: *see* **Share' Magles el-Sha'b**. Logically speaking, one would expect the name of this street to have changed in step with that of Share' Magles el-Sha'b, off which it branches (*see* next entry), thus Haret Magles el-Umma, etc. However, no confirmation of this has been found.

Magles el-Sha'b, Share' (el-Munira)

'People's Assembly Str.' Since 1972, after the lower house of parliament, located on this street, as mandated by the 1971 constitution.

> From 1956 to 1972: **Share' Magles el-Umma** ('National Council Str.'), after the unicameral house mandated by the 1956 constitution.

> From 1926 to 1956: **Share' Magles el-Nuwwab** ('Council of Deputies Str.'), after the name for the lower house of parliament mandated by the 1923 constitution. The 2014 constitution restores this name to the chamber but the name of the street has yet to be changed.

> From no earlier than 1924 to 1926: **Share' Dar el-Neyaba** ('Chamber of Deputies Str.'), perhaps after a popular term for the lower house of parliament (though not one found in any of the preceding constitutions). In any event, the authorities moved fast to replace it (*see above*).

> By 1908 to at least 1924: **Share' el-Sheikh Yusef** ('Sheikh Yusef Str.'); this name still applies to the street west of Share' Qasr el-'Eini (*see* main entry for Share' el-Sheikh Yusef).

Mahattet Helwan, Share' (el-Munira)

'Helwan Station Str.' Since 1894 or soon after, after a branch of the Tura–Helwan light rail system that terminated here, just south of today's el-Sayyeda Zeinab Metro station; this short street dead-ends at the abandoned platform. The Tura–Helwan railway was a state-owned enterprise—"Cairo's first mechanized mass-transit system," as historian of Cairo Samir Raafat points out—and was inaugurated in 1877. In 1888, the Suarès group (*see* former Midan

Sawares, *under* Midan Mustafa Kamel) bought the concession for the line from the state, with permission to extend it to central Cairo, which the group did, making its terminus at Bab el-Luq (*see* Share' Mansur). In 1904, the new line was sold in turn to the Delta Light Railway Company, allied to the Delta Land Company that was developing the new suburb of el-Ma'adi, and in 1914 it was sold again by the latter to Egyptian State Railways. Thereafter it was nationalized and ultimately became part of Line One of today's Metro system. This station was named after the line's destination rather than its location, in the same way that Alexandria's main station, Mahattet Masr, for example, references Cairo.

el-Mahdi, 'Atfet (el-Munira)
Date unknown; unidentified. *See* Haret el-Mahdi.

el-Mahdi, Haret (el-Munira)
Date unknown; unidentified. El-Mahdi (literally, 'the Guided One') may be a family name, perhaps that of early residents; it is not a reference to Muhammad Ahmad ebn 'Abdallah, the Sudanese leader ('the Mahdi') who between 1882 and 1885 drove Egyptian forces out of his country.

el-Mahdi, Share' (el-Azbakiya)
By 1888, after el-Sheikh Muhammad el-Mahdi el-Hefni (c.1742–1815). Born Hebat Allah ebn Ebifaneyus, a Copt, he converted to Islam at the hands of a certain Sheikh el-Hefni, whose name he adopted, and became a scholar at the mosque–university of el-Azhar. Intimate of the Mamluk elite, he acquired wealth and built himself a mansion in the neighborhood of this street. Following the arrival of the French in 1798, he made himself useful to them, serving on their Council of Notables, translating their decrees, and acting as a go-between between them and the population, a position for whose ambiguities he paid when his house was burned down by the mob during the second uprising against French occupation, in 1800. El-Mahdi continued to flourish under Muhammad 'Ali, taking the latter's side against 'Umar Makram and accompanying his son Tusun on his campaign in the Hejaz, a mission for which he was unanimously nominated by his fellow sheikhs. He failed, however, in his ambition to become Sheikh of el-Azhar.

Maher Basha, 'Atfet (el-Munira)
Date unknown; perhaps after any of three related men from a prominent Circassian–Egyptian family: Muhammad Maher Basha, sometime governor of Cairo and undersecretary at the ministry of war; his son, Ali Maher Basha (1881–1960), four-time prime minister and the first prime minister after the 1952 revolution; or the latter's brother, Ahmad Maher Basha (1888–1945), two-time prime minister, assassinated in the parliament building by a member of the National Party.

Mahmud Basyuni, Share' (Downtown)
Since 1950, after Mahmud Ebrahim Basyuni (1874–1944), a Wafdist politician and a leader of the 1919 revolution, famed for his oratory. Basyuni was twice elected president of the Lawyers' Syndicate and served as minister of religious endowments and president of the Upper House of the Egyptian parliament. (A Bassiouni Street in Chicago, USA, close to DePaul University campus, is named in honor of Cherif Bassiouni (1937–2017), Mahmud's grandson, often recognized as "the father of international criminal law," who taught there.)

> From 1913 to 1950: **Share' el-Antikkhana el-Masriya**
> ('Egyptian Museum Str.'), using the old name (*antikkhana*, 'house of antiquities') for the Musuem of Egyptian Antiquities, which moved to its present site, to which this street leads, in 1902. This name, though only officially decreed in 1913, is already found on earlier maps.

> From at least 1908 to 1913: **Share' el-Antikkhana**
> ('Museum Str.'); *see above*. The street is still sometimes referred to by this name.

Mahmud Mukhtar, Share' (el-Gezira)
Since 1966, after Mahmud Mukhtar (1891–1934), Egypt's pioneering sculptor. Mukhtar graduated in 1911 from the School of Fine Arts in Cairo, then completed his studies at the École Supérieure des Beaux Arts in Paris. His most famous work, the massive granite *Nahdet Masr* (Egypt's Awakening, 1920), which stands at the start of the approach to Cairo University in Giza,

is said to be the first statue by an Egyptian sculptor to represent a concept rather than a person, while his statue of Sa'd Zaghlul (1938), in front of the Opera House grounds in el-Gezira, reflects his admiration for the Wafdist leader (as does his other statue of Zaghlul, in Alexandria). A museum of his work was opened on this street, near Kubri el-Galaa', in 1962.

> From 1929 to 1966: **Share' el-Ma'rad** ('Exhibition Str.'), after the exhibition grounds to the south of the street. First laid out to showcase the activities of the Royal Agricultural Society (which held its first exhibition in a specially designed building there in 1900), the grounds are now home to the Cairo Opera House, the Museum of Modern Egyptian Art, and the Hanager theater space. Older attractions, such as the Cotton Museum, a swimming pool, and a planetarium, have disappeared or no longer function.

Mahmud Sedqi, Share' (el-Zamalek)

Since c.1928, after either Mahmud Sedqi Basha (1851–1924), a physician in government service who studied at the School of Medicine, was sent on mission to France, and returned in 1878, rising later to become governor of Alexandria (1899) and then of Cairo (1906–09), or a namesake, an engineer, who was minister of public works from 2 December 1924 to 13 March 1925.

> From 1930 to c.1928: **Share' el-Ser Garesten** after Sir William Edmund Garstin (1849–1925), a British irrigation and civil engineer whose career began in India. He succeeded Sir Colin Scott Moncrieff (*see* former Share' el-Ser Munkerif, *under* Share' el-Mansur Muhammad) as director of irrigation. During his tenure, in 1894, the decision was made to build the first Aswan Dam; his 1904 report following his survey of the White Nile established the parameters of Nile irrigation in Egypt for the next twenty years.

el-Mahrani, Share' (Downtown)

By 1912, after Mamluk commander Seif el-Din Balban (or Yalban or Balbay) el-Mahrani of the era of Sultan el-Malek el-Zaher Beibars (r.1260–77) who founded a housing compound (*manshiya*) on the land exposed during the thirteenth century by the Nile's shift to the west. The naming of a street in Downtown after this person in not historically accurate: the original Manshiyet el-Mahrani was located farther south, between today's Midan Fumm el-Khalig and the neighborhood of Qasr el-'Eini (*see* Share' Sekket el-Manshiya). Some early sources refer to the street as **Share' Seif el-Din el-Mahrani**. This and surrounding streets were pedestrianized in the early 1990s.

el-Maktab, 'Atfet ('Abdin)
By 1904; the name is said by residents to refer to a former school on the street for teaching young children the Qur'an and basic literacy skills (more commonly called a *kuttab*).

el-Malek el-Afdal, Share' (el-Zamalek)
By 1913, after el-Malek el-Afdal ('the Most Virtuous King') ebn Naser el-Din Yusef Salah el-Din (r.1186–96), a son of Saladin and second Ayyubid ruler of Damascus. El-Afdal led the Ayyubid forces in the Battle of Cresson (1187) when the Crusaders were routed, but was later exiled to the Hawran by a rival family member.

el-Malek el-Naser, Share' (el-Munira)
By 1914, in historical evocation of the Mamluk-dynasty three-time (1293–94, 1299–1309, and 1310–41) ruler el-Malek el-Naser ('Victorious King') Muhammad ebn Qalawun, who established, in the area formerly known as Genan el-Zuhri (*see* Share' Genan el-Zuhri), a space for equestrian exercises and training (1320) and a palace (1329). This space, called Midan el-Mahari ('Swift Camel Sq.'), and the palace were located in the quadrant bounded today by Share' Muhammad Mu'ezz el-Arab on the north, Share' Kheirat on the east, Share' Game' el-Esma'ili on the south, and Share' Mansur on the west, to the south of el-Berka el-Nasriya (*see* Share' el-Berka el-Nasriya) and together make up the heart of the el-Nasriya neighborhood.

el-Mallah, 'Atfet (el-Munira)
'Salt Seller's (or Maker's) Alley.' Date unknown; unidentified.

Ma'mal el-Barud, Share' (Fumm el Khalig)
'Gunpowder Factory Str.' By 1921, after a facility, originally established under Muhammad 'Ali Basha (r.1805–48) as a military

school but converted by 'Abbas Helmi I Basha (r.1848–54) to produce gunpowder. The area contained saltpeter works but was otherwise undeveloped.

el-Mamarr el-Tugari (Downtown)
'Commercial Passage.' By 1920; this warren of pedestrian alleyways filled with shops was once home to the Greek Club.

el-Manakh, Sekket (Downtown)
'Camel-ground Connecting Str.' Probably since 1888, when former Share' el-Manakh (*see* Share' 'Abd el-Khaleq Sarwat Basha), into which it runs, was named.

el-Manshiya (or el-Munshah), Sekket (Fumm el-Khalig)
'Compound Connecting Str.' By 1935, after a *manshiya* or housing compound established in 1272 by Seif el-Din Balbay (or Balban or Yalbay) el-Mahrani, Master of the Horse to Mamluk ruler el-Zaher Beibars. Manshiyet el-Mahrani ('el-Mahrani's Compound') occupied approximately the same space as the older Manshiyet el-Fadel, being defined by the el-Khalig el-Masri canal to the east, today's Share' Bustan el-Fadel to the north, and the el-Manyal channel of the Nile to the west. There el-Mahrani built himself, in addition to a mosque, a mansion, and was imitated in this by as many as forty other Mamluk commanders. Over the centuries, the district developed into one of Cairo's most popular pleasure spots, largely because of its proximity to the Canal Inlet (Fumm el-Khalig), where an earthen dam was broken each year, to great celebration, to admit the Nile's water into el-Khalig el-Masri, marking the peak of the flood. The area later became known as Qasr el-'Eini (*see* Share' Qasr el-'Eini).

Manshiyet (or Munshat) el-Fadel, Share' (Downtown)
'El-Fadel's Compound Str.' By 1911, after a *manshiya* or housing compound established c.1174 by Muhy el-Din Abu 'Ali 'Abd el-Rahim ebn 'Ali el-Bisani el-Asqalani el-Masri, commonly referred to as el-Qadi el-Fadil ('the Learned Judge'), statesman, model of elegant epistolary style, poet, and head of chancery to Salah el-Din (Saladin) and his two immediate successors. As his name shows, the judge's father was from Bisan, in Palestine, while he himself was born in Asqalan, also in Palestine, but moved to

Cairo, where he assisted in the transition from the Shiite Fatimid caliphate to the rule of the Sunni Ayyubids. The naming of a street in Downtown after this settlement is not historically accurate: the actual Manshiyet el-Fadel and its associated plantation (*see* Share' Bustan el-Fadel) were located farther south, in the area between Share' Muhammad 'Ezz el-'Arab on the north and Share' Esma'il Serri on the south, and Share' Qasr el-'Eini on the west and Share' Bur Sa'id and Share' Nubar on the east. The settlement disappeared in 1252, during a ten-year-long eastward incursion by the Nile. The street is one of four, in this and other parts of the city, whose names allude to el-Qadi el-Fadel (*see* Introduction, page 16).

Manshiyet el-Kataba, Share' (Downtown)

'Chancellery Clerks' Compound Str.' By 1934, in historical evocation of a *manshiya* or housing compound constructed on the bank of the Khalig el-Maghrabi canal (*see* Introduction page 3) following the draining by that canal of a pond known as Berket Qarmut ('Qarmut's Lake') that had once been part of the plantation of Ebn Ta'lab (*see* Share' Ebn Ta'lab) and occupied the western ends of Share' Qasr el-Nil, Share' 'Adli, and Share' 'Abd el-Khaleq Sarwat. The new quarter was largely occupied by chancellery clerks (top administrative officials), and the topographer el-Maqrizi (1364–1441) wrote of it that, as a youth, he "never passed through it without noticing signs of affluence in every home—smells of frying onions from the kitchens, scent of aloe-wood incense and frankincense, fumes of wine, pounding of pestles"; even by the time el-Maqrizi wrote, however, the quarter had been abandoned and had fallen into ruin.

Manshiyet el-Mahrani, Share' (Downtown)

'El-Mahrani's Compound Str.' By 1911, in historical evocation of a *manshiya* or housing compound established in the late thirteenth century by Seif el-Din Balbay (or Balban or Yalbay) el-Mahrani, a Mamluk of the era of Sultan el-Malek el-Zaher Beibars (r.1260–77). The naming of a street in Downtown after this compound is not historically accurate: the actual Manshiyet el-Mahrani was located farther south, in an area close to today's Qasr el-'Eini (*see* Sekket el-Manshiya). This name is unusual in that the street that it denotes encircles, rather than forming a single side of, a block.

Mansur, Share' (Downtown)

Since at least 1888, after (Yehya) Mansur Basha Yakan (1837–1913). The Yakans were in-laws of Muhammad 'Ali Basha's family, a bond that was strengthened by Mansur's marriage to Tawhida, daughter of Khedive Esma'il in 1869; their former palace, Qasr el-Ensha—since 1964 the Ministry of War Production—occupies the block between Share' Mansur and Share' el-Falaki at their intersection with Share' Esma'il Abaza. Mansur Yakan held several government posts, including minister of education, religious endowments, and the interior. The street was constructed along with and ran on either side of the Bab el-Luq–Helwan light rail line (opened 1889), whose first terminus was on this street north of Share' Muhammad Mahmud; when the line was incorporated into the underground Metro system in 1987, the street attained its full usable width. Before 1987, the street was also known as **Share' Sekket Hadid Helwan** ('Helwan Railway Str.') and **Share' Masr–Helwan** or **Share' Helwan**, after the railway, its route, and its destination respectively.

> In 1912, **Share' el-Suq el-Gedid** ('New Market Str.') appears in an official source, as the name of Share' el-Mansur south of Midan el-Falaki to Share' Muhammad Mahmud, where the Bab el-Luq food market had recently opened. The name seems not to have continued in use.

el-Mansur Muhammad, Share' (el-Zamalek)

By 1913, after el-Malek el-Mansur ('the King Granted Victory by God') Naser el-Din Muhammad (r.1198–1200), third Ayyubid sultan of Egypt.

> From at least 1937 to at least 1973: during this period, the northern (newer) extension of the street (from Share' Esma'il Muhammad to Share' Bahgat 'Ali) was named **Share' el-Ser Munkerif**, after Sir Colin Campbell Scott Moncrieff. Recruited from India by Lord Cromer to serve as director-general of irrigation (1884–87), Scott Moncrieff restored the system, which had fallen into disrepair during the Dual Control period. He was the uncle of Charles Kenneth Scott Moncrieff, translator of Marcel Proust's *Remembrance of Things Past*.

el-Manyal, Kubri (Fumm el-Khalig)

'El-Manyal Bridge,' or **Kubri Mathaf el-Manyal** ('el-Manyal Museum Bridge') or **Kubri Nafezet Sheyam el-Shafʿi** ('Sheyam el-Shafʿi Pedestrian Overpass Bridge'). From no earlier than after 1962; the name **Kubri el-Manyal** alludes to a district on the island of el-Roda named after the nilometer (an ancient device for measuring the height of the Nile flood) at the island's southern tip. This bridge joins the island to the mainland just north of the French Wing of the Qasr el-ʿEini hospital. **Kubri Mathaf el-Manyal** alludes to the palace of Prince Muhammad ʿAli Tawfiq (1875–1955), youngest son of Khedive Esmaʿil and heir apparent from 1936 until 1952; known for its extensive gardens filled with exotic trees and its exceptional collection of Islamic, and especially Ottoman, treasures, the palace was turned into a museum at the prince's death, in accordance with his will. The name **Kubri Nafezet Sheyam el-Shafʿi** is also applied to this bridge in some sources, after a pedestrian overpass that formerly crossed Shareʿ ʿAli Ebrahim, of which the bridge is an extension (*see* former Shareʿ Nafezet Shiyam el-Shafeʿi, *under* Shareʿ ʿAli Ebrahim).

> From after 1935 to at least 1962: **Kubri el-Sayyala** or **Kubri Sayyalet el-Roda**, after the body of water that separates the island of el-Roda (on which the district of el-Manyal is located) from the eastern bank of the Nile. Following the renaming of the bridge, at some point after 1962, this name appears to have been transferred to former Kubri Fumm el-Khalig to its south.

Manzaret el-Sukkara, Shareʿ (el-Munira)

'Sugar Candy Viewing Stand Str.' By 1918, in historical evocation of a facility, constructed by the Fatimid caliph el-ʿAziz be-llah (975–96), from which each year the caliph would view, in conditions of pomp and luxury, the cutting of the earth dam that held back the waters of the Nile and their release into the el-Khalig el-Masri canal, signaling that the annual flood had reached its peak. Historians point out, however, that the area to which modern authorities assigned this street name was under water during the Fatimid period and for a hundred years more,

and that the original Manzaret el-Sukkara would have been
farther north, at the southern end of Share' el-Nasriya. *Suk-
kara*, meaning 'piece of sugar candy,' may have evoked sweetness
and luxury.

el-Maqrizi, Share' (el-Zamalek)
By 1913, after Taqi el-Din Ahmad ebn 'Ali ebn 'Abd el-Qader
ebn Muhammad el-Maqrizi, (1364–1442), Mamluk-era topographer and historian best known for his exhaustive description
of the city of Cairo, generally known as his *Khitat* (Topography).
He also wrote a history of the Fatimids, from whom he believed
himself to be descended.

Mariette, Share' *see* Mirit, Share'

el-Maris, Share' (el-Munira)
Since 1911; according to medieval topographer el-Maqrizi, *maris*
means 'infertile sandy ground,' and was applied to the area of Bustan
el-Khashshab (*see* Share' Bustan el-Khashshab) after the latter
became unproductive.

Ma'ruf, Share' (Downtown)
Since 1887, after the neighborhood of which this is the main street
and which in turn takes its name from the Sufi saint Sidi Ma'ruf,
whose shrine is on the north side of nearby Share' el-Sheikh Ma'ruf.

Masged el-Sherif, Mamarr (Downtown)
'El-Sherif Mosque Passage.' Date unknown, after the mosque on
the passage. The relationship between the 'el-Sherif' to whom the
mosque is dedicated and the various Sherifs who have lent their
names to nearby streets (Share' Sherif, Share' el-Sherifein, etc.) is
unclear. The sign at the entrance to the passage is not standard-is-
sue and may be unofficial.

el-Mashhadi, Haret (Downtown)
From at least 1913, after an unidentified individual, perhaps an
early resident. In 1913, what had been the western end of Haret
el-'Awayed was annexed to this street; at the same time, the annex-
ation of the western, widened, end of Haret el-Mashhadi to Share'

el-Mashhadi was confirmed. For more on this block, whose street pattern has been unusually disrupted, *see* former Haret el-Fawwala, *under* Share' el-Sayyed Muhammad Taher.

el-Mashhadi, Share' (Downtown)
By 1913; *see* Haret el-Mashhadi.

Masr–Helwan, Share' *see* Helwan, Share'

Matar, Share' (el-Zamalek)
Since 1975; unidentified. Matar is a family name, perhaps that of early residents. This street has long been closed at one end and is used for parking.

Mathaf el-Manyal, Kubri *see* el-Manyal, Kubri

el-Mawardi, Share' (el-Munira)
By 1918, probably after the district of 'Eshash el-Mawardi ('el-Mawardi's Shacks'), which occupied the area to the east of this street in the 1920s and which took its name from el-Sheikh Muhammad el-Mawardi, a Sufi saint of whom nothing but the name is known and whose tomb is situated opposite the end of nearby Share' Maqam el-Mawardi ('el-Mawardi's Tomb Str.'; out of area) to which it was moved from the east side of Share' el-Khalig el-Masri when the latter was widened, around 1899.

el-Mekhallelatiya, Darb (el-Azbakiya)
'Pickle-makers Side Street.' By 1801.

el-Meligi, Share' (el-Azbakiya)
By 1888, after el-Meligi el-Nahhas ('el-Meligi the Coppersmith'), whose house was here at this date.

el-Melkein, Haret (el-Azbakiya)
'Two Properties Lane.' By 1905.

el-Mergawi, Haret ('Abdin)
Probably c.1904, according to residents, after a certain Muhammad Ahmad Mahmud el-Mergawi, an early resident of the street.

el-Midan el-Kebir, Share' (el-Munira)

'Big Square Str.' By 1914, in historical evocation of the ground for equestrian exercises and training created in 1329 by the Mamluk ruler el-Malek el-Naser Muhammad ebn Qalawun (*see* Share' el-Malek el-Naser), who added a palace alongside it in 1329. However, the deployment of the name here may be an error, as some historians claim that the space created by el-Malek el-Naser and originally called by him Midan el-Mahari ('Swift Camels Sq.') was the same as Midan el-Nashshaba ('Archers' Sq.'), that is, well to the west of this street (*see* former Share' Madrab el-Nashshab, *under* Share' Mudiriyet el-Tahrir).

Mirit, Share' (Downtown)

By 1907, after François Auguste Ferdinand Mariette (1821–81), French Egyptologist, excavator, and founder of the Museum of Egyptian Antiquities, which opened on its present site in 1902. Mariette was also the first director of the Egyptian Department of Antiquities. Among his excavations were the Serapeum at Saqqara and the temples of Abydos and Dendera. Mariette's brief plot line written for Khedive Esma'il eventually became the scenario for Verdi's opera *Aida*. He is buried in a sarcophagus in the garden of the Egyptian Museum, watched over by his own statue.

> From at least 1888 to no later than 1907: **Share' el-Qushlaq** ('Barracks Str.') or **Share' Qushlaq Qasr el-Nil** ('Qasr el-Nil Barracks Str.'), after the Qasr el-Nil barracks (*see* Share' Qasr el-Nil). Not to be confused with Share' Qushlaq 'Abdin near Midan 'Abdin.

From 1913 to after 1953, the space formed by the intersection of Share' Shambuliyon, Share' Qasr el-Nil, and Share' Bustan with this street was called **Midan Mirit**, the name also being extended in some maps from southeast of the Egyptian Museum to Midan el-Tahrir. The square fronted the main gate of the Qasr el-Nil barracks (demolished 1953).

> From at least 1886 to 1913, the same space was called **Midan Qasr el-Nil**. Confusingly, this name was also used on some maps to refer to today's Midan Tal'at Harb.

Mishil Lutfallah, Share' (el-Zamalek)

Since 1973, after Michel Lutfallah (c.1880–1961), an Egyptian banker of Levantine background active in post–First World War Arab politics (he founded the Syrian Union Party, which opposed the French mandate in Syria, and funded the Syrian–Palestinian Congress). He inherited the Saray el-Gezira palace from his father, Habib Lutfallah (*see* former Share' Lutfallah, *under* Share' el-Shahid Zakariya Rezq). Following Michel Lutfallah's death, the building was sequestrated and turned into the government-owned Hotel Omar Khayyam (now the Marriott).

Mudiriyet el-Tahrir, Share' (Garden City)

'Liberation Directorate Str.' Since 1953 or soon after, after an experimental land-reclamation area with special administrative status in the Western Desert south of Alexandria. Liberation Directorate was inaugurated in 1953 as a national project with the intention of showcasing socialism by attracting and providing livelihoods for the rural poor from other parts of the country. By the 1970s, this plan was deemed to have failed, the area reclaimed falling far short of the original goal of 1.2 million faddans, and that at exorbitant cost to the state; since then, plots have been assigned to graduates from agriculture faculties and the state farms have been privatized. The name was chosen because the scheme's first administrative headquarters were located on this street.

> From at least 1935 to at least 1953: **Share' Madrab el-Nashshab** ('Bull's-eye Str.'), in historical evocation of a ground for archery training created by Mamluk sultan el-Malek el-Naser Muhammad ebn Qalawun in the thirteenth century. The original ground, however, was located to the east rather than the west of the road that is now Share' Qasr el-'Eini, as is made clear in the map made for the *Description de l'Égypte,* compiled no later than 1801.

el-Mugamma', Share' (Downtown)

'Government Complex Str.' Since c.1951, after the government's central administrative services facility, el-Mugamma' ('the Complex'), built between 1946 and 1951. Conversion of the building to other purposes began in 2016.

Muhammad ʿAbd el-Wahhab, Shareʿ *see* el-Musiqar Muhammad ʿAbd el-Wahhab, Shareʿ

Muhammad ʿAli, Haret (ʿAbdin)

Probably by 1908; unidentified. Muhammad ʿAli is a given name, perhaps that of an early resident, but certainly not that of the founder of Egypt's modern monarchy.

Muhammad ʿAli, Shareʿ

From 1875 to 1954 and from an unknown date after 1954 to the present (partial): after Muhammad ʿAli Basha (before 1768–1849), Ottoman viceroy of Egypt and effectively the country's independent ruler from 1805 until his abdication in 1848. The street was conceived of by Muhammad ʿAli as a way of providing access, unobstructed by the winding lanes of the city's old quarters, from the traditional seat of government at the Citadel to the ruler's palaces at el-Azbakiya. The order for the laying out of the street was issued in 1846 but it was completed only in 1874, by which time more than 700 large houses, mosques, and other structures, as well as a large cemetery (Turab el-Manasra), had been demolished to make way for it. In 1847, an order, not implemented at that time, was issued by the Cairo Town Planning Council (Magles Tanzim el-Mahrusa) naming the street-to-be Shareʿ el-Qalʿa. The building of Shareʿ Muhammad ʿAli, with its continuation, Shareʿ Kulut (Clot) Beih, and the widening of Shareʿ el-Muski (out of area), foreshadowed the Esmaʿiliya project. The street, of the same width today as when first laid out, was originally lined, in imitation of Paris's Rue de Rivoli, with arcades, a few of which survive. It was the first street in Cairo to have an electric streetcar line (from 1896, running from the Citadel to Bulaq). From the late nineteenth through the early twentieth centuries, the street was famous for its newspaper and journal offices, and also, in the stretch between Midan el-ʿAtaba el-Khadra and Midan Bab el-Khalq, for its cafes frequented by musicians seeking work, leading to its nickname of **Shareʿ el-ʿAwalim**, or the Street of the Almahs (women leaders of troupes of singers and dancers); later, the musicians were supplemented by film extras. The street shares with Shareʿ Kulut Beih the honor of being modern Cairo's first officially named street.

From 1954 to an unknown later date, the name **Share'
el-Qal'a** applied to this street plus its extension east from
Midan el-'Ataba to Midan Bab el-Khalq (out of area). At
that unknown date, the stretch west of Midan Bab el-Khalq
(out of area) to Midan el-'Ataba reverted to its former name
(*see* main entry for Share' el-Qal'a).

Muhammad 'Ali Genah, Share' (Garden City)
Since 1970, after Muhammad 'Ali Jinnah (1876–1948), lawyer,
politician, and founding father of Pakistan.

From at least 1935 to 1970: **Share' el-Bergas** ('Archery-
on-Horseback Str.'), after a form of mounted combat
training developed by the Mamluks that involved archery
and perhaps javelins. The name evokes, and may correspond
accurately to, the Mamluk military exercise grounds that
once existed in the area; *see also* former Share' Madrab
el-Neshab, *under* Share' Mudiriyet el-Tahrir, into which this
street ran.

Muhammad el-Alfi, Share' *see* Muhammad Beih el-Alfi, Share'

Muhammad Anis, Share' (el-Zamalek)
By 1937, probably after Muhammad Anis Basha, Counselor of the
State Lawsuit Authority (Hay'et Qadaya el-Dawla), an institution,
founded in 1875, that acts for the state in legal matters. Anis was
the second to hold this highest position in the Authority.

From at least 1919 to no later than 1937: **Share' el-Madrasa**
('School Str.'), after Zamalek Girls' College, formerly the
Collège de la Mère de Dieu, associated with the Roman
Catholic Convent of the same name, located on this street.

From c.1910 for a few years, the western end of this street,
between Share' Yusef Kamel and Share' Abu el-Feda, may
have been called **Sekket Geziret Arawi** ('Arawi Island Connecting Str.'), after the original name of el-Gezira el-Wusta,
one of the three islands that coalesced to form the present
island of el-Gezira.

Muhammad Beih el-Alfi, Share' (el-Tawfiqiya)

Since 1935, after Muhammad Beih el-Alfi el-Kebir ('the Great') (1751–1807), a leading member of the Mamluk clique that ruled Egypt during the decades before the French invasion; *alfi* means 'purchased for a thousand pieces' or, according to some, 'purchased for a thousand *ardabb*s of wheat,' the story being that el-Alfi's master presented him to the leading Mamluk Murad Beih, who rewarded the man with gifts to this value. In 1798, el-Alfi built the last of his many palaces beside the lake at el-Azbakiya, at the eastern end of today's street; he lived in it, however, for only sixteen days before the forces of the French Expedition arrived, confiscated the palace, and made it their seat of government and Napoleon's residence; Kléber, his successor as commander of the expedition, was assassinated in its garden (*see* Share' Seliman el-Halabi). El-Alfi's subsequent attempts to involve the British in the restoration of Mamluk rule led to an abortive invasion by the former in 1807, ironically just after el-Alfi fell sick and died. Rebuilt in the early years of Muhammad 'Ali's rule, the palace was occupied, from 1837, by an important school for the training of Muhammad 'Ali's reformist cadres (*see* Share' Madraset el-Alsun) and, later still, by the first iteration of Shepheard's Hotel. The street was pedestrianized in the 1990s.

From at least 1912 to 1935: **Share' el-Alfi,** *see above.*

From 1908 to no later than 1912: **Share' Halim,** after Sa'id Halim Basha (*see* Share' Halim, main entry).

From 1890 to 1908: **Share' Tawfiq** or **Share' el-Tawfiqiya,** the first name referring to Khedive Muhammad Tawfiq (r.1879–92), successor to Khedive Esma'il, who initiated the development of the Tawfiqiya district north of Share' Sitta w-'Eshrin Yulyu to accommodate overflow from the Esma'iliya quarter, the second (perhaps less official) referring to the district itself. Later, this name was reassigned to the street that enters Midan 'Urabi from the north (now Share' 'Urabi). Not to be confused with nearby Share' Suq el-Tawfiqiya.

During this earlier period, the street was apparently also known unofficially as **Shareʿ el-Temsah** ('Crocodile Str.'), the name being officially quashed in favor of Shareʿ el-Alfi in 1916.

Muhammad ʿEzz el-ʿArab, Shareʿ (el-Munira)

Since 1951, after Sheikh Muhammad ʿEzz el-ʿArab Beih (d.1934), a lawyer, best known for persuading the courts, in 1904, to annul the betrothal of ʿAli Yusef (*see* Shareʿ el-Sheikh ʿAli Yusef) to the daughter of el-Sheikh el-Sadat (head of a prominent family of descendants of the Prophet Muhammad) at the woman's father's request, on the grounds that the groom was a journalist, and therefore of insufficiently respectable status (the marriage went ahead in 1905 following the intervention of persons of good will). ʿEzz el-ʿArab lived at #7.

> From 1950 to 1951: **Shareʿ el-Sheikh ʿAli Yusef** (*see* main entry). In 1951, this name was reassigned to former Shareʿ el-Munira, in the same district but at right angles to this street. The replacement of ʿAli Yusef by his would-be nemesis Muhammad ʿEzz el-ʿArab is noteworthy.

> From 1888 to 1950: **Shareʿ el-Mubtadayan** ('Primary School Str.'), after a school that was transferred in 1868 from earlier quarters in Abu Zaʿbal, north of Cairo, to a mansion at the eastern end of this street, originally that of Muhammad ʿAli Basha's Mamluk ally ʿUsman Beik el-Bardisi (1758–1806), and subsequently an official guest house. The school offered a three-year cycle of instruction, in Arabic and Turkish, that made up the first stage of Khedive Esmaʿil's revived national education program. The word *mubtadayan*, meaning 'beginners,' is Turco-Persian and dates to Muhammad ʿAli's initial attempts to modernize Egyptian education. The building is still a school and the street is still widely referred to by this name.

Muhammad Farid, Midan (Downtown)

Since 2011, after Muhammad Beih Farid, nationalist politician (*see* Shareʿ Muhammad Farid), whose statue was relocated to this site

from the Azbakiya Gardens in 2005. This square was the site of the
original Bab el-Luq, the gate in the city's western wall that lent its
name to the district (*see* Midan Bab el-Luq *below*). Two popular
names are also found: **Midan Abu Zarifa**, after a celebrated *ful*
and *taʿmiya* (stewed bean and bean patty) restaurant located just off
the square (the first shop on Shareʿ el-Raʾis ʿAbd el-Salam ʿAref to
the west, now an apothecary's) during the 1960s (and perhaps earlier), and **Midan Muhammad Nagib**, after the subway station on
the square named for Brigadier General Muhammad Nagib Yusef
Qutb el-Qashlan (1901–84), Egypt's first president (1953–54),
which opened in 1996.

> From 1967 to 2011: **Midan el-Raʾis ʿAbd el-Salam
> ʿAref** ('President ʿAbd el-Salam Aref Sq.'), after the Iraqi
> president (1963–66) of that name, who in 1964 signed
> with President Gamal ʿAbd el-Naser an agreement to pave
> the way for full union between Iraq and Egypt, a project
> thwarted by ʿAref's death.

> From 1961 to 1967: **Midan el-Bustan** ('Plantation Sq.'),
> after Shareʿ el-Bustan, which enters the square from the west.

> From after 1948 to 1961: **Midan Talʿat Harb**, after the Egyp-
> tian national capitalist (*see* Midan Talʿat Harb, main entry).

> From 1847 to at least 1948: **Midan Bab el-Luq** ('Silt Gate
> Sq.'), after the gate in the city's western wall that lent its name
> to the district; present at the time of the French occupation
> (1798–1801), it had disappeared, like all the other western
> gates, by the time of the Esmaʿiliya project. The same name is
> often popularly applied today to the square officially known as
> Midan el-Falaki and probably has been since that square was
> created, reflecting the newer square's importance as the main
> hub of the Bab el-Luq district. This gave rise to a confusion
> that older maps solved by referring to what is now Midan
> Muhammad Farid as the "*Rondpoint* (Roundabout) *de*" Bab
> el-Luq and to what is now Midan el-Falaki as the "*Place*
> (Square) *de*" Bab el-Luq. The word *luq* means alluvial silt that
> is soft enough to be cultivated without plowing. At some point

during this period, the name **Midan el-Sanafiri** seems also to have been used, after former Share° el-Sanafiri, which enters it from the east; this name was officially quashed in 1913.

Muhammad Farid, Share° (Downtown)
Since 1941, after Muhammad Beih Farid (1868–1919), lawyer, writer, and nationalist politician, founder with Mustafa Kamel in 1907 of the National Party (el-Hizb el-Watani), whose slogan was "Egypt for the Egyptians" and of which he became leader on Kamel's premature death. Threatened with arrest during the uprising against the British in 1919, Farid fled to Europe, where he died in poverty. Appropriately, **Share° Muhammad Farid** intersects with **Midan Mustafa Kamel**, while the two men's remains are buried next to one another in a mausoleum close to the Citadel. #147 (originally the home of Swiss architect Lepori, who designed the hippodrome; on which *see* Midan Mustafa Kamel) and #149 (originally the home of the Russian consul) are said to be the oldest surviving buildings of the original Esma°iliya district.

From at least 1888 to 1941: **Share° Emad el Din**, after a saint of that name (*see* main entry for Share° Emad el-Din).

Muhammad Haggag, Share° (Downtown)
By 1915; unidentified. Muhammad Haggag is a man's name, perhaps that of an early resident.

Muhammad Hasan el-Geziri, Share° *see* el-Duktur Muhammad Hasan el-Geziri, Share°

Muhammad Helmi Ebrahim, Share° (Downtown)
Since 1967, after an unidentified individual.

From no earlier than 1946 to 1967: **Share° el-Hegg** ('Pilgrimage Str.'). The reason for the choice of name is not known.

From at least 1918 to at least 1946: **Share° el-Madrasa el-Faransawi** or **Share° el-Madrasa el-Faransawiya** ('French School Str.'), after the École française du Caire (the French School of Cairo), founded in 1880 as a counterpart to the French archaeological missions in Athens and Rome. It adopted its current name of Institut Français d'Archéologie Orientale (IFAO, the French Institute of Eastern Archeology) in 1898 and moved from here to its present location on Share' el-Sheikh 'Ali Yusef in 1907.

Muhammad Mahmud, Share' (Downtown)

Since 1945, after Muhammad Mahmud Basha (1877–1941), a leader of the 1919 Revolution, one of the founders of the Liberal Constitutionalist Party and its leader following the death of 'Adli Yakan, cabinet minister, and twice prime minister (1928–29, 1937–39); during his first premiership, he drew up the agreement dividing the waters of the Nile between Egypt and Sudan. Mahmud owned a mansion with large grounds on cross-street Share' el-Falaki and it was in this house, on 18 September 1918, that Sa'd Zaghlul and other leaders of what would become the Wafd (Delegation) Party met to devise a strategy for the presentation of Egypt's case for independence to the Versailles Peace Conference; Mahmud later visited the United States in search of support. When, however, 'Adli Yakan (*see* Share' 'Adli) split with Sa'd Zaghlul, Mahmud followed the former out of the Wafd to form the new party. A contemporary noted that the Oxford-educated Mahmud resembled an Englishman in every respect except that he did not wear a bowler hat, disliked marmalade, and did not sing in his bath. The red-brick café at the corner with Share' Mansur was from 1938 to 1984 the ticket office of Bab el-Luq station, on the Masr–Helwan light rail line (opened 1889, now incorporated into the Metro system), and sported a large, handsome, and much-consulted clock on its northern façade. In November 2012, the street witnessed violent and sustained clashes between security forces and protesters.

From at least 1914 to 1945: **Share' el-Qased**, after the tomb of Sufi saint Sheikh Muhammad el-Qased (dates unknown), and its associated cemetery, located between Midan 'Abdin and Share' Mansur; the tiny tomb itself is on Share' 'Abd el-'Aziz Gawish, beneath the Burg el-Atibba building. Originally, the street did not reach Midan el-Tahrir on the west, and access to the square was via Share' el-Amir Qadadar; between 1936 and 1938, however,

Share' el-Qased was extended to link to Midan el-Tahrir, eliminating parts of the gardens of the Lycée Français and the American University in Cairo.

Muhammad el-Mar'ashli, Share' (el-Zamalek)

By 1937, for Muhammad el-Mar'ashli Basha, a civil and hydraulic engineer who was governor of el-Beheira in 1866, minister of public works and irrigation for just over a month (17 August to 23 September) in 1879, and chief engineer of coastal forts in 1882, when the British fleet bombarded Alexandria. Though his birth and death dates are not known, his active period seems to preclude residence in el-Zamalek, which was undeveloped until after 1906, and his assignment of a street there appears to be part of the homage paid to hydraulic engineers through the names of its streets.

From at least 1919 to no later than 1937: **Share' Diyakunu**; unidentified (Diacono?), presumably after an early foreign resident.

Muhammad Mazhar, Share' (el-Zamalek)

By 1937, after Muhammad Mazhar Basha, one of the first students sent by Muhammad 'Ali Basha (in 1826) to Paris, where he trained as a marine engineer and mathematician. Upon his return sixteen years later, Mazhar was made principal of the artillery academy at Turah, south of Cairo, and served (c.1866) as undersecretary to the ministry of public works and irrigation, when he oversaw the expansion of the port of Alexandria and built the lighthouse at Ras el-Tin. He also worked with Mougel to build barrages on the Nile (*see* former Share' Murgeil, *under* Share' el-Duktur Muhammad Hasan el-Geziri).

Late 1920s to no later than 1936: **Share' Mariyu Russi** or **Share' el-Duktur Russi**, after Mario Rossi (1897–1961), a prominent and prolific Italian architect whose house was on this street. As chief architect to the Ministry of Religious Endowments from 1929 to 1954, Rossi designed many well-known mosques, including that of 'Umar Makram (*see* Share' 'Umar Makram) and of Mursi Abu el-'Abbas in Alexandria.

From after 1906 to the late 1920s: **Shareʿ el-Gabalaya**
('Little Mountain Str.'), an earlier name of Shareʿ Hasan
Sabri, of which this street may be considered the northern
extension. Until the 1940s, the name **Shareʿ el-Amir Saʿid**
('Prince Saʿid Str.'), now Shareʿ el-Shaʿer ʿAziz Abaza, may
also have been applied informally to this street as it forms the
latter street's northern extension.

Muhammad Mazlum, Shareʿ (Downtown)

By 1912, after the owner of the mansion that stood until at least
1908 at the southwest corner of this street and Shareʿ Rushdi.
Muhammad Mazlum was minister of religious endownments
in the mid-nineteenth century. His better-known son, Ahmad
Mazlum (1858–1928), a later occupant of the palace, served as
a lawyer, judge, governor of the Canal Zone, chief of protocol to
Khedive Esmaʿil, minister (justice, finance, religious endowments),
member of the Chamber of Deputies, and speaker of parliament.

From at least 1908 to before 1912 (from Midan el-Falaki to
Shareʿ Muhammad Sabri Abu ʿAlam only): **Shareʿ el-Subki**;
unidentified. El-Subki is a family name (meaning 'from the
town of Subk,' in Lower Egypt), perhaps that of early residents.

Muhammad el-Qasabgi, Shareʿ (Downtown)

Since 1966, after Muhammad Ahmad el-Qasabgi (1892–1966),
lutenist and innovative composer who wrote for and performed
with many of the greatest singers of his day, from Salah ʿAbd
el-Hayy, Leila Murad, and Asmahan to Umm Kulsum. He is often
to be seen seated behind the latter in her filmed concerts.

From at least 1888 to 1966: **Shareʿ el-Tubgi** (*see* Shareʿ
el-Tubgi, main entry); this name, which formerly applied
both east and west of Shareʿ el-Gumhuriya, was changed on
the west side to the above.

Muhammad Sabri Abu ʿAlam, Shareʿ (Downtown)

Or **Shareʿ Sabri Abu ʿAlam**. Since 1951, after (Muhammad)
Sabri Abu ʿAlam Basha (1893–1947), from a major landowning
family, head of the Lawyers' Syndicate, secretary-general of the

Wafd Party (1943–47), publisher of its main organ *Sawt el-Umma* (Voice of the Nation), parliamentarian, and twice minister of justice (1936–37, 1942–44). During his first term in that post, he prepared the law abolishing the special legal status of foreigners, while during his second he prepared the Judicial Independence Act (1943) and was signatory to the Alexandria Protocol that established the Arab League (1944).

> 1893 to 1951: **Share' Game' Sharkas** ('Mosque of Sharkas Str.'), after the mosque of that name (also spelled Jarkas) at the corner of this street and Share' Muhammad Mazlum. Nothing is known of the builder of the mosque (from his name, a Mamluk), which was in ruins in 1888 and later rebuilt. The mosque was also formerly known as that of Ebrahim el-Sufi, a saint whose tomb it contains.

> 1887 to 1893: **Share' Seliman Basha**, after Seliman Basha el-Faransawi, a name re-assigned in 1893 to today's Share' Tal'at Harb (*see* former Share' Seliman Basha, *under* the latter).

Muhammad Saqeb, Share' (el-Zamalek)

Since c.1928, after Muhammad Saqeb, an irrigation engineer who had studied under government sponsorship in Europe. Saqeb participated in the construction of the barrages north of Cairo, designed to control water flow to the Delta, and became Inspector of Irrigation for Upper Egypt; he is credited with contributing to the planning of Zamalek.

Muhammad Sedqi, Share' (Downtown)

Since 1927, after Muhammad Sedqi Basha, a lawyer and counselor at the Courts of Cassation and briefly (1924–25) minister of religious endownments. The Muhammad Sedqi Building, which he constructed in the late 1920s and where he lived for a period, still stands at the corner with Share' Huda Sha'rawi.

Muhammad Shawqi, Share' (el-Munira)

From after 1984, after Muhammad Shawqi, stage name of Muhammad Ebrahim Ebrahim (1915–84), theater and movie actor, who began his career with the comedy troupes of ʿAli el-Kassar (*see* Shareʿ ʿAli Kassar) and Shekuku and acted in more than 250 plays, movies, and TV series.

> By 1935: **Shareʿ Talʿat**; unidentified. Talʿat is a given name, perhaps that of an early resident. Not to be confused with another Shareʿ Talʿat or with Shareʿ Ahmad Talʿat, both of which are nearby; however, it is possible that all three names refer to the same person.

Muhammad Tawfiq Deyab, Shareʿ *see* Tawfiq Deyab, Shareʿ

Muhammad Musa, Haret (Downtown)
Probably c.1887; unidentified. Muhammad Musa is a man's name, perhaps that of an early resident.

el-Muhandes ʿAli Labib Gabr, Shareʿ (Downtown)
'Eng. ʿAli Labib Gabr Str.' Since 1966, after a leading architect (d.1965) who designed several of Cairo's iconic buildings, including the Lebanese Embassy and the Indian ambassador's residence, both in Zamalek, and the National Research Center, in el-Duqqi. He was awarded the State Recognition Prize in 1962.

> From 1936 to 1966: **Mamarr Behlar** ('Baehler Passage'), created when Charles Baehler (1868–1937), Swiss speculative builder and, by 1925, controller of most of Egypt's luxury hotels, tore down the Savoy Hotel (British Army headquarters during the First World War) and built, between 1927 and 1929, an apartment building, known as the Baehler Building. The 'passage' (in fact, a substantial street) appears not to have been made until 1936. Baehler also built the Metropolitan (now the Cosmopolitan) Hotel on Shareʿ Ebn Taʿlab and the King David Hotel in Jerusalem (1929), and played a major role in the development of el-Zamalek, including the construction there of another set of luxury apartment buildings, known as Baehler's Mansions, on the north side of the eastern end of Shareʿ Setta w-ʿEshrin Yulyu. The street is still generally known by this name.

Muharram, Haret (el-Munira)
Date unknown; unidentified. Muharram (the first month of the Islamic year) is a male given name, perhaps that of an early resident.

Mukhles, Haret (el-Munira)
Date unknown; unidentified. Mukhles is a male given name (literally, 'Sincere'), perhaps that of an early resident.

Mu'nes Afandi, Share' (el-Munira)
'Mu'nes Effendi Str.' By 1948, after Muhammad Mu'nes Afandi (d. c.1900), a calligrapher whose school most later Egyptian calligraphers would follow.

> From at least 1920 to no later than 1948: **Share' el-Nattata**. The word *nattata* means 'something that jumps up and down, or bounces' or 'something that causes another thing to jump up and down, or bounce.' Though we have no positive evidence for what was intended, we speculate that this may be 'Flea Street.'

Munshat . . . *see* Manshiyet . . .

Muntazah el-Gezira, Share' (el-Gezira)
'Gezira Park Str.' Since at least 1922, after the park, at first called Muntazah el-Kubri ('Bridge Park'), now called Muntazah el-Hurriya ('Freedom Park'), created at the southern tip of Gezira island after completion of the first Aswan Dam (1902) allowed the construction of a permanent embankment.

el-Muqaddam, Darb (el-Azbakiya)
By 1888; *muqaddam* is an obsolete mid-level military rank with no direct modern equivalent.

el-Mursalin, Share' (el-Zamalek)
'Missionaries' Str.' Since c.1884, after the priests of the Roman Catholic congregation of the Comboni Fathers, whose school and other facilities still exist in the surrounding area (*see* former Share' Kumbuni, *under* Share' Hasan Asem).

el-Musiqar Muhammad 'Abd el-Wahhab, Share' (el-Zamalek)
'Musician Muhammad 'Abd el-Wahhab Str.' Since after 1991,
after Muhammad 'Abd el-Wahhab (1901–91), singer, composer,
producer, and actor, sometimes called the Father of Modern Egyptian Music.

> From 1934 to after 1991: **Share' Saray el-Gezira** ('Gezira
> Palace Str.'), after the palace built in 1869 by Khedive Esma'il
> to accommodate guests attending the opening of the Suez
> Canal. Among those who stayed there were Empress Eugénie
> of France and Emperor Franz-Joseph of Austria. The area
> covered some 62 acres and contained a *haramlek* (private
> quarters), two salamliks (reception and public quarters), a
> kiosk, fountains, and a grotto. Bought when Khedive Esma'il's
> assets were sold following his bankruptcy and exile in 1873,
> the palace was converted into the Gezira Palace Hotel. The
> palace became a private residence again in c.1919 and, in
> 1962, once more a hotel, first called the Omar el-Khayyam,
> now the Marriott (*see* Share' Mishil Lutfallah).

Mushtuhur, Share' (Downtown)
By 1863; unidentified. Mushtuhur is a male given name, perhaps
that of an early resident.

Mustafa 'Abd el-Razeq, Haret (Downtown)
Probably c.1914; according to local lore, Mustafa 'Abd el-Razeq
was the owner of the house to which the street's only sign is
attached.

Mustafa Abu Heif, Share' (Downtown)
Since after 1946, after a member of a family whose descendents
still live on this street. Mustafa was the brother of 'Abd el-Latif
Abu Heif (1929–2008), recognized as the Marathon Swimmer of
the Century by the International Swimming Hall of Fame in 2001.

> From 1887 to at least 1946: **Haret el-Daramalli**, after
> Hesein Basha el-Daramalli (*see* 'Atfet el-Daramalli), whose
> mansion was on the land between this street and Share'
> Tal'at Harb. Originally, this name applied not only to

today's Share' Mustafa Abu Heif but also to Share' Bustan
ebn Qureish (south of Share' el-Tahrir).

Mustafa Ahmad, 'Atfet (Downtown)
Probably by 1887; unidentified. Mustafa Ahmad is a man's name,
perhaps that of an early resident.

Mustafa Kamel, Midan (Downtown)
Since 1940, after Mustafa Kamel Basha (1874–1908), journalist,
politician, and nationalist hero. In 1900, following legal studies
and political agitation for Egypt's independence in France, Kamel
began publication of a newspaper called *el-Lewaa'* (The Banner). In
1907, he founded the National Party (el-Hizb el-Watani), which
demanded the immediate evacuation of all British troops, the uni-
fication of Egypt and the Sudan under the Egyptian crown, and
constitutional rule. The National Party saw Egypt as an integral
part of an Ottoman and Islamic order, in distinction to the Waf-
dists, who saw it as an independent entity. Kamel's remark "If I
weren't an Egyptian I would have wished to be one" is well known.
His statue, made in France and delivered in 1913, was unveiled
here in 1940 (*see also* Share' Mustafa Kamel), the political rivalries
of the day having prevented its immediate installation. The square
is crossed by Share' Muhammad Farid, named after Kamel's close
collaborator, who succeeded him as leader of the party.

From c.1900 to 1940: **Midan Sawares**, after the Suarès
della Pegna family, bankers who came to Egypt from Leg-
horn, Italy, in the early nineteenth century and were active in
the financing of land development, railways, and water supply.
The family mansion was located in the area of the square and
a horse- or mule-drawn omnibus company owned by them—
the first public transport company in Cairo—had its terminus
there; the buses (themselves known as *sawares*) were discontinued in 1940.

From 1870 to c.1900: **Midan el-Badrum**. The name was
a corruption of French *hippodrôme* and referred to a race-
course-cum-circus located to the northwest of the square,
on the northern half of Share' Gawad Husni. Situated amid

villas and gardens, the hippodrome may have been, from its construction in 1870 until its demolition in the 1880s, the most conspicuous building in el-Esmaʿiliya.

Mustafa Kamel, Shareʿ (ʿAbdin)

By c.1940, after Mustafa Kamel Basha (*see* Midan Mustafa Kamel). The street may have been named in coordination with the erection of Mustafa Kamel's statue in Midan Mustafa Kamel (1940). A school named after Kamel stands on this street and presumably is an avatar of the school he founded in Haret Barguwan in the medieval city, where his statue was first housed on its arrival from France in 1913.

> By 1908 to c.1940: **Shareʿ el-Sheikh ʿAbdallah** ('Sheikh ʿAbdallah Str.'); *see* Haret el-Sheikh ʿAbdallah.

Mustafa Khalil, Shareʿ *see* el-Duktur Mustafa Khalil, Shareʿ

el-Mustashar Muhammad Fahmi el-Sayyed, Shareʿ (Garden City)

'Counselor Muhammad Fahmi el-Sayyed Str.' Since at least 1975, after Muhammad Fahmi el-Sayyed (d.1964), legal advisor to President Gamal ʿAbd el-Naser.

> From at least 1933 to no later than 1975: **Shareʿ Rustum Basha,** perhaps after Hasan Rustum Basha, briefly speaker of parliament (18 May to 6 July 1879) under Khedive Esmaʿil, who probably had a house on this street.

el-Mustashar Muhammad Fathi Nagib, Shareʿ (Garden City)

'Counselor Muhammad Fathi Nagib Str.' Since 2007, after Muhammad Fathi Nagib (1938–2003), lawyer. Nagib was a member of the legal team that successfully asserted Egypt's claim to Taba in 1988. In July 2001, he was appointed head of the Court of Cassation and in September 2001 president of the Supreme Constitutional Court.

> From at least 1925 to 2007: **Shareʿ el-Hadiqa** ('Garden Str.'), after gardens belonging to the el-Qasr el-ʿAli palace

complex, on whose grounds Garden City is built. As late as the Second World War, maps show the area between this street and Share' Qasr el-'Eini as empty of buildings and, in some cases, adorn it with (presumably symbolic) palm trees. Despite this, a historical topographer, writing in 1925, claims that the street is not in the same place as the historical garden.

Mustashfa el-Talaba, Share' (Fumm el-Khalig)
'Students' Hospital Str.' After 1935, after a hospital dedicated to the treatment of students that formerly occupied the site of today's Ministry of Health–run Egypt Children's Hospital.

Muwaffaq el-Din, Share' (Fumm el Khalig)
From after 1948, probably after Muwaffaq el-Din Abu el-'Abbas, born 1198 in Cairo (or 1203 in Damascus), died 1270 in Syria. Often called Ebn Abi Useibe'a, Muwaffaq el-Din is best known for his book *Well-springs of Information about Physicians by Generation* (*'Uyun el-Anbaa' fi Tabaqat el-Atibbaa'*), in which he documents the lives of more than four hundred physicians of varying (Muslim, Christian, Jewish, etc.) traditions. The choice of name was probably suggested by the street's proximity to the Qasr el-'Eini teaching hospital.

N

el-Nabarawi, Share' (Downtown)
By 1912, probably after Ebrahim Beih el-Nabarawi (1817–62), a pioneering Egyptian surgeon who taught at the Qasr el-'Eini hospital. Born to a peasant family in Nabaroh in the Delta's el-Gharbiya province, el-Nabarawi is said to have run away away from home when he failed to get a good price for the family's watermelons. He attached himself to the mosque–university of el-Azhar, then entered the army medical school at Abu Za'bal, where he studied for five years, at the end of which he was sent by the government to France for further studies, returning in 1838. Appointed thereafter to teach at the medical school (now at Qasr

el-'Eini), he eventually became personal physician to Muhammad 'Ali Basha and his successor, 'Abbas Helmi I Basha. 'Ali
Mubarak said of him that he was "the finest surgeon of his generation, courageous enough to undertake tasks no others dared
to attempt" and that he was known as "the doyen of doctors."
El-Nabarawi wrote a book on surgery and translated others into
Arabic from French.

el-Nadwa el-Saqafiya, Mamarr (Downtown)
'Cultural Seminar Passage.' Probably since 1955, when the still-ex-
isting café from which it takes its name was established.

Nafezet Sheyam el-Shaf'i, Kubri *see* el-Manyal, Kubri

el-Naggar, Haret ('Abdin)
Perhaps by 1888; unidentified. Literally, 'Carpenter's Lane'; however, el-Naggar is also a family name, perhaps of early residents.

el-Naggar, Haret (el-Munira)
Date unknown; unidentified. Literally, 'Carpenter's Lane'; however,
el-Naggar is also a family name, perhaps of early residents.

Nagib el-Rihani, Share' (el-Tawfiqiya)
Since 1949, after the comic actor and playwright of Iraqi–Lebanese
parentage (1892–1949) known for his satirical social comedies.
El-Rihani founded his first troupe (with 'Aziz 'Id) in 1915, having 'Rose' el-Yusef (*see* Share' Fatma el-Yusef) as the lead actress.
However, he is best known for his collaborations with poet Badi'
Kheiri, with whom he created the popular character Kishkish Beih,
a rich but naïve landowner from the countryside who falls willing
prey to the fleshpots of the city. El-Rihani starred in seven movies
and wrote more than fifty plays. The choice of name alludes to the
presence in this neighborhood, primarily on nearby Share' 'Emad
el-Din, of the theaters in which Nagib el-Rihani and others of
Egypt's golden age of comic and satirical theater worked.

> From 1944 to 1949: **Share' Qantaret el-Dekka** ('Bench
> Bridge Str.'); *see below and* Share' el-Gumhuriya and Haret
> Qantaret el-Dekka.

Earlier, the street bore two names, as follows:

East of Shareʿ el-Gumhuriya:
From 1885 to 1944: **Shareʿ Wishsh** (or **Wagh**) **el-Berka**
('Top of the Lake Str.'), as it ran along the northern shore of
Berket el-Azbakiya ('el-Azbakiya Lake') before the latter was
drained in 1848. *Wagh* is the literary equivalent of colloquial
Wishsh; when street signs were first put up, starting in 1847,
Wagh was used.

West of Shareʿ el-Gumhuriya:
From 1905 to 1944: **Shareʿ Qantaret el-Dekka** ('Bench
Bridge Str.'), reassigned from the northern stretch of Shareʿ
el-Gumhuriya (*see also* Haret Qantaret el-Dekka).

Shareʿ Wishsh el-Berka and (after 1905) Shareʿ Qantaret
el-Dekka met at former **Midan Qantaret el-Dekka**, then
an important square, now an unnamed intersection.

el-Nahhas, ʿAtfet (ʿAbdin)
Probably by 1888; unidentified. El-Nahhas means literally 'coppersmith,' but is also a family name, perhaps that of early residents.

el-Naʿim, Shareʿ (el-Zamalek)
'Heaven-on-Earth Str.' Since 1936, one of several street names in
the area chosen presumably for their pleasing associations (*see also*
Shareʿ el-Ferdos, Shareʿ el-Nesim, etc.). Until after 1964, when the
Aswan High Dam was completed, allowing stabilization of the
river bank, most of the land between this street, Shareʿ Muhammad Mazhar on the west, and the tip of the island on the north was
devoted to agriculture.

Naqib el-Sahafiyin Kamel Zuheiri, Shareʿ (el-Zamalek)
'President of the Journalists' Syndicate Kamel Zuheiri Str.' Since
2013, after Muhammad Kamel Muhammad ʿAli (el-)Zuheiri (1927–
2008), president of the Egyptian Journalists Syndicate (1968–71 and
1979–81) and of the Arab Journalists' Union (simultaneously with
the foregoing). During his career, Zuheir worked for *Roz el-Yusef* and
el-Helal magazines, and for *el-Gumhuriya* daily newspaper.

From after 1937 to 2013: **Share' el-Narges** ('Narcissus Str.');
one of a series of small streets connecting Share' Yusef Kamel
with Share' Bahgat 'Ali whose names celebrate flowers.

Naser el-Din, Share' (Downtown)
By 1912, in historical evocation of three-time (1293–94, 1299–
1309, and 1310–41) Mamluk ruler el-Malek el-Naser ('Victorious
King') Muhammad ebn Qalawun.

Nasra, 'Atfet ('Abdin)
By 1888, after a female saint, Setti Nasra, whose tomb (no longer in
existence) was situated on this street and who gave her name to Berket
Setti Nasra ('Lady Nasra's Lake,' also known as Berket el-Saqqayin,
'Water Carriers' Lake'), alongside which this street once ran.

el-Nasriya, Share' ('Abdin)
Since 1847, reflecting the street's status as the main artery of the
district of the same name; *see* Share' el-Berka el-Nasriya.

Nasyet el-Ekhsas, Share' (el-Zamalek)
'Hovel Corner Str.' By 1910, probably after the shacks or huts whose
removal was called for in a petition by the better-off residents of the
area (reported in *el-Ahram* of 7 December 1928), on the grounds that
they constituted a health hazard. These 'hovels' may have belonged
to descendants of the fishermen who are said to have been present
when Khedive Esma'il built Saray el-Gezira in 1869, or of Upper
Egyptians who are said to have settled in the area sometime in the
second half of the nineteenth century, or of Nubians brought in by
the British in the early twentieth century to guard an army camp
near Share' Abu el-Feda. In some maps, and on the sign, the name is
given as **Share' Nasyet el-Ekhtesas** but this is a corruption of the
original. At least one official source refers to the presence, in 1910, of
a **Sekket el-Ekhsas**, which was probably the same street.

Nubar, Share' (el-Munira, Downtown, 'Abdin)
Since 1933, after Nubar Basha Nubarian (1825–99), Egypt's first
prime minister, a post he held three times. Nubar's family migrated to
Egypt from Armenia via Izmir and his father (or, according to other
sources, his uncle) worked for Muhammad 'Ali, initially as a translator

and later as his agent, first in Anatolia, then in Paris. His older brother, Shafiq, also worked for Muhammad ʿAli as his personal secretary and translator. Nubar likewise began his career as a royal interpreter, became private secretary to Muhammad ʿAli's heir, Ebrahim Basha, and went on to serve all of Egypt's rulers up to and and including Khedive Esmaʿil. Regarded by many Europeans of his day as the effective power in the country, he also became one of its richest men. Before 1933, this name applied to another street (*see* Shareʿ el-Gumhuriya).

> From 1874 to 1933: **Shareʿ el-Dawawin** ('Government Offices Str.'), after the government divans, or offices, established here following Khedive Esmaʿil's abandonment in 1874 of the Citadel as the seat of government. After the renaming of the rest of the street as Shareʿ Nubar in 1933, the short stretch between Shareʿ el-Tahrir and Shareʿ el-Bustan appears to have retained its original name for a while until eventually becoming (by 1946) the southern end of Shareʿ Sherif.

O

For names whose first letter is sometimes given elsewhere as 'O,' *see under* 'U.'

P

For names whose first letter is sometimes given elsewhere as 'P,' *see under* 'B.'

Philips, Mamarr *see* Filibs, Mamarr

Q

Qadadar, Shareʿ *see* el-Amir Qadadar, Shareʿ

el-Qadi el-Fadel, Share' (Downtown)

By 1908, after Muhy el-Din Abu 'Ali 'Abd el-Rahim ebn 'Ali el-Bisani el-'Asqalani el-Masri (1135–1200), commonly referred to as el-Qadi el-Fadil ('the Learned Judge'), statesman, model of elegant epistolary style, poet, and head of chancery to Salah el-Din (Saladin) and his two immediate successors. As his name shows, the judge's father was from Bisan, in Palestine, while he himself was born in Asqalan, also in Palestine, but moved to Cairo, where he assisted in the transition from the Shiite Fatimid caliphate to the rule of the Sunni Ayyubids. The assignment of the name of el-Qadi el-Fadel to this location is not historically accurate: the plantation and settlement established by el-Qadi el-Fadel were located farther north, in the area between Share' Muhammad 'Ezz el-'Arab on the north and Share' Esma'il Serri on the south, and Share' Qasr el-'Eini on the west and Share' Bur Sa'id and Share' Nubar on the east. The street is one of four, in this and other parts of the city, whose names allude to el-Qadi el-Fadel (*see* Introduction, page 16).

el-Qal'a, Share'

'Citadel Str.' Since 1954, after Qal'et el-Gabal ('the Citadel of the Mountain') to the southeast, to which this street ultimately, under another name, leads. The citadel in question was built by Salah el-Din (Saladin), founder of the Ayyubid dynasty between 1176 and 1193 to protect the city against possible attack by the Crusaders; captive Crusaders were used as labor. It served as the ruler's residence and the seat of government until the reign of Khedive Esma'il, when government offices began to move to Share' el-Dawawin, while the royal residence was transferred to 'Abdin Palace.

> From 1875 to 1954 and from an unknown date after 1954 to the present: **Share' Muhammad 'Ali.** This name originally applied to the entire length of this street from Midan el-'Ataba to Midan el-Qal'a (out of area) but the street was renamed following the fall of the monarchy; later, the stretch between Midan el-'Ataba and its intersection with Midan Bab el-Khalq (out of area) reverted to this name (*see* main entry for this street name).

el-Qammah, Haret ('Abdin)
'Wheat Seller's Lane.' By 1913; earlier, the lane was treated as part
of Haret Selim.

el-Qammah, Zuqaq (el-Munira)
'Wheat Seller's Cul-de-sac.' Date unknown.

Qantaret el-Dekka, Haret (el-Tawfiqiya)
'Bench Bridge Lane.' By 1801, after a bridge over a canal that took
water into the northwest tip of Berket Batn el-Baqara ('Cow's Belly
Lake,' *see* Share' Saray el-Azbakiya) during the Nile flood. The canal
in question was originally called Khalig el-Dakar, after Mamluk
commander Badr el-Din el-Turkumani (d.1338), known as el-Dakar
(meaning perhaps 'the Man of Action'), who had it dug and built the
bridge, known then as Qantaret el-Dakar. By 1475, the canal had
silted up, as had the lake, and both, along with the bridge, were rehabilitated by Mamluk commander Azbak men Tutukh, after which
the lake became known as Berket el-Azbakiya (*see* Share' Saray
el-Azbakiya). The 'bench' in question was a platform, built on the
bridge, for viewing the initial surge of the waters into the depression,
which then gradually dried out over the year. This narrow, almost
invisible, alley is the sole remaining witness to the Qantaret el-Dekka
area, the scene of great pomp and circumstance during the Mamluk
period and a major commercial center from the mid-nineteenth to at
least the mid-twentieth century, when it was home to both a Share'
Qantaret el-Dekka and a Midan Qantaret el-Dekka.

el-Qased, 'Atfet ('Abdin)
Probably by 1904, after a Sufi saint, Sheikh Muhammad el-Qased;
the sheikh's tomb is nearby on Share' 'Abd el-'Aziz Gawish, on the
other side of Share' Muhammad Mahmud. Sheikh el-Qased gave
his name to the cemetery that occupied much of the land in this
vicinity until cleared during the reign of Khedive Esma'il (1863–
79), and hence also to former Share' el-Qased (*see under* Share'
Muhammad Mahmud).

Qasem, Zuqaq (el-Munira)
Probably by 1935; unidentified. Qasem is a male given name, perhaps that of an early resident.

Qasr el-ʿEini, Kubri (Garden City, Fumm el-Khalig)
Since 1954, after Shareʿ Qasr el-Eini, which the bridge joins to the
island of el-Manyal on the west.

> 1908 to 1954: **Kubri el-Amir Muhammad ʿAli**, after Prince
> Muhammad ʿAli Tawfiq (1875–1955), heir presumptive
> (1892–99) and president of the Council of Regency during
> the minority of King Faruq (1937–39), whose palace was
> situated some two hundred meters to its south (*see* Kubri
> Mathaf el-Manyal). The bridge was opened simultaneously
> with Kubri ʿAbbas (connecting the western side of the island
> of el-Manyal to el-Giza; out of area) and Kubri el-Malik
> el-Saleh (connecting el-Manyal to Old Cairo; out of area);
> previously, the island had not been connected to the rest of
> the city by bridges, and no more were built until after 1954.

Qasr el-ʿEini, Shareʿ (Fumm el-Khalig, el-Munira, Garden City)
ʿEl-ʿEini's Palace Str.,' or **Shareʿ el-Qasr el-ʿEini** ('el-ʿEini Palace
Str.'). Since 1900, after the palace of that name built in 1466 at
the southern end of the modern street, in the area then known as
Manshiyet el-Mahrani (*see* Shareʿ Sekket el-Manshiya) by Shehab
el-Din ebn Ahmad ebn ʿAbd el-Rahim ebn Badr el-Din Mahmud
el-ʿEini (d. c.1503), whose last name means 'from Ayntab'—
today's Gaziantep, in Turkey—the birthplace of his grandfather,
a celebrated scholar of religion. Placed as a young man in charge
of market supervision, then becoming chief Hanafi judge and a
favorite of the Mamluk rulers, el-ʿEini was given military rank and
promoted to be Commander of the Pilgrimage and Master of the
Horse; indeed, he became so rich and powerful during the first
decades of his career that he was popularly known as ʿAziz Masr
('the Lord of Egypt'); later, however, he was dogged by imprison-
ment, and the wealth he had amassed in the first half of his career
was lost to the extortions of Egypt's rulers during the second. He
died as a fugitive in Medina, at which point his palace became the
property of the state. Mamluk and Ottoman rulers used the palace
as a guesthouse, as housing for dismissed officials, and as a personal residence. By the nineteenth century, the neighborhood had
become best known for its Bektashi dervish convent next door to
the palace, where a certain Sheikh el-ʿEini was said to be buried.

Around 1836, Muhammad ʿAli Basha established a medical school
and hospital in the area, and these are still in existence. In 1900,
Shareʿ Qasr el-ʿEini included today's Shareʿ Talʿat Harb from
Midan el-Tahrir to Midan Talʿat Harb; in 1913, its domain was
truncated, so that it now ends at Midan el-Tahrir.

> From at least 1861 to 1900: **Shareʿ el-Qasr el-ʿAli** ('High
> Palace Str.'), after the palace complex created by Ebrahim
> Basha (1789–1848) on an area of sand, swamps, and hillocks
> next to the Nile. The complex consisted of two major build-
> ings—a *haramlek* (private family quarters) and a *salamlek*
> (public reception building), some hundreds of yards apart,
> in addition to buildings such as a sugar refinery (*see* Shareʿ
> Maʿmal el-Sukkar). Work appears to have started in 1835.
> Ebrahim's *haramlek* lay to the north, and eventually became
> the palace of his son, Ahmad Refʿat (*see* Shareʿ Ahmad
> Refʿat). His *salamlek* lay to the south, and, restored by
> Khedive Esmaʿil, became, in 1863, the home of the latter's
> mother, Khushyar (Hoshiar) Kadinafandi (*see* former Shareʿ
> Walda Basha, *under* Shareʿ ʿAysha el-Teimuriya). Maps gen-
> erally refer to the first as "the Palace of Ibrahim Basha" and
> to the second as "the Palace of the Khedive's Mother." Later,
> the name Shareʿ el-Qasr el-ʿAli was reassigned to the stretch
> of today's Shareʿ Kurnish el-Nil that borders Garden City on
> the west (*see* Shareʿ Kurnish el-Nil).

> From some point during this same period until 1913, the
> name **Shareʿ Masr el-ʿAtiqa** or **Shareʿ Masr el-Qadima**
> ('Old Cairo Str.') was popularly used of the entire thorough-
> fare today covered by Shareʿ Qasr el-Eini and Shareʿ Talʿat
> Harb up to Shareʿ Setta w-ʿEshrin Yulyu, after the settle-
> ment on the Nile south of modern Cairo to which it led.
> The southern portion of the road was also sometimes called
> **Shareʿ Fumm el-Khalig** ('Canal Inlet Str.'). These names
> also appear on some maps.

el-Qasr el-Kebir, Haret (el-Munira)

'Big Palace Lane.' By 1935, in historical evocation of a palace built
in 1329 by the Mamluk ruler el-Malek el-Naser Muhammad

ebn Qalawun (*see* Share' el-Malek el-Naser) alongside a ground for equestrian exercises and training. The use of this name for this street may, however, be mistaken, as the palace and the training ground, originally called Midan el-Mahari ('Swift Camel Sq.'), in fact covered an area well to the west and were defined, in terms of today's streets, by Share' Bur Sa'id on the south, Share' el-Komi on the east, Share' Mu'ezz el-'Arab on the north, and Share' Helwan on the west. The area where today's street runs would have been covered, in the days of el-Malek el-Naser, seasonally at least, by the waters of el-Berka el-Nasriya (*see* Share' el-Berka el-Nasriya).

Qasr el-Nil, Kubri (Downtown)

'Nile Palace Bridge.' From 1871 (completed) to 1933, from 1953 to 1970, and from an unknown subsequent date (*see* Kubri Gamal 'Abd el-Naser *below*) to the present, after the Qasr el-Nil barracks just to its north on the east bank of the Nile (*see* Share' Qasr el-Nil); in its earlier years, it was also known as **Kubri el-Gezira** ('el-Gezira Bridge'), after the island at its western end, or simply as **el-Kubri** ('the Bridge'; name officially quashed in 1913), reflecting the fact that it was, at the time of its construction, the first and only permanent non-railway crossing over the Nile in Egypt (or elsewhere in Africa). The original bridge was 406 meters long and made of iron girders. Originally intended primarily to allow passage between the palaces of 'Abdin on the east and Saray el-Gezira on the west, it was designed for pedestrian and horse-drawn traffic, though reinforced to take automobiles in 1913; it charged a toll. The bridge was designed by Louis Maurice Adolphe Linant de Bellefonds (1799–1883), chief engineer of the Suez Canal, better known as Linant Pasha, and the bronze lions on either side of each end of the bridge (originally intended for the statue of Muhammad 'Ali in Alexandria) were made by French sculptor Alfred Jacquemart and installed in 1881. The original bridge, which had become unsound, was replaced between 1931 and 1933 by the present structure, a steam ferry operating in the interim.

> 1970 to an unknown date: **Kubri Gamal 'Abd el-Naser**, after the leader of the 1952 revolution and Egypt's second president (r.1956–70). However, the name seems never to have gained traction, either popularly or officially, and may be

considered defunct (*compare* former Midan Anwar el-Sadat, *see under* Midan el-Tahrir).

1933 to 1953: **Kubri el-Khedeiwi Esma'il** ('Khedive Esma'il Bridge'), opened by King Fu'ad on 6 June 1933 following the replacement of the original bridge, and named by him in honor of his father.

Qasr el-Nil, Share' (Downtown)

'Nile Palace Str.' Since 1888, after Qasr el-Nil ('the Nile Palace'), referring to either of two palaces at the western end of the street. The first was built by Muhammad 'Ali Basha (r.1805–48) for his daughter Nazli Hanem immediately to the north of Kubri Qasr el-Nil; this was bought in 1853 by Muhammad Sa'id Basha (r.1854–63) who, on becoming ruler, demolished the palace and replaced it, on a larger area, with the Qasr el-Nil barracks, begun in 1854 and completed in 1863. This in turn became the headquarters of the Egyptian Army and, from 1882, of the British armed forces in Egypt. While demolishing the first, Muhammad Sa'id built, in 1857, a second palace, with the same name, just north of the barracks; this was extensively remodeled by Khedive Esma'il in 1863 and 1869. Eventually, it would become a British military hospital. The barracks, which abutted directly onto the river on the west, and the hospital, were demolished between 1953 and 1954, allowing for the laying out of the corresponding section of Share' Kurnish el-Nil. The barracks themselves were replaced by the Nile Hilton hotel (now the Nile Ritz-Carlton), the Arab League headquarters, and the headquarters of the Arab Socialist Union (after 1962), which later (1978) became the headquarters of the National Democratic Party (gutted by fire 2011, demolished 2016).

From at least 1863 to before 1908, the eastern end of this street, between Midan Mustafa Kamil and Share' el-Gumhuriya, was called **Share' Game' el-Kekhya**, after the mosque built by 'Usman Kekhya (d.1736) at its eastern end.

el-Qeblawi, Haret (Fumm el-Khalig)

By 1935; unidentified. El-Qeblawi (literally, 'from the south') may be a family name, perhaps that of early residents.

Qenawi, 'Atfet (el-Munira)
By 1888; unidentified. Qenawi (literally, 'from Qena') may be a given name, perhaps that of an early resident.

el-Qummus, Haret (Fumm el-Khalig)
'Archpriest's Lane.' From an unknown date; Christian cemeteries and churches exist in the area.

Qushlaq 'Abdin, Share' ('Abdin)
"'Abdin Barracks Str.' Since at least 1914, after barracks built during the reign of Khedive Tawfiq (r.1879–92) to house the royal guard attached to 'Abdin Palace.

R

el-Ra'is 'Abd el-Salam 'Aref, Share' (Downtown)
'President 'Abd el-Salam 'Aref Str.' Since 1966, after Iraq's second president (from 1963 to his death in 1966). In 1964, 'Aref signed an agreement with President Gamal 'Abd el-Naser, a personal friend and a political ally, paving the way for full union between Iraq and Egypt, a project thwarted by 'Aref's death. This name is often ignored in popular usage in favor of Share' el-Bustan (*see below*), especially for the street west of Midan el-Falaki, and even official sources vary in their usage.

The chronology for the different sections of the street is:

From Midan el-Tahrir to Midan el-Falaki:

From at least 1888 to 1933: **Share' el-Bustan** ('Plantation Str.'), after the Saray el-Bustan palace (built 1868, demolished 1980), built as a residence for Khedive Esma'il in the new quarter named after him, and the birthplace and residence of King Fu'ad (1868–1936) before he ascended the throne; later, it served various purposes, including: from 1924 to 1935 that of headquarters of the Foreign Ministry, from 1945 to 1960 that of the first headquarters of the League of Arab States, and from 1961 to 1980 the Science Museum. The palace no doubt took its name in turn from the *bustan* ('plantation') of Ebn Ta'lab (*see* Share' Ebn Ta'lab) or another of the plantations that occupied much of this area from the Ayyubid period. The site of the palace is now occupied by the el-Bustan Center multi-story car park and shopping mall. This name is still frequently used (*see above*).

From Midan el-Falaki to Midan Muhammad Farid:

From 1933 to 1966: **Share' el-Bustan** (*see above*).

From the inception of the Esma'iliya project to 1933: **Share' Kubri Qasr el-Nil.** Until 1933, the names Share' el-Bustan and Share' Kubri Qasr el-Nil (today's Share' el-Tahrir) were reversed east of Midan el-Falaki to Midan Muhammad Farid, so that Share' el-Bustan exited Midan el-Falaki from its southeastern corner, while since 1933 it has exited from its northeastern corner.

From Midan Muhammad Farid to Share' el-Gumhuriya:

From at least 1863 to 1933: **Share' el-Sawwafa** ('Wool Merchants Str.'); this length of the street predates the Esma'iliya project and was formed by the unplanned westward expansion of the city during the earlier part of the nineteenth century.

Ramez, Haret (el-Munira)
Probably by 1908; unidentified. Ramez is a male given name, perhaps that of an early resident.

el-Rammah, Haret ('Abdin)
'Lancer's Lane.' By 1887, after the mosque of Qani Bay el-Seifi, known as el-Rammah ('the Lancer') after his skill with that weapon, who was Master of the Horse during the reigns of Mamluk Sultan Qayit Bay (1468–96) and his son el-Malek el-Naser

Muhammad (1496–98). The mosque, designed to serve also as a school, was completed in 1502 and appears on the LE200 banknote.

Ramsis, Midan (el-Tawfiqiya, el-Azbakiya)

From 1914 to before 1920 and from 1956 to the present, after the colossal statue of Ramsis (Ramesses) II discovered in 1820 at Mit Rahina (ancient Memphis, twenty kilometers south of Giza) that presided over the square from 1954 to 2006. Use of the name is discontinuous: Viscount Kitchener (British agent and consul-general in Egypt from 1911 to 1914) planned to bring the statue to the square and was the first to give it this name (Baedeker's Guide, English edition, 1914, p.78). The project was aborted by the eruption of the First World War, and by 1920 the name had disappeared from the maps. Kitchener's project was eventually realized in February 1954, when the statue was brought to the square and the name restored. In 2006, amid fears of the impact on it of pollution and vibration, the statue was moved again, to the Giza Plateau, where it is slated for installation at the Grand Egyptian Museum.

> From 1928 to 1956: **Midan Nahdet Masr** (Egypt's Awakening Sq.), popularly **Midan el-Nahda,** after the celebrated statue by Mahmud Mukhtar, unveiled there in 1928, showing Egypt as a woman raising her veil with her right hand and placing her left on the head of a seated sphinx. In 1955, following the installation of the statue of Ramsis II, Muhktar's statue was moved to its present location in el-Giza, at the entrance to the avenue (thereafter Share' Nahdet Masr) that leads to Cairo University.

> From at least 1912 to 1928 two names were used: **Midan el-Mahatta** ('Station Sq.') designated the northern part of the square, **Midan Bab el-Hadid** its contiguous southern portion. This followed a reconfiguration of the spaces in front of the station and at the end of Share' el-Gumhuriya that was made possible by the filling in of the Esma'iliya Canal and the creation of the streets known today as Share' Ramsis and Share' el-Galaa'. The name Midan el-Mahatta reflected the presence of the terminus of the Cairo–Alexandria railway line (the first in Africa; the station was opened in 1856 and rebuilt

in 1893 following a fire). The name Midan Bab el-Hadid
maintained the ancient designation (*see below*). Both names
continue to be used informally for the square as a whole.

From 1914 to before 1920: **Midan Ramsis** (*see* main entry
above).

Anciently to 1914 (and informally to the present): **Midan
Bab el-Hadid** ('Iron Gate Sq.'), after the westernmost
bastion of the city wall built by Salah el-Din (Saladin), which
stood, until 1281, on the banks of the Nile and which marked
Cairo's limit in that direction until the end of the eighteenth
century. Though the gate (located at the entrance of today's
Share' Kulut Beih) was demolished in 1847, the name Midan
Bab el-Hadid has continued to be used, at least informally,
throughout the square's subsequent history, irrespective of the
name(s) given on maps. During the earlier period, and especially on maps of the last quarter of the nineteenth century,
the square was sometimes also referred to as **Midan el-Faggala** ('Radish Farmers' Sq.'), after the quarter to its east.

Ramsis, Share' (Downtown, el-Tawfiqiya)
Since 1956, simultaneously with the naming of Midan Ramsis, to
which it leads.

From 1954 to 1956: **Share' Nahdet Masr** ('Egypt's Awakening Str.'), after the square to which it led (*see* former Midan
Nahdet Masr, *under* Midan Ramsis).

From 1950 to 1954: **Share' el-Maleka** ('Queen Str.'). Following a falling-out between King Faruq and his mother (*see*
Share' el-Maleka Nazli *below*) over the latter's support for her
daughter's marriage to a Copt, the name was changed, leaving
the street in a state of generic regality.

From at least 1927 to 1950: **Share' el-Maleka Nazli**
('Queen Nazli Str.'), after Nazli Sabri, second wife, from 1919
until his death in 1936, of King Fu'ad and mother of King
Faruq (r.1936–52).

From 1893 to at least 1926: **Share' 'Abbas, or el-Share'
el-'Abbasi,** after Khedive 'Abbas Helmi II (r.1892–1914),
during whose reign the Esma'iliya Canal (*see below*) was filled
in from the Nile to the new district of el-'Abbasiya (also
named in the khedive's honor). This name was confirmed by
official notice in 1916, despite, or because of, Khedive Abbas's
dethronement by the British in 1914.

From 1863 to 1893: **Share' Ter'et el-Esma'iliya**
('Esma'iliya Canal Str.'), an unpaved road running parallel
to the Esma'iliya Canal on its southern side. The canal, also
known as the Sweet Water Canal, made use, at its western
end, of the remains of el-Khalig el-Naseri and was inaugurated in 1863. It took water from inlet points at what is now
Midan 'Abd el-Men'em Reyad and at Shubra and conveyed
it to the city of el-Esma'iliya and other communities along
the Suez Canal (both inlets were filled in in 1910 and the
Esma'iliya Canal now draws its water from an inlet at Shubra
el-Kheima). The canal was also, probably from 1874, a source
of piped water (*see* Share' Wabur el-Meyah), supplanting the
city's two ancient canals as a source of drinking water for the
city's new areas; as such it played an essential role in their
development. Share' Ter'et el-Esma'iliya marked the boundary between Cairo and Bulaq. The street is sometimes referred
to as **Share' el-Ter'a el-Esma'iliya** ('Esma'il's Canal Str.'),
after the khedive rather than the city.

el-Rashidi, Share' (el-Munira)
By 1948, after either Dr. Ahmad Hasan el-Rashidi (d.1865), who
taught medicine at the Abu Za'bal medical school and wrote several
books in that field, or Dr. Hesein Ghanem el-Rashidi, a contemporary of the former. Both men worked as language editors at the Abu
Za'bal medical school in the late 1820s or 1830s and both were
then sent by the government to study medicine in France.

From at least 1918 to no later than 1948: **Share' Gohar
el-Qa'ed** ('General Gohar's Str.'), in historical evocation of
Abu el-Hasan Jawhar ebn 'Abd Allah el-Seqelli (d.992), a
slave who rose to become general of the Fatimid armies in

their drive to conquer North Africa (the last element of his name means 'the Sicilian,' though recent research suggests he was Dalmatian). Gohar conquered Egypt in 969 and ruled it as viceroy for the Fatimids until 972, during which period he founded the city of Cairo and built the mosque of el-Azhar; after further campaigns, he was again viceroy from 975 to 979. A major street in the medieval city also bears this name.

By 1908: **Share' Meleka**. The name appears only in European-language maps and the transliteration (as shown here) does not give a clear meaning. Perhaps what is meant is 'Malaka,' a female given name, perhaps that of an early resident.

Reda Basha, Share' (el-Munira)
Probably by 1935; unidentified, but likely the same person who gave his name to nearby Share' (Reda) el-Hakim.

Reda el-Hakim, Share' *see* el-Hakim, Share'

Rushdi, Share' (Downtown)
Since 1938, after Hesein Basha Rushdi (1863–1928), a French-trained lawyer who held numerous government positions between 1908 and 1921, including those of chairman of the committee that drafted the 1922 constitution, minister of foreign affairs, and, four times, premier; in the latter capacity he declared war in 1914 against the German–Ottoman alliance, thus severing Egypt's ties to the Ottoman sultan, its former suzerain. Rushdi was a major player in the struggle for Egyptian independence from British protection, both resigning the premiership (3 December 1918) in protest at Britain's refusal to allow an Egyptian delegation to go to the Paris peace conference and later (April 1919) forming the 'Cabinet of Seven,' popularly maligned for its willingness to work under the British protectorate. Between 1938 and 1948, the street ended on the west at former Share' el-Sheikh Abu el-Seba' (*see under* Share' el-Shahid Gawad Husni); thereafter, it was extended to Share' Sherif, displacing the name Share' Muhammad Mazlum from that part of the street.

From at least 1906 to 1938: **Share' el-Saha** ('Enclosure Str.'), after a donkey market on land that was formerly part

of Bustan Ebn Taʿlab (*see* Shareʿ Ebn Taʿlab) that stretched
from this street to Shareʿ el-Raʾis ʿAbd el-Salam ʿAref on the
south and from Shareʿ Muhammad Farid on the west to Shareʿ
el-Gumhuriya on the east. The market was held daily after the
afternoon prayer until at least 1888; the enclosure also held two
plaster kilns. **Shareʿ Suq el-ʿAsr** ('Afternoon Market Str.'),
gazetted for ʿAbdin in 1885, may refer to this street.

S

el-Saʿayda, Haret or ʿAtfet (ʿAbdin)
'Upper Egyptians' Lane' (or Alley). By 1885.

el-Sabaʿ Seqayat, Shareʿ (Fumm el Khalig)
'Seven Watering Points Str.' By 1920, in historical evocation of
seven water distribution points served by a single well that were
constructed and dedicated as endowments for the public good by
the Ekhshidid-dynasty vizier Jaʿfar ebn el-Fadl ebn el-Furat (tenth
century). The naming of this street after Ebn el-Furat's installations, however, appears to be an error: their originals were located
some two kilometers away, near the Ebn Tulun mosque, and the
site of this street was under water when they were built.

Sabet, Darb (el-Munira)
Probably since after 1935; unidentified. Sabet is a family name,
perhaps that of early residents of the street.

Sabri Abu ʿAlam, Shareʿ *see* Muhammad Sabri Abu ʿAlam,
Shareʿ

Saʿd Zaghlul, Midan (el-Gezira)
Since 1938, after the 16-meter-tall statue of nationalist leader Saʿd
Zaghlul (1859–1927) that dominates the square and is the twin
of that in the square of the same name in Alexandria. The statue,
sculpted by Mahmud Mukhtar and paid for by public subscription,
was unveiled on 27 August 1938. On some maps, the name is given
as **Midan el-Ubera** ('Opera Sq.'), after the Cairo Opera House in

the adjacent grounds; however, this does not seem to have official standing and risks confusion with the Downtown square of the same name.

> From at least 1929 to 1938: **Midan el-Gezira** ('Island Sq.'), after the Island (*el-Gezira*, the Island of Bulaq) to which the square functioned as the point of entry from the southeast. This name continues to appear on some maps.

Sa'd Zaghlul, Share' (el-Munira)
Since 1914, after Sa'd Ebrahim Zaghlul Basha (1859–1927), nationalist politician and founder–leader of the Wafd (Delegation) Party, established to argue for the independence and unity of Egypt and the Sudan at the Paris Peace Conference of 1918. For refusing to give up his political agitation against them, the British exiled Zaghlul to Malta and then to the Seychelles, leading to the popular uprising of 1919. Zaghlul returned to Egypt in 1923 and won the 1924 elections by a landslide. Zaghlul's house, Beit el-Umma ('the House of the Nation'), still stands at #2 on this street and has been turned into a museum and arts space.

> By 1908 to 1914: **Share' Helmi Basha**; unidentified.

el-Sadd el-Barrani, Share' (Fumm el Khalig)
'Outer Levee Str.' Since 1885, after a levee, also known historically as el-Gisr el-A'zam ('the Great Dyke'), built to direct the waters of the Nile flood to the fields to the southeast of the levee and to protect the city to its northwest. The levee followed the course of the Nile before the river shifted to the west in the twelfth and thirteenth centuries and thus predates the Esma'iliya project.

Sa'd el-Din, Share' (el-Munira)
By 1935; unidentified. Sa'd el-Din is a given name, perhaps that of an early resident.

el-Safa, Share' (el-Zamalek)
'Felicity Str.' By 1928; one of several street names in the area chosen presumably for their pleasing associations (*see also* Share' el-Ferdos, Share' el-Ward, etc.).

Safiya Zaghlul, Shareʿ (el-Munira)

By 1948, after Safiya Mustafa Fahmi (1876–1946), daughter of two-time prime minister Mustafa Basha Fahmi and wife of nationalist leader Saʿd Basha Zaghlul (*see* Shareʿ Saʿd Zaghlul), whose name she took. Safiya Zaghlul was a political and social activist in her own right and became known as 'Mother of the Egyptians' for her encouragement of demonstrators during the events of 1919; she remained politically active after her husband's death in 1927.

> From at least 1908 to no later than 1948: **Shareʿ el-Ensha**, either after the Qasr el-Ensha palace built by Khedive Esmaʿil for his daughter Princess Tawhida (Tefida), wife of Mansur Basha Yakan, or after the district between Shareʿ Muhammad ʿEzz el-ʿArab on the south and Shareʿ el-Sheikh Rihan on the north that was known, until at least the 1950s, as el-Ensha (literally, 'the construction'), perhaps because of the building work that went on there (Khedive Esmaʿil built at least two other palaces for other daughters in the same neighborhood). The district is now generally treated as a part of el-Munira, a name that formerly applied south of Shareʿ Muhammad ʿEzz el-ʿArab only.

Salah el-Din, Sekket (el-Zamalek)

By 1910, after Salah el-Din Ayyub (*see* Shareʿ Salah el-Din).

Salah el-Din, Shareʿ (el-Zamalek)

By 1913, after el-Malek el-Naser ('Victorious King') Salah el-Din Yusef ebn Negm el-Din el-Ayyubi (r.1169–93), known in English as Saladin, effectively the first Ayyubid sultan of Egypt and Syria and founder of the Ayyubid dynasty (his predecessor, his uncle Sherkuh, died almost immediately after gaining possession of Egypt). Salah el-Din, a Sunni Muslim of Kurdish background, put an end to the Shiite state of the Fatimids in Egypt while successfully fighting the Crusaders in Palestine. His sultanate included Egypt, Syria, Upper Mesopotamia, the Hejaz, Yemen, and parts of North Africa.

Salah Taher, Shareʿ (el-Zamalek)

Since 2013, after Salah Taher (1911–2007), a painter of the realist, and later the abstract, schools, also known for his portraits (for example, of presidents Gamal ʿAbd el-Naser and Anwar el-Sadat). From 1954, he served in several positions in the arts bureaucracy, including that of director of the Cairo Opera House (1962–66).

> From 1936 to 2013: **Shareʿ el-Nesim** ('Breeze Str.'), one of several names in the area presumably chosen for their pleasing associations (*see also* Shareʿ el-Ferdos, Shareʿ el-Naʿim, etc.).

Saleh ʿArafa, Haret (el-Munira)
Perhaps from c.1918; unidentified. Saleh ʿArafa is a man's name, perhaps that of an early resident.

el-Saleh Ayyub, Shareʿ (el-Zamalek)
By 1913, after el-Malek el-Saleh ('the Righteous King') Negm el-Din Ayyub (r.1240–49), the last Ayyubid ruler of Egypt to wield effective power. His wife, Shagaret el-Durr, married a Mamluk, who became the first ruler of the Mamluk era (*see* Shareʿ Shagaret el-Durr).

Saleh Selim, Midan (el-Gezira)
Since 2003; as for Shareʿ Saleh Selim.

Saleh Selim, Shareʿ (el-Gezira)
Since 2003, after Saleh Selim (1930–2002), soccer player. Selim played for el-Nadi el-Ahli ('the National Club') from 1944—with a brief intermission as a professional with Graz, Austria—until 1967, after which he continued his association with the club by serving as president from 1980 to 1988 and from 1990 to 1992.

> From 1976 to 2003: **Shareʿ el-Andalus**, after the el-Andalus Garden, laid out in 1897, to the north of Qasr el-Nil bridge at the entrance to el-Gezira and opposite this more recently created street. El-Andalus is the Arabic name for the parts of the Iberian Peninsula that were under Muslim rule from the eighth to the fifteenth centuries and is the origin of 'Andalusia.'

Salem, Haret (ʿAbdin)
By 1888, after Salem Basha Salem (1832–93), called el-Hakim ('the Doctor'), who owned a house on the street. Son of a celebrated

Azhari scholar, Sheikh Salem el-Sharqawi, Salem was educated at the Madraset el-Alsun (*see* Share' Madraset el-Alsun), then joined the Qasr el-'Eini medical school. In 1850, he was sent by the government to study medicine in Germany and on his return, after first being assigned to the army, became attached to the royal court as Khedive Tawfiq's private physician. He authored works on internal medicine and on the therapeutic qualities of mineral water.

Sameh Ahmad el-Sayyed, Share' (el-Zamalek)
Probably from the mid-1970s, after a businessman who built an apartment block on the street.

Sami, Share' ('Abdin)
By 1887, after a certain Ya'qub Beih Sami, whose house was on the street at the date given.

Samir Zaki, Share' (el-Zamalek)
Since at least 1973, perhaps after Samir Zaki 'Abd el-Qawi, chairman of the board of the Sixth of October Company for Reclamation and Development, though he is not believed to have lived on this street.

> From at least 1930 to no later than 1972: **Share' Jan Bunfur** ('Jean Bonfour (?) Str.'). Unidentified; perhaps an early resident of the street.

Sanduq el-Tawfir, Share' (Downtown)
'Savings Fund Str.' Since after 1946, after the National Savings Bank, run by the Post Office (which has facilities on and close to this street). The change in name neatly replaces the sense of the street's former name (*see below*) with its opposite.

> From c.1920 to at least 1946: **Share' Sanduq el-Dein** ('Public Debt Fund Str.'), after the building constructed in 1889 to house the Caisse de la Dette Publique ('Public Debt Fund'), an office established by Khedive Esma'il in 1876 to supervise the repayment of Egypt's debts to foreign creditors. The Caisse was abolished in 1940 and the building, which occupies part of the site of a large palace built by 'Ali Beih el-Kebir, Egypt's

de facto ruler from 1760 to 1772, now houses Cairo's Health Directorate (entrance on Share' el-Beidaq).

el-Saqqayin, Share' ('Abdin)

'Water Sellers' Str.' By 1888, an extension of the older Haret el-Saqqayin ('Water Sellers' Lane,' officially named in 1847; out of area). The association with water sellers may be due to the presence in the vicinity until the second half of the nineteenth century of a seasonal pond, el-Berka el-Nasriya (*see* Share' el-Berka el-Nasriya), also called Berket el-Saqqayin ('Water Sellers' Lake'), one of several from which water sellers drew their water, especially during the three months following the peak of the annual flood. Some water sellers sold water wholesale, bringing it on donkey- or camel-back to fill cisterns beneath houses, others retail, in the street, from skins carried on their backs. The number of water sellers was estimated in 1870 at 3,876, divided into five guilds, each covering an area of the city. Their numbers declined rapidly following the introduction of piped water.

Saray el-Azbakiya, Haret (Downtown)

'El-Azbakiya Palace Lane.' Since 1935, after Share' Saray el-Azbakiya, which this short street connects to Share' Setta w-'Eshrin Yulyu.

Saray el-Azbakiya, Share' (el-Tawfiqiya)

'El-Azbakiya Palace Str.,' or **Share' el-Azbakiya** ('el-Azbakiya Str.'). Since 1935, after a palace built by Muhammad 'Ali Basha for his daughter Zeinab Hanim on the western bank of Berket el-Azbakiya ('el-Azbakiya Lake'), replacing an earlier palace belonging to Muhammad Beih el-Alfi (1751–1807) (*see* Share' Muhammad Beih el-Alfi); or, in the case of the alternative name, for the district of el-Azbakiya as a whole, which takes its name from Mamluk commander Azbak (Turkish Özbek) men Tutukh (literally, 'Azbak-who-was-purchased-from-Tutukh'; d.1498 or 1499), who built his palace there in 1476, starting a fashion followed by other Mamluk grandees, and rehabilitated an existing seasonal lake, Berket Batn el-Baqara ('Cow's Belly Lake'). This was filled in in 1848. Reference is often made to the 1869 make-over of the resulting park, henceforth known as Geneinet el-Azbakiya ('the el-Azbakiya

Garden'), by a French garden designer in imitation of Paris's Park Monceau, ordered by Khedive Esmaʿil to impress guests invited for the opening of the Suez Canal. Even before that, however, a contemporary could describe it as "Cairo's largest park for the common people, with extensive peripheries, full of trees with interlacing branches and sweet-smelling herbs and flowers, as well as of paths geometrically arranged encircling Frankish cafes where, from as soon as the sun declines to the time of the evening prayer, natives and globetrotters, be they Franks or Arabs or Turks or of any other nation, meet." Originally a kilometer in length and half a kilometer in breadth, the park has been reduced in size numerous times and only a fraction of it survives. Until late in the nineteenth century, the el-Azbakiya district was Cairo's modern center and the residential district most favored by Europeans. The street was pedestrianized in the late 1990s.

> From at least 1912 to 1935: **Shareʿ el-Telleghraf** ('Telegraph Str.'), after the headquarters of the Egyptian Telephone and Telegraph Company, established in 1881. The first telegraph line in Egypt was set up in 1854, to serve the railroad.

el-Sawwafa, Haret (Downtown)
'Wool Merchants' Lane.' By 1904, presumably after the profession of its first residents; formerly, this lane led off Shareʿ el-Sawwafa (*see* Shareʿ el-Ra'is ʿAbd el-Salam ʿAref). Until 1913, when it was officially quashed, the name **Sekket el-Sawwafa** ('Wool Merchants' Connecting Str.') appears also to have been used of this and surrounding lanes.

el-Sayes, Haret (el-Munira)
'Groom's Lane.' Probably by 1863; A *sayes* or 'syce' not only looked after horses but also ran in front of or at the stirrup of important persons when they drove or rode through the city.

el-Sayyala, Kubri (Fumm el-Khalig)
'Channel Bridge,' or **Kubri Sayyalet el-Roda** ('el-Manyal Channel Bridge'). By 1962, after the water channel (Arabic *sayyala*) that separates the island of el-Roda (or el-Manyal) from the eastern bank of the Nile close to the Tumor Institute.

From after 1954 to no later than 1962: **Kubri Fumm el-Khalig** ('Canal Inlet Bridge'), after the entry point for water into the el-Khalig el-Masri canal; the canal was filled in in 1899 but its name survives in Midan Fumm el-Khalig ('Canal Inlet Square'), just south of the bridge. This name is still used in some recent maps.

el-Sayyed el-Bakri, Share' (el-Zamalek)

Since 1954, probably after el-Sayyed Muhammad Tawfiq el-Bakri (1870–1932), poet, prose writer, and reformist who in 1881 led the first, short-lived, attempt at the creation of an Arabic language academy. El-Bakri was a member of a distinguished family of *sayyed*s, or descendants of the Prophet Muhammad and of the first caliph, Abu Bakr el-Seddiq; he was appointed head of the Sufi orders of Egypt and representative of the descendants of the Prophet, both posts traditionally held by members of the Bakri family.

From 1913 to 1954: **Share' el-Amir Kamal** ('Prince Kamal Str.'), after Prince Kamal el-Din Hesein (1874–1932), son of Sultan Hesein Kamel. An avid explorer, particularly of the Western Desert, Prince Kamal gave the plateau known as el-Gelf el-Kebir its name. He was also a collector of oriental art and antiques and reportedly an adherent of the Bektashi Sufi order. Uniquely in the history of the Egyptian monarchy, he renounced his right to succeed his father in October 1917, possibly in protest at the British occupation; this led to the ascension to the throne of his uncle, Sultan (later King) Ahmad Fu'ad I (r.1917–36). This area of el-Zamalek—immediately north of Khedive Esma'il's palace of Saray el-Gezira and extending to Share' Setta w-'Eshrin Yulyu—is home to twelve streets formerly named after princes of the ruling family. Of these, six were the sons of Khedive Esma'il (not represented were two who died young plus his second son, Muhammad Tawfiq, later to become khedive and have the whole district of el-Tawfiqiya named after him), the others his cousins or grandsons.

Sayyed Darwish, Share' *see* el-Sheikh Sayyed Darwish, Share'

el-Sayyed Muhammad Taher, Share' (Downtown)
Probably by 1973; unidentified. Despite the large size of this street and its relative newness, it has proved impossible to find any information about the person after whom it is named.

> From at least 1801 to probably no later than 1973: **Haret el-Fawwala** ('Bean Sellers' Lane'), after the old neighborhood of el-Fawwala (Ard el-Fawwla, 'Bean Sellers' Ground'), which itself took its name from Berket el-Fawwala ('Bean Sellers' Lake'), which at the start of the nineteenth century stretched north to today's Share' Setta w-'Eshrin Yulyu and into the el-Tawfiqiya district. Starting in 1911 and continuing until recently, the el-Fawwala block (between Share' Muhammad Farid on the west, Share' el-Gumhuriya on the east, Share' Qasr el-Nil on the north, and Share' Rushdi on the south) was largely reconfigured, most of its streets being either replaced by much wider and longer streets, as in this case, or eliminated altogether. Streets that disappeared in their entirety are: Haret el-Kafarwa north of Share' Rushdi, Haret Awlad She'eib ('Sons of She'eib Lane'), 'Atfet Awlad She'eib ('Sons of She'eib Alley'; by 1863), Zuqaq Zaher el-Lon ('Resplendent Color Cul-de-sac'), Zuqaq el-Sahbi, Zuqaq Farag, Zuqaq el-Nesha ('Starch Cul-de-sac'), Darb el-Manakh ('Camel-ground Side Street'), 'Atfet el-Makhbaz ('Bakery Alley'), Rahabet el-Tebn ('Straw Field'; previously called, from at least 1863 until at least 1913, Share' Sahet el-Hemir, 'Donkey Enclosure Str.'), and 'Atfet Abu Haggag.

Sayyed Taha, Share' (Downtown)
Probably from the 1960s, after Brigadier General Sayyed Mahmud Taha (1915–51), 'the Black Hyena,' leader of Egyptian forces in Palestine during the 1948 war. Besieged, along with Gamal 'Abd el-Naser and other members of the secret Free Officers organization, at the southern Palestinian village of Faluja from October 1948 until the end of February 1949, Taha withdrew under the armistice arrangements but did not suffer defeat. The Siege of Faluja was celebrated during the subsequent era as a symbol of heroism and as an incubator of the demand for change that led to the revolution of 1952.

From at least 1946 to probably the 1960s: **Share' N. Museiri,** after Nesim Museiri (Nissim Mosseri) (1848–97), prominent member of a Jewish money-lending and banking family of Italian origin, who in 1876 founded the bank J.N. Mosseri et Fils Cie.

el-Sayyeda Umm Kulsum, Share' (el-Gezira)
'Lady Umm Kulsum Str.' Since 1975, after Fatma Ebrahim el-Sayyed el-Beltagi (1898 or 1904–1975), known as Umm Kulsum (and popularly as el-Sett, or 'the Lady'), *diva* and actress. Regarded by some as the greatest Arab singer of all time, her monthly Thursday-night broadcast concerts in the period after 1967 were listened to throughout the Arab World. Her statue, by Tareq el-Komi, stands where her villa once stood on Share' Abu el-Feda. This name applies to the entire length of the street along the western bank of el-Gezira Island from its southern end to the beginning of Share' Abu el-Feda in the north.

From at least 1962 to 1975, **Share' el-Gabalaya** ('Little Mountain Str.'); this followed the transfer of this name from the street that runs to the east of the grotto known as the Fish Garden to that which runs to its west, on the renaming of the eastern street as Share' Hasan Sabri (*see* Share' Hasan Sabri, main entry).

Before 1962, this thoroughfare was treated for naming purposes as two streets of roughly equal length, the first from the southern end of the island to the intersection with today's Share' el-Gezira/ Share' Hasan Sabri, the second from the same intersection north to the beginning of Abu el-Feda at the intersection with Share' Setta w-'Eshrin Yulyu. The names evolved as follows:

Southern section:
From at least 1954 to no later than 1962: **Share' Hasan Sabri,** that is, this street was regarded as the southern section of today's Share' Hasan Sabri (*see* main entry).

From at least 1937 to no later than 1954: **Share' el-Gabalaya** ('Little Mountain Str.'), former name of Share' Hasan Sabri

and, by the same logic, the same thoroughfare's southern
section (*see* Share' Hasan Sabri, main entry).

By 1897 to before 1937: **Share' el-Gezira** ('Island Str.'), that
is, this street was regarded as the southern section of today's
street of the same name. In 1897, no named streets existed
north of the point where the street turns inland. *See also*
Share' el-Gezira, main entry.

Northern section:
From c.1907 to before 1962, **Share' el-Bahr el-A'ma**
('Blind River Str.'), after the channel that separates el-Gezira
from el-Duqqi, el-'Aguza, and Embaba which originally
filled only during the annual flood. Dredging of the channel
was completed in 1871, allowing a year-round flow of water.
Dim lighting and ease of access to the river's bank, hidden
behind trees and bushes, gave this street a reputation as a
lovers' lane.

el-Sayyeda Zeinab, Midan (el-Munira)
'Lady Zeinab's Sq.' Since soon after 1898, after el-Sayyeda Zeinab
(d. c.681), daughter of the Prophet Muhammad's daughter Fatima
el-Zahraa' and his son-in-law and nephew 'Ali ebn Abi Taleb, and
the mosque that is dedicated to her and that is said to hold her
tomb. Historians agree that el-Sayyeda Zeinab died and was buried in Medina, in the Hejaz, and that there is no evidence that
her remains were brought to Egypt. Notwithstanding that, popular
sentiment appears to have insisted, starting from the later Mamluk
period, that el-Sayyeda Zeinab was in fact buried in Cairo, rival
claims being made for tombs at Bab el-Nasr (out of area) and
close to Qanater el-Seba' (*see below*). Sufi saint 'Ali el-Khawass
clinched the matter with a dream in favor of the latter in the early
sixteenth century, and the tomb has remained a site of intense popular piety ever since. The mosque took on its present form, after
numerous enlargments, demolitions, and rebuildings, in 1942. The
square itself took on its present form following the filling in of
the el-Khalig el-Masri canal in 1898 to accommodate a streetcar
line, and the consequent demolition of old houses built against the
mosque that had hidden it from view from the west.

From the third quarter of the thirteenth century to soon after 1898, **Midan Qanater el-Seba'** ('Lions' Bridges Sq.'), after two bridges over the el-Khalig el-Masri canal that were built by Mamluk sultan el-Malek el-Zaher ('Resplendent King') Beibars (r.1260–77) and decorated with reliefs of lions, his personal emblem. Though this square fell on the west side of the canal while the mosque of el-Sayyeda Zeinab was located to its east, it was this expanse that contributed the greater part to today's square, following the filling in of the canal.

Seif, Haret (el-Munira)
Date unknown; unidentified. Seif (literally, 'sword') is a male given name, perhaps that of an early resident.

Seif el-Din el-Mahrani, Share' *see* el-Mahrani, Share'

Sekket Hadid Helwan, Share' *see* Helwan, Share'

Selim, Haret ('Abdin)
By 1904, after Selim Beih (later, Basha) Fathi, appointed governor of Sudan in 1851, who had a mansion here. Not to be confused with Haret Selim (el-Munira).

Selim, Haret (el-Munira)
Probably by 1918; unidentified. Selim is a male given name, perhaps that of an early resident. Not to be confused with Haret Selim ('Abdin).

Seliman el-Halabi, Share' (el-Tawfiqiya)
By 1962, after Seliman ebn Muhammad Amin (c.1777–1800), the theology student from Aleppo (Halab) who assassinated French general Jean-Baptiste Kléber, commander of the French occupation forces in Egypt following Napoleon's departure, in the garden of his headquarters at el-Azbakiya on 14 June 1800. El-Halabi, who stated that he had come to Egypt with the intention of committing this act, was executed on 17 June 1800 (his right hand was burned to the bone, after which he was impaled and his body left to rot) at the public execution area formerly located at the intersection of Share' Muhammad 'Ezz el-'Arab and Share' el-Munira, an area

now shared by the Dar el-'Ulum Garden and the grounds of the
Institut Français d'Archéologie Orientale. His skull and his dagger
are on display at the Musée de l'Homme in Paris.

> From at least 1875 to at least 1948: **Share' Dubreih**, prob-
> ably after Yusef Beih Dubreih (1838– after 1890), chief of
> secret police under Khedive Tawfiq; the name is spelled on
> maps in a variety of ways, and might in origin be Dubray, or
> Dupré, or Debray. According to his contemporary biographer,
> lawyer and journalist Yusef Asaf, Yusef's father, whose name
> is given in Arabic as Eskandar (that is, Alexandre), came to
> Egypt from France in 1830 as one of the twenty young doctors
> who accompanied Clot Beih when the latter was invited by
> Muhammad Ali Basha to organize a health system for the mil-
> itary (*see* Share' Kulut Beih). Yusef was born in Cairo, educated
> at foreign schools, and thereafter alternated between working
> as a translator (between 1858 and 1864 he was employed by
> the Suez Canal Company to translate for De Lesseps, builder
> of the Suez Canal) and engaging in ultimately unsuccessful
> commercial ventures. He joined the police force as a translator
> in the 1870s and in 1880 reached the rank of second inspec-
> tor. His big break came in 1882, when he remained loyal to
> Khedive Tawfiq in the face of Ahmad 'Urabi's mutiny and fled
> with twenty-six other police officers to Port Said, from which
> the khedive brought them to Alexandria by boat. In Alexan-
> dria, Dubreih was given the task of organizing the police force
> there, and, following 'Urabi's defeat, in Cairo. In 1883, he was
> promoted to first inspector and in 1885 was charged with orga-
> nizing, under the ministry of the interior, a secret police force,
> of which he was then appointed director. Dubreih introduced
> a system for the recording of prior offences "for every person
> in Egyptian territory" and of taking photographs of offenders
> that could then be circulated to police stations, passport offices,
> and ports. Asaf notes that he "distributed secret police agents
> throughout Egypt to keep an eye on things."

Sengar, Share' (Fumm el Khalig)
After 1948; according to residents, after the Singer Sewing
Machine company, its first agency in Cairo having opened on this

street. However, the presence of a Singer Sewing Machine agency in Goad's 1904 insurance map of el-Azbakiya, on Share' el-Bawaki (out of area), throws doubt on this, and perhaps on the connection to sewing machines in general.

Senteral, Mamarr (Downtown)

Since 1927, when the candy store named Centrale, which gives its name to the passageway and is still in operation, opened. An alternative name for the same passageway is **Mamarr Babik**, after the watch and smoking accessories store at its north end (opened in the same year), which itself evokes the Bebek Palace in Istanbul, on the shores of the Bosphorus, gifted by the Ottoman sultan in 1894 to the Egyptian royal family and now the Egyptian consulate.

Seri Lanka, Share' (el-Zamalek)

Since 1983, in recognition of the presence on the street of the Embassy of Sri Lanka.

> From no earlier than 1937 to 1983: **Share' Yehya Basha Ebrahim**, after Yehya Ebrahim (1861–1936), lawyer and politician, who held several ministries, including education, and was prime minister from 15 March 1923 to 27 January 1924, during which time he secured the return from exile of nationalist leader Sa'd Zaghlul, whose Wafdist Party then proceeded to defeat Ebrahim's government by a landslide. Ebrahim's refusal to contest the election strengthened the election's credibility and his own reputation for integrity. In 1925, Ebrahim became the first president of the Hezb el-Ettehad ('Union Party'), allied to the palace. This name is still found on signs on the street.

> From 1913 to at least 1937: **Share' el-Amir Hesein**, after Prince Hesein Kamel (1853–1917), a son of Khedive Esma'il who became sultan of Egypt in 1914 following the deposition by the British of his nephew Khedive 'Abbas Helmi II and the severing of ties between Egypt and the Ottoman Empire, with which Britain was at war. By the time this name was changed, Hesein Kamel had been commemorated—as sultan,

rather than prince—with another, larger, street (*see* former Shareʿ el-Sultan Hesein Kamel, *under* Shareʿ el-Sheikh Rihan). This area of el-Zamalek—immediately northeast of Khedive Esmaʿilʾs palace of Saray el-Gezira and extending to Shareʿ Setta w-ʿEshrin Yulyu—is home to twelve streets named after princes of the ruling family. Of these, six are the sons of Khedive Esmaʿil (not represented were two who died young and his second son, Muhammad Tawfiq, later to become khedive and have the whole district of el-Tawfiqiya named after him) and the others his grandsons or cousins.

el-Serugi, Haret (el-Munira)
'Saddler's Lane.' Probably by 1918.

Setta-ktobar, Kubri (Downtown, el-Gezira)
'6th of October Bridge.' Begun in 1969 and finished in 1996, the 'bridge' consists of a 20.5-kilometer-long elevated highway running from Nasr City in the east (out of area) to the vicinity of the Agricultural Museum in el-Duqqi in the west (out of area), overpassing Midan ʿAbd el-Menʿem Reyad and the district of el-Gezira on the way. The name commemorates the start of the 1973 Arab–Israeli War, though the bridge's first and shortest phase (from el-Gezira to el-Aguza) had been completed by that date.

Setta w-ʿEshrin Yulyu, Shareʿ (Downtown, el-Tawfiqiya)
'26th of July Str.' Since 1954, in commemoration of the abdication and departure into exile of King Faruq (r.1936–52), three days after the Free Officers' coup of 23 July 1952. The street, which until the early twentieth century started at Shareʿ el-Gumhuriya in the el-Azbakiya district on the east and ended at the east bank of the Nile, had been extended, by no later than 1913, to cross the Nile to el-Gezira/el-Zamalek and now also crosses the river on the western side of the island to continue to Tariq Eskenderiya el-Sahrawi ('the Alexandria Desert Road') in el-Giza.

> Between el-Azbakiya and the east bank of the Nile:
> From 1926 to 1954: **Shareʿ Fu'ad (el-Awwal)** ('Fu'ad (I) Str.'), after Sultan, later King, Ahmad Fu'ad I (r.1917–36); this name is still sometimes used.

From at least 1874 to 1926: **Share' Bulaq,** after the street's western terminus, Cairo's northern port of Bulaq Abu el-'Ela (so called to distinguish it from the town of Bulaq el-Dakrur on the west bank of the Nile), then a settlement divided from the city by open land. This important artery was reinforced with material taken from the ancient refuse mounds on the northern and northwestern edges of the city, which was also used to fill in the low-lying areas that flanked it.

In el-Gezira/el-Zamalek (the street divides el-Zamalek to the north from el-Gezira to the south):

From 1926 to 1954: **Share' Fu'ad (el-Awwal)** ('Fu'ad (I) Str.'), after Sultan, later King, Ahmad Fu'ad I (r.1917–36); this name is still sometimes used (*see above*).

From at least 1913 to 1926: **Share' Sherkuh,** after Asad el-Din Sherkuh ebn Shadi (d.1169), who assumed the post of vizier in Egypt in 1169 at the invitation of the Fatimid caliph. Sherkuh died two months later and was succeeded by his nephew Salah el-Din Yusef ebn Negm el-Din el-Ayyubi (Saladin), who put an end to Fatimid rule and initiated the Ayyubid dynasty. The street was also popularly known as **Share' el-Zamalek,** after the district of which it is the main artery, and this name appears on maps of the period.

el-Seyaha, Mamarr (Downtown)
'Tourism Passage,' or **Mamarr Shurtet el-Seyaha** ('Tourist Police Passage'). Date unknown; after a building on the passage that now houses offices of the Hotels and Tourist Installations department of the Ministry of Tourism. The same offices were formerly occupied by the Tourist Police.

el-Sha''ar, 'Atfet ('Abdin)
'Barley Seller's Alley.' Since 1913.

From at least 1887 to 1913: **Haret el-Hekr** ('Land Grant Lane'), a name that still applies to the east–west street that forms a T-junction with 'Atfet el-Sha''ar to the north.

el-Sha'er 'Aziz Abaza, Share' (el-Zamalek)

'Poet 'Aziz Abaza Str.' Since 1973, after (Muhammad) 'Aziz Abaza (1898–1969), an Egyptian poet best known for his verse dramas with a Pan-Arabist message who lived at #17 on this street. After training as a lawyer, Abaza spent most of his career in government service, rising to serve as a provincial governor. He was also elected to parliament. He was awarded the State Merit Award for Arts in 1965.

> From 1954 to 1973: **Share' el-Ma'had el-Sewesri** ('Swiss Institute Str.'), after the Swiss Institute for Egyptian Architectural and Archaeological Research, located on the street at #11. This privately-funded institute was founded in 1931 as the Ludwig-Borchardt Institute, named after a leading German archaeologist; it was placed under Swiss patronage on Borchardt's death in 1938 to prevent it from falling into British hands during the Second World War.

> From 1913 to 1954: **Share' el-Amir Sa'id** ('Prince Sa'id Str.'), after Sa'id Halim Pasha (1865–1921), a grandson of Muhammad 'Ali. Like several members of his family, Sa'id served in the Ottoman government, holding the post of grand vizier of the Ottoman Empire from 1913 to 1917. This name may also have applied informally to the street's northern continuation, now Share' Muhammad Mazhar. This area of el-Zamalek—immediately north of Khedive Esma'il's palace of Saray el-Gezira and extending to Share' Setta w-'Eshrin Yulyu—is home to twelve streets formerly named after princes of the ruling family. Of these, six were the sons of Khedive Esma'il (not represented were two who died young plus his second son, Muhammad Tawfiq, later to become khedive and have the whole district of el-Tawfiqiya named after him), the others his cousins or grandsons.

Shaf'i, 'Atfet (el-Azbakiya)

Since 1965, after Dr. Muhammad Beih Shaf'i; *see* Haret Shaf'i.

> From before the Esma'iliya project to 1965: **'Atfet Muhammad Shaf'i**. The change to plain 'Atfet Shaf'i was

presumably made to harmonize the name with that of Haret Shaf'i (*see below*), referring to the same person.

Shaf'i, Haret (Downtown)

By 1888, after Dr. Muhammad Beih Shaf'i (d.1860), who lived on this street. Shafe'i studied medicine at the medical school at Abu Za'bal and was sent to France by the government for further studies in 1826. On his return in 1838, he was appointed professor of internal medicine at Abu Za'bal and, later, Qasr el-'Eini hospital, of which he went on to become the director. He authored several books on medicine and translated works by Clot Beih (*see* Share' Kulut Beih).

Shafiq Mansur, Share' (el-Zamalek)

Since 1954, after Shafiq Beih Mansur (1856–90), lawyer and mathematician, and son of Mansur Basha Yakan (*see* Share' Mansur). Shafiq Mansur, who studied in France and Switzerland, worked on his return at the Native Tribunals. He translated French legal and mathematical works into Arabic and participated in the 1888 translation into French of 'Abd el-Rahman el-Jabarti's celebrated history of Egypt.

> From 1913 to 1954: **Share' el-Amir Ebrahim** ('Prince Ebrahim Str.'), probably after Prince Ebrahim Hasan (1879–1918), a grandson of Khedive Esma'il. Educated at the Theresianum (Vienna), Harrow, and Sandhurst, Prince Hasan was a member of several scientific societies, including the Ligue de Prophylaxie Sanitaire et Contre la Traite des Blanches, and author of *L'Île de Ceylan*. He married several times, including actress Pearl Ola Jane Humphrey, noted for her role in *The Prisoner of Zenda*. This area of el-Zamalek—immediately northeast of Khedive Esma'il's palace of Saray el-Gezira and extending to Share' Setta w-'Eshrin Yulyu—is home to twelve streets named after princes of the ruling family. Of these, six are the sons of Khedive Esma'il (not represented were two who died young and his second son, Muhammad Tawfiq, later to become khedive and have the whole district of el-Tawfiqiya named after him) and the others his grandsons or cousins.

Shagaret el-Durr, Share' (el-Zamalek)

By 1913, after Shagaret el-Durr ('Tree of Pearls'; d.1257), the only
Muslim woman to rule Egypt. Shagaret el-Durr was the wife of
el-Salih Ayyub, last Ayyubid ruler of Egypt, and, faced by a Cru-
sader invasion, concealed his death for three months in collusion
with his chief army commanders. Eventually recognized publicly,
she ruled as sultan for some three months in 1250, after which she
abdicated in favor of her new husband, the Mamluk 'Ezz el-Din
Aybak, thus ushering in the Mamluk dynasties that were to rule the
country for the next two hundred and fifty years. Shagaret el-Durr
quarreled with Aybak and had him murdered but, imprisoned, was
in turn beaten to death with wooden clogs in the bathhouse by the
serving women of her co-wife, the mother of Aybak's successor.

el-Shahid Ahmad Nabil, Share' (el-Zamalek)

'Martyr Ahmad Nabil Str.' Since after 1973, after Captain Ahmad
Nabil Hasan el-Sayyed Qora (1949–73), who gave his life for his
country in the 1973 war against Israel and was posthumously
awarded the Star of the East (Military).

> After 1937 to after 1973: **Share' Kulumbaruli**, after Fr.
> Angelo Colombaroli (1863–1922), sometime Father General
> of the Verona Fathers Institute, from which was born the
> congregation of the Comboni Fathers, to whom the land
> once belonged (*see* former Share' Kumbuni, *under* Share'
> Hasan 'Asem).

el-Shahid Eshaq Ya'qub, Share' (el-Zamalek)

'Martyr Eshaq Ya'qub Str.' From after 1956, after First Lieutenant
Eshaq Ya'qub Hasanein, Supply Corps, who gave his life for his
country on 2 December 1956 in the fight against the Tripartite
Aggression of Israel, Britain, and France. This street is close to that
of Zakariya Rezqallah, another first lieutenant who died on the
same day (*see* Share' el-Shahid Zakariya Rezq).

> From 1913 to 1954(?): as a (discontinuous) extension of
> Share' el-Sheikh el-Marsafi, the street bore the same former
> name as the latter, that is, **Share' el-Amir Tusun** ('Prince
> Tusun Str.'), after Muhammad Tusun Basha (1853–76), a son

of Muhammad Sa'id Basha (r.1854–63). This area of el-Zamalek—immediately northeast of Khedive Esma'il's palace
of Saray el-Gezira and extending to Share' Setta w-'Eshrin
Yulyu—is home to twelve streets formerly named after
princes of the ruling family. Of these, six were the sons of
Khedive Esma'il (not represented were two who died young
plus his second son, Muhammad Tawfiq, later to become
khedive and have the whole district of el-Tawfiqiya named
after him), the others his cousins or grandsons.

el-Shahid Gaber Salah (Jika), Share' ('Abdin)
'Martyr Gaber Salah (Jika) Str.' Since 2013, after sixteen-year-old
activist Gaber Salah, nicknamed Jika, who was shot dead on 25
November 2012 during clashes between protesters and police in
Share' Muhammad Mahmud, of which this street is an extension.
During the demonstrations themselves, the name **Share' Jika** was
applied by the protesters to Share' Yusef el-Gendi.

> From c.1908 to 2013: **Share' Qawala** or **Share' Kawala**,
> after Kavala in northeastern Greece, birthplace of Muham-
> mad 'Ali Basha, founder of Egypt's modern monarchy. This
> name formerly applied to Share' el-Gumhuriya from Midan
> 'Abdin to Midan el-Ubera. Following its reallocation to
> this street and until 1945, the name applied from Share'
> Sheikh 'Abd el-'Aziz Gawish east to Midan el-Gum-
> huriya. With the renaming of Share' el-Qased as Share'
> Muhammad Mahmud, the latter was extended to apply up
> to Share' Muhammad Farid and the domain of this name
> was reduced to the block between the latter and Midan
> el-Gumhuriya.

el-Shahid Gawad Husni, Share' (Downtown)
'Martyr Gawad Husni Str.' Since 1961, after Gawad Husni (1935–
56), a Syrian student at Cairo University killed defending Port Said
during the Tripartite Aggression against Egypt of Britain, France,
and Israel.

> From 1944 to 1961: **Share' Tal'at Harb**, after Muhammad
> Tal'at Harb (*see further* Share' Tal'at Harb, main entry),

founder of Bank Misr, whose first headquarters opened in
1920 at #15. The bank moved to Share' Muhammad Farid
in 1927.

From at least 1863 to 1944: **Share' el-Sheikh Abu el-Seba'**,
after 'Abd el-Rahman Abu el-Seba', a Sufi saint of unknown
history, whose tomb and mosque (1895) are located on nearby
Haret Bab el-Luq (*see also under* Share' el-Batal Ahmad 'Abd
el-'Aziz).

el-Shahid Kamal el-Din Salah, Midan (Qasr el-Dubara)
'Martyr Kamal el-Din Salah Sq.' Since 1966, after Muhammad
Kamal el-Din Salah (1910–57); *see* **Share' el-Shahid Kamal
el-Din Salah**. The square consists largely of an off-ramp leading
to Kubri Qasr el-Nil; this destroyed the villa of Adolphe Qat-
tawi Beih (1865–1925), second son of Ya'qub Qattawi Beih (*see*
Share' Qattawi Beih) and sometime secretary of the Royal Egyp-
tian Geographical Society; the villa was sold after his death to
Qut el-Qulub el-Demardashiya, eccentric literary hostess and
French-language novelist.

From at least 1912 to 1957: **Midan Elhami,** after Ebrahim
Elhami Basha (1836–60), son of Abbas Helmi Basha I.

el-Shahid Kamal el-Din Salah, Share' (Qasr el-Dubara)
'Martyr Kamal el-Din Salah Str.' Since 1957, after Kamal el-Din
Salah, a diplomat, Egypt's representative on the United Nations
Advisory Council for the Trust Territory of Somaliland under Italian Occupation, who was assassinated in Mogadishu on 16 April
1957. The street was no doubt chosen as his memorial because of its
closeness to the old Foreign Ministry building on Share' el-Tahrir
west of Midan el-Tahrir.

From at least 1912 to 1957: **Share' el-Sheikh Barakat,**
after the mosque and tombs of Sufi saints el-Sheikh Barakat
and el-Sheikh Mansur (dates unknown); the mosque was
built in 1897 on this street at #17, east of Midan Simon Bulifar but is now demolished. This name still applies to the street
west of Midan Simon Bulifar.

el-Shahid Kamal Khalil, Share' (el-Zamalek)
'Martyr Kamal Khalil Str.' By 1998, probably after Captain Kamal Khalil Ebrahim el-Sharqawi (1939–67) of the Tank Corps, who gave his life for his country in its 1967 war with Israel.

el-Shahid Muhammad Mustafa Esma'il, 'Atfet (Downtown)
'Martyr Muhammad Mustafa Esma'il Alley.' Since 1962; *see* Haret el-Shahid Muhammad Mustafa Esma'il *below*.

> From at least 1904 to 1962: **'Atfet Fahmi**, after 'Ali Fahmi Basha; *see* former Share' Fahmi, under Share' 'Abd el-Megid el-Remali.

el-Shahid Muhammad Mustafa Esma'il, Haret (Downtown)
'Martyr Muhammad Mustafa Esma'il Lane.' Since 1962, after an Egyptian who gave his life for his country, probably in its 1948 war with Israel.

> From at least 1904 to 1962: **Haret Fahmi**, after 'Ali Fahmi Basha; *see* former Share' Fahmi, under Share' 'Abd el-Megid el-Remali.

el-Shahid Zakariya Rezq, Share' (el-Zamalek)
'Martyr Zakariya Rezq Str.' Since after 1956, after First Lieutenant Zakariya Rezqallah, Infantry, who gave his life for his country on 2 December 1956 in the fight against the Tripartite Aggression of Israel, Britain, and France. This street is close to that of Eshaq Ya'qub, another first lieutenant, who gave his life on the same day (*see* Share' el-Shahid Eshaq Ya'qub).

> From c.1940 to after 1956: **Share' Lutfallah**, after Prince Habib Lutfallah (fl. first quarter of the twentieth century), a Greek Orthodox merchant and landowner of Levantine origin. Supposedly one of the richest men in Egypt, his title was bestowed by Sherif Hussein bin 'Ali, Hashemite King of the Hejaz, in gratitude for financial services. Lutfallah bought the Gezira Palace Hotel, formerly the Saray el-Gezira palace (*see* former Share' Saray el-Gezira, under Share' el-Musiqar Muhammad 'Abd el-Wahhab) in 1919 or

1922 for LE115,000 and turned it into a residence; *see also* Share' Mishil Lutfallah.

Shaljiyan, Share' (Downtown)
Since at least 1946, after the Leon Chaldjian Building, at the corner of Share' Tal'at Harb and Share' el-Muhandis 'Ali Labib Gabr, which contained the premises of a well-known men's bespoke tailoring house of the same name.

Shalabi, Haret (el-Azbakiya)
By 1888, after a certain Tadrus Shalabi, whose house stood at one end of the street at the date given.

Shambuliyon, Share' (Downtown)
Since 1923, after Jean François Champollion (1790–1832), the French scholar who in 1822 laid the foundations of modern Egyptology by deciphering the inscriptions on the Rosetta Stone. The street was likely given this name in commemoration of the centenary of that event.

> From 1874(?) to 1923: **Share' Wabur el-Meyah** ('Water Pump Str.'). The Cairo Water Company was founded in 1865 and won the concession to provide the city with piped water in the same year, when it was granted land, according to one account, in Fumm el-Khalig to build a pumping station and settlement tanks. This project underperformed, according to this account, and the pumps and tanks were re-established here, on the site of today's High Court and judges' and journalists' syndicate buildings. According to other sources, however, the company started work here in 1867. The pumps lifted water from the Esma'iliya Canal and provided most of downtown with its first piped water.

> The history of the northern end of this street, where it meets Share' Setta w-'Eshrin Yulyu, is different from the rest, as the street split just before reaching the latter, and in so doing defined the western and southern sides of a large public garden (*see* Share' Geneinet el-Musallas *below*).

The western branch of the street continued to carry the name Share' Wabur el-Meyah until the land was taken in the mid-1920s for the construction of a new Mixed Tribunals (now High Court) complex (inaugurated 1931), at which point it ceased to exist.

The eastern branch had its own names until at least 1934, as follows:

> From 1912 to 1934: **Share' Muwiyar**, after Louis Pierre Mouillard (1834–97), pioneer theorist of aviation who studied bird flight in Cairo, opined in his work on gliders *L'Empire de l'Air* that human flight would "result in the rapid removal of nationalities," and died in poverty there. With the reconfiguring of the land for the new High Court buildings and the reduction of the former garden to the size of the present court car park, the north end of this street was incorporated into former Share' Fu'ad el-Awwal, and the rest into Share' Shambuliyon itself.

> From at least 1887 to no later than 1924: **Share' Geneinet el-Musallas** ('Triangle Garden Str.'), after the public garden that once occupied the site of the car park in front of the High Court and a part of the High Court grounds.

Shams, Mamarr (el-Tawfiqiya)
'Sun Passage.' Probably since 1910, after the el-Shams el-Gedida ('New Sun') café, known for its murals, by an unknown artist, depicting scenes from the Egyptian coutryside.

el-Shams, Share' (Qasr el-Dubara)
'Sun Str.' Since c.1948, after the Al Chams apartment building erected by the Compagnie Al Chams between this street and Midan Simon Bulifar on the site and grounds of the Qasr el-Dubara palace, demolished and subdivided in 1947. The word *shams* means 'sun' but is also a partial anagram of the Arabic name of the property company, el-Shareka el-Mesriya le-l-Mabani el-Hadisa, founded in 1946, that built this and other luxury apartment buildings in Cairo and el-Giza in the late 1940s and 1950s.

el-Sha'rawi, Haret ('Abdin)
Probably by 1918; unidentified. El-Sha'rawi is a family name, perhaps that of early residents.

el-Sharekat, Share' (Downtown)
'Companies' Str.' Probably by 1973, after the many public-sector
companies created by Bank Misr (headquartered on nearby Share'
Muhammad Farid and with many other buildings in the area) whose
headquarters are on this street, such as the Holding Company for
Cotton and Textile Industries, the Nile Public Company for Desert
Highways, and the Alexandria Company for Pharmaceuticals and
Chemical Products. For more on this block, whose street pattern
has been unusually disrupted, *see* former Haret el-Fawwala, *under*
Share' el-Sayyed Muhammad Taher.

el-Sharq, Mamarr (Downtown)
'The East Insurance Company Passage.' Probably since 1931, after
the company, founded in that year, whose headquarters occupy its
east side on Share' Qasr el-Nil. The passage is also known widely
but informally as **Mamarr Esturil** ('Estoril Passage'), after the
long-established restaurant of that name on its west side.

el-Sharqawi, 'Atfet ('Abdin)
By 1888, possibly related to the Hosh el-Sharqawi ('el-Sharqawi's
Courtyard') south of Midan Bab el-Khalq (out of area), which was
close to the tanneries at the beginning of the nineteenth century.

el-Shawarbi, Haret (el-Tawfiqiya)
Probably by 1934, after 'Abd el-Hamid Basha el-Shawarbi (*see*
Haret 'Abd el-Hamid el-Shawarbi).

el-Shawarbi, Share' (Downtown)
Since 1901, after Muhammad Ahmad el-Shawarbi Basha (1841–?),
a landowner from Qalyub, in the Delta, member of the Chamber of Deputies in 1882 and later member and then speaker of
the Senate. El-Shawarbi was famed as a philanthropist, building
a charity hospital and a mosque in his home town and supporting
religious institutions. Vestiges of el-Shawarbi's villa (built in 1872
and a rare survivor of those built under the original el-Esma'iliya

development plan) may be seen behind, and obscured by, the first building on the left when entering the street from Share' 'Abd el-Khaleq Sarwat. During the 1970s, the street became famed for the otherwise unobtainable foreign clothing and accessories that were sold there; soon after, it was pedestrianized, and it continues to be dominated by retail clothing outlets.

el-Shay el-Hindi, Mamarr (Downtown)

'Indian Tea Passage.' Probably since 1963, after the Indian Tea House (now closed) on the passage, and its proprietor, the Tea Board of India, around the corner on Share' Tal'at Harb. The Indian Information Center and Library also opened on the passage in 1963, to be followed in 1992 by the Indian Cultural Center. Both relocated to Zamalek in 2014.

el-Sheikh 'Abdallah, Sekket or 'Atfet ('Abdin)

By 1904; *see* Haret el-Sheikh 'Abdallah. Signs with both names are to be found on the street. The sign giving the name as 'Atfet el-Sheikh 'Abdallah presumably pre-dates the extension of the *'atfa,* or alley, forming part of a *hara,* through to Share' Muhammad Mahmud and its conversion into a *sekka,* or connecting street.

el-Sheikh 'Abdallah, Haret ('Abdin)

By 1904, after Sheikh 'Abdallah el-Hasani, a Sufi sheikh along the north side of whose mosque and tomb the lane runs. Sheikh 'Abdallah is said by some to have been a son of Sheikh Rihan, from whose street the lane branches.

el-Sheikh 'Abd el-Aziz Gawish, Share' ('Abdin)

By 1973, after 'Abd el-Aziz Khalil Hasan Gawish (1876–1929), political journalist. Gawish was editor of *el-Liwaa',* organ of Mustafa Kamel's National Party (el-Hezb el-Watani) and from that platform attacked the British occupation, the khedive, and the government.

> From at least 1888 to no later than 1973: **Share' 'Abd el-Dayem**, after an otherwise unknown Sufi saint whose mosque and tomb are on the street. The mosque, though much rebuilt, dates to c.1766, before which only the tomb existed.

el-Sheikh ʿAbd el-Latif Deraz, Share (Garden City)

From no earlier than 1977, after Sheikh ʿAbd el-Latif Deraz (1890–1977), a cleric and political activist who was among the first to participate in the 1919 uprising against the British, for which he was interned or confined to his home village on more than one occasion. He served as a member of the lower house of parliament in 1929 and 1948 and in the single-chamber parliament following the 1952 revolution, when he was also appointed *wakil* (undersecretary) for el-Azhar. He was active in support of the Palestinian cause and founded, in 1954, the Struggle Group for the Liberation of the Islamic Peoples.

> From at least 1935 to no earlier than 1977: **Share Hod el-Laban** ('Milk Basin Str.'), apparently after a dairy serving the needs of the el-Qasr el-ʿAli palace complex, on whose grounds the larger part of Garden City was built.

el-Sheikh ʿAli el-Ghayati, Share (Downtown)

From 1962, after ʿAli el-Ghayati (1885–1956), Azhari sheikh, Islamist activist, and journalist–poet opposed to British occupation and the monarchy; his poetry collection *Wataniyati* ('My Nationalism') was banned in 1910, leading him to flee in disguise to Turkey, then Geneva, from which he returned in 1937.

> From at least 1863 to 1962: **Share el-Kafarwa**, after the surrounding neighborhood (*see* Haret el-Kafarwa). Before the construction of this street, this name is applied in some maps to Haret el-Kafarwa.

el-Sheikh ʿAli Yusef, Share (el-Munira)

Since 1951, after Sheikh ʿAli Yusef (1863–1913), pioneer of the Egyptian press and developer of a new journalistic writing style that eschewed the formerly predominant use of rhymed prose. ʿAli Yusef published the widely circulated daily newspaper *el-Muʾayyad* (1889–1915), which allied itself with the National Party (el-Hezb el-Watani) founded by Mustafa Kamel, which opposed British occupation (*see* Midan Mustafa Kamel); *el-Muʾayyad* also campaigned for the abolition of forced peasant labor and encouraged the purchase of locally made goods to support the Egyptian economy.

'Ali Yusef gained popular support when put on trial for publishing a leaked military telegram in 1896 and notoriety when taken to court in 1905 by his prospective father-in-law (*see* Share' Muhammad 'Ezz el-'Arab). He owed his title of 'sheikh' to his appointment as head of the Wafa'i clan of descendants of the Prophet Muhammad. Not to be confused with Share' el-Sheikh Yusef.

> From at least 1918 to 1951: **Share' el-Munira**, after the surrounding district, which is said to take its name from the brilliance of the lights at the forty-day wedding celebration held by Khedive Esma'il for four of his sons and three of his daughters (*see* former Share' Afrah el-Angal, *under* Share' Fatma el-Yusef).

el-Sheikh Barakat, Share' (Downtown, Qasr el Dubara)
By 1914, after the mosque and tombs of Sufi saints el-Sheikh Barakat and his companion el-Sheikh Mansur (dates unknown), which was built in 1897 on this street at #17, east of Midan Simon Bulifar. Until 1957, this name also applied also to the continuation of the street east of Midan Simon Bulifar.

el-Sheikh Farag, Haret ('Abdin)
By 1863, after the mosque and tomb of a saint of that name, still present on the street. The name **Sekket el-Sawwafa** ('Wool Merchants' Connecting Street') appears also to have been used of this and surrounding alleys until 1913, when it was officially quashed.

el-Sheikh Ma'ruf, Share' (Downtown)
Since no earlier than 1914, after Sidi Ma'ruf, the Sufi saint buried inside the mosque that bears his name on the north side of the street; ironically, nothing is known of the history of this saint, even though his name means, literally, 'Well Known.' Not to be confused with nearby Share' Ma'ruf.

el-Sheikh el-Marsafi, Share' (el-Zamalek)
Since 1954, probably after Sheikh Hesein el-Marsafi (1815–90), writer, teacher, and public intellectual, who studied at el-Azhar but when appointed professor of Arabic linguistics at Dar el-'Ulum in 1872 championed Western methods of teaching the classical

language. He was the first to formulate the concept of the *nahda* ('renaissance,' as applied to the nineteenth-century Arab intellectual revival) and in 1881 published a treatise defining eight newly-coined terms critical to Arab discourse: *umma* (nation), *watan* (homeland), *hukuma* (government), *'adl* (justice), *seyasa* (politics), *hurriya* (freedom), and *tarbiya* (education). Blind from the age of three, he learned Braille and taught at the School for the Blind.

> From 1913 to 1954: **Share' el-Amir Tusun** ('Prince Tusun Str.'), after Muhammad Tusun Basha (1853–76), a son of Muhammad Sa'id Basha (r.1854–63). The small square approximately halfway down the street does not bear a name of its own at present but before 1954 appears to have been known as **Midan el-Amir Tusun**. This area of el-Zamalek—immediately northeast of Khedive Esma'il's palace of Saray el-Gezira and extending to Share' Setta w-'Eshrin Yulyu—is home to twelve streets named after princes of the ruling family. Of these, six are the sons of Khedive Esma'il (not represented were two who died young and his second son, Muhammad Tawfiq, later to become khedive and have the whole district of el-Tawfiqiya named after him) and the others his grandsons or cousins.

el-Sheikh Rihan, 'Atfet ('Abdin)
By 1888, an appendage of Haret el-Sheikh Rihan.

el-Sheikh Rihan, Haret ('Abdin)
By 1888, after the saint of that name (*see* Share' el-Sheikh Rihan) whose humble tomb is on this street; children who are late in speaking are given water to drink from the well next to the tomb.

el-Sheikh Rihan, Midan ('Abdin)
Since 1954: *see* Share' el-Sheikh Rihan.

> From 1938 to 1954: **Midan el-Sultan Hesein Kamel**; *see* Share' el-Sheikh Rihan.

> From at least 1908 to 1938: **Midan Ragab** (or **Ragheb**?) **Agha**. Curiously, Arabic sources spell the name (in fact, two distinct names) differently; *see also* Share' Game' 'Abdin.

el-Sheikh Rihan, Share'

(Qasr el-Dubara, el-Munira, Downtown, 'Abdin)
By1888, after a saint who according to some was a freedman of
the Prophet Muhammad named Abu Rihana, according to others
a descendent of el-Husayn, grandson of the Prophet, and according to yet others simply unknown. His tomb is located on Haret
el-Sheikh Rihan, a lane running north from this street. A Sheikh
Rihan Gate in the city's western wall existed until at least 1861, and
a road exited the city at that point and ran westward between fields
toward the river, stopping just short of it. To the east, the street
originally ended in a warren of alleys just short of Share' Bur Sa'id
but was lengthened in 1915 to reach that street. At various times,
parts of it have been renamed, only to revert, as follows:

> From Midan Qasr el-Dubara to Midan el-Tahrir:
> From after 1871 to 1938: **Share' Saray el-Esma'iliya**
> ('Esma'iliya Palace Str.'), after the palace of that name built
> by Khedive Esma'il in or soon after 1871 for his third wife,
> Jaham Afat (d.1907), and later the residence of the repre-
> sentative of the Ottoman Porte. The palace was demolished
> (starting 1938) to make way, on the south, for the Mugamma'
> (a governmental administrative complex) and, on the north,
> for a widening of the square.

> From Midan el-Tahrir to the intersection with Midan
> el-Gumhuriya:
> From 1938 to 1954: **Share' el-Sultan Hesein Kamel** ('Sul-
> tan Husein Kamel Str.'), after the ruler (1914–17) imposed by
> the British to replace Khedive Abbas Helmi II, who refused
> to renounce allegiance to the Ottoman sultan at the start of
> the First World War. His sympathy toward Egypt's rural poor
> caused him to be known as 'Father of the Peasants.' Hesein
> Kamel occupied the Saray el-Esma'iliya palace at the west-
> ern end of the street from an unknown date until 1885. In
> 1954, following the 1952 Revolution, the name of the street
> reverted to Share' el-Sheikh Rihan.

> From Midan el-Gumhuriya to Share' Bur Sa'id:
> From at least 1918 to 1940: **Share' el-Mabduli** (*see* Midan

el-Gumhuriya); after 1940, this name was reallocated to a
street at right angles to Share' el-Sheikh Rihan (out of area).

el-Sheikh Saleh, 'Atfet (Downtown)
By 1913, after an otherwise unknown Sufi sheikh of that name.

el-Sheikh Sayyed Darwish, Share' (el-Tawfiqiya)
Since 1970, after composer–singer Sayyed Darwish (1892–1923),
a prominent figure in the early twentieth-century renaissance of
Egyptian and more widely Arabic music. He owed the title of
sheikh to his early training in Qur'anic recitation but was influ-
enced by the music of Aleppo, where he spent some time, and
also adapted Western features to Arab musical practice. During a
working life of only ten years, he composed numerous songs in
both popular and religious modes, many of which are still sung, and
wrote the music for some twelve musicals. He is generally credited
with setting to music the song *Biladi, Biladi* ('My Country, My
Country'), now the national anthem.

> From 1887 to 1970: **Share' Zaki**, after Muhammad Zaki
> (fl. late nineteenth century), who lived on this street and was
> minister of public works (1890) and chief of protocol to the
> khedive.

el-Sheikh Yusef, Midan *see* el-Sheikh Yusef, Share' (Qasr el Dubara)

el-Sheikh Yusef, Share' (Qasr el-Dubara)
Since at least 1907, after the small mosque containing the tomb
of a Sufi saint who lived during the first quarter of the nineteenth
century and is said to have been a highwayman in his youth; on the
arrest of his associates, who hid their crimes behind a pretence of
holiness, he sought refuge with Muhammad Lazughli (*see* Midan
Lazughli), who pardoned him. His small mosque, to the west of
Share' Qasr el-'Eini, contains both his remains and Lazughli's. In
some maps, this crescent-shaped street is called **Midan el-Sheikh
Yusef** ('Sheikh Yusef Sq.'). The name formerly applied both west
and east of Share' Qasr el-'Eini, but now applies west of that street
only, while the eastern section of the street is now named Share'
Magles el-Sha'b.

Sherif, Share ̒ (Downtown)

Since 1941, after Muhammad Sherif Basha (1828–87), a soldier, initially, and statesman, who supported the transformation of Egypt into a constitutional monarchy with a representative parliament and who sought to limit foreign influence. Sherif was born in Cairo to a family of descendants of the Prophet Muhammad that had been brought to Istanbul by the Ottomans following their conquest of the Hejaz: at the time of his birth, his father, Ahmad Sherif Afandi, was serving as Qadi ̒Askar, or chief judge, of Egypt. Though the family returned to Istanbul in 1842, Ahmad Afandi, while passing through Egypt later to assume a post in the Hejaz, consigned his son to the guardianship of Muhammad ̒Ali Basha, who had the youth educated with the royal princes, whom he accompanied on a military training mission to France that lasted from 1844 to 1849. Sherif's witnessing of the revolutionary events that shook Europe in 1848 no doubt shaped his later support for constitutionalism. On his return, Sherif was appointed aide-de-camp to the chief of staff to the Egyptian army, Seliman Basha, whose daughter Nazli he eventually married. Later, he held several key ministerial positions, including that of foreign minister (in which capacity in 1877 he signed, on behalf of Egypt, the treaty banning the slave trade), of interior minister, and, three times, of prime minister: in 1879 (until the exile of Khedive Esma ̒il), from 1881 to 1882 (on the insistence of ̒Urabi Basha during the latter's struggle with Khedive Tawfiq, during which period he oversaw the creation of the first Chamber of Deputies), and again from 1882 to 1884 (when he resigned in protest at the evacuation of the Sudan with the pronouncement, "Though we should leave the Sudan, the Sudan will never leave us"). He also acted as regent of Egypt during four absences of Khedive Esma ̒il. His palace (bought by him in 1872) was located close to the old Broadcasting Building, and its gardens began at today's Midan Tal ̒at Harb and extended to Share ̒ el-Sherifein; the palace and grounds were sold eventually to the Qattawi family (*see* former Share ̒ Musa Qattawi Basha, *under* Share ̒ Abu Bakr Kheirat). This street name originally applied to the much smaller street now known as Share ̒ Sherif el-Sughayyar, which ran up to the gate of the palace.

From 1888 to 1941: **Share ̒ el-Madabegh**, after the tanneries (*madabegh*) formerly located in Bab el-Luq near Share ̒

Huda Sha'rawi and Share' el-Ra'is 'Abd el-Salam 'Aref, to
which this street led; the tanneries were moved to Fustat in
1866. The street was created by the filling in of the el-Khalig
el-Naseri canal, known at this point as Khalig el-Maghrabi
(*see* former Share' el-Maghrabi, *under* Share' 'Adli), in accordance with the Esma'ilyya project plan.

el-Sherif el-Edrisi, Share' (el-Zamalek)
Since 1954, after Abu 'Abd Allah Muhammad ebn Muhammad ebn 'Abd Allah ebn Edris el-Hammudi el-Hasani el-Edrisi
(1100–65 or –66), known as el-Sherif el-Edrisi, a descriptive geographer and cartographer and an advisor to Roger II, Norman king
of Sicily, for whom he wrote his best-known work, an ambitious
geographical text popularly known as the *Book of Roger*.

> From 1913 to 1954: **Share' el-Amir Gamal el-Din** ('Prince
> Gamal el-Din Str.'), after Prince 'Ali Gamal el-Din (1875–
> 93), ninth son of Khedive Esma'il, who died while attending
> cavalry school in Vienna. This area of el-Zamalek—immedi-
> ately northeast of Khedive Esma'il's palace of Saray el-Gezira
> and extending to Share' Setta w-'Eshrin Yulyu—is home
> to twelve streets formerly named after princes of the ruling
> family. Of these, six were the sons of Khedive Esma'il (not
> represented were two who died young plus his second son,
> Muhammad Tawfiq, later to become khedive and have the
> whole district of el-Tawfiqiya named after him), the others
> his cousins or grandsons.

Sherif el-Sughayyar, Share' (Downtown)
'Lesser Sherif Str.' Since 1941, after Muhammad Sherif Basha
(*see* Share' Sherif *above*), to whose palace this led. The adjective
el-Sughayyar ('the Lesser'), whose official status is unclear but
which is consistently used by residents, was presumably added
when the adjacent former Share' el-Madabegh was renamed Share'
Sherif. The street was pedestrianized in the late 1990s.

> From at least 1906 to 1941: **Share' Sherif** (*see* main entry).
> The only sign on the street retains this name and may date to
> before the change.

el-Sherifein, Share῾ (Downtown)

'Two Sherifs Str.' Since 1887, after two unrelated men each of whom bore the name Sherif and each of whom had a mansion on this street, namely 1) Muhammad Sherif Basha (1826–87), who gave his name to nearby Share῾ Sherif, and 2) ῾Ali Sherif Basha (1834–97), son of Muhammad Sherif Basha el-Kebir ('the Older'), so called to distinguish him from (1). ῾Ali Basha Sherif was educated in military schools in Egypt and France, and on his return was appointed a colonel in the artillery. Though he held various government offices, he is best known as a breeder of Arabian horses, several of the purest blood lines of which he is credited with saving. At his death, he owned more than four hundred animals, some of which Lady Anne Blunt purchased for her Arabian stud farm in England. The exact location of his mansion on the street is no longer known. The current Cairo Stock Exchange building opened on this street in 1928, one year before the Great Wall Street Crash. This and surrounding streets were pedestrianized in the early 1990s.

Sherket el-Sukkar, Mamarr (Downtown)

'Sugar Company Passage.' Probably by 1926, after the semi-monopolist Egyptian Sugar Company, established in the 1880s by the Suarès family (*see* former Midan Sawares, *under* Midan Mustafa Kamel). The largest industrial enterprise in Egypt until the late 1920s, it was nationalized in 1956. Its headquarters still stand at the corner of this street with Share῾ Gawad Husni (entrance on the latter). To some locals, the street is known as **Mamarr Sherif**, after Share῾ Sherif, from which it branches.

Shetat, ῾Atfet (Abdin)

Probably from after 1935; unidentified. The meaning of the word is unclear; it may be a family name, perhaps of early residents.

Shiha, Haret (Abdin)

By 1888; unidentified. Shiha is a male given name, perhaps that of an early resident.

el-Shuqafatiya, Haret (῾Abdin)

'Potters' Lane.' By 1887. In today's Egyptian Arabic, the word *shuqaf*, from which the name is derived, is limited to *broken* pottery.

However, the fourteenth-century dictionary *el-Qamus el-Muhit* defines it also as plain 'pottery' and cites other places in Cairo in whose names the word occurs.

el-Shuqafatiya, Kemalet Haret (ʿAbdin)
'Potters' Lane Extension.' Since 1913; *see* Haret el-Shuqafatiya. The name was created probably to provide an address for the short, northern end of Haret el-Shuqafatiya when it was severed from its longer, southern part by the running through of Shareʿ el-Saha (before 1906). Previously, this lane had been part of former Shareʿ Sahet el-Hemir el-Qadima.

Shurtet el-Seyaha, Mamarr *see* el-Seyaha, Mamarr

Sidi ʿAbd el-Haqq (el-Sunbati), Darb *see* Sidi ʿAbd el-Haqq (el-Sunbati), ʿAtfet

Sidi ʿAbd el-Haqq (el-Sunbati), ʿAtfet or Darb (el-Azbakiya)
'My Master ʿAbd el-Haqq (el-Sunbati) Alley' or 'Side Street.' By 1863, after ʿAbd el-Haqq ebn Muhammad ebn ʿAbd el-Haqq el-Sunbati (1436–c.1526), a judge of the Shafeʿi school and a noted transmitter of prophetic traditions, whose mosque (Mamluk, of unknown date) is on the street.

Sidi ʿAbd el-Haqq (el-Sunbati), Shareʿ (el-Azbakiya)
'My Master ʿAbd el-Haqq (el-Sunbati) Str.' From at least 1912, after ʿAbd el-Haqq el-Sunbati, whose mosque is on a nearby street (*see* ʿAtfet Sidi ʿAbd el-Haqq el-Sunbati).

Sidi ʿAbd el-Qader, Shareʿ (el-Azbakiya)
Since 1913, after a Sufi saint buried inside el-ʿEzam mosque (*see below*).

> From c.1874 to 1913: **Shareʿ Gameʿ el-ʿEzam** ('Mosque of the Bones Str.'), after the mosque at the corner with Shareʿ ʿAbd el-ʿAziz. This mosque was built over a pit in which bones from two graveyards (the Cemetery of el-Azbak and Sheikh Salama's Mound), removed during the creation of the original Midan el-Ataba el-Khadra, were interred; preeminent among their owners was the Sufi saint ʿAbd el-Qader

el-Desuqi, brother of the better known Ebrahim el-Desuqi (1295–96), founder of the Desuqi Sufi order, and a tomb was built for him inside the mosque, which is sometimes also called by his name.

Simon Bolivar, Midan *see* Simon Bulifar, Midan

Simon Bulifar, Midan (Qasr el-Dubara)

Since 1960, after General Simon Bolivar (1783–1830), leader of independence movements in Bolivia, Columbia, Ecuador, Panama, Peru, and Venezuela. The square's six-foot bronze statue of the general by Venezuelan sculptor Carmelo Tabaco was presented to Egypt by Venezuela and unveiled on 11 February 1979 in recognition of Egypt's struggle for independence from Britain. The baroque villa at #1 on the square, known as Villa Emanuel Casdaghli and now a school, was home to the United States Embassy from 1934 to 1939. For a few years during the 1990s, the square carried a sign bearing the name **Midan Simone de Beauvoir**.

> From at least 1912 to 1960: **Midan Qasr el-Dubara** ('Twine Palace Sq.'), after a palace built by Muhammad ʿAli Basha before 1843 as the chief residence of his wives. Later it was lived in by Princess Amina Elhami (1858–1931), mother of Khedive Abbas Helmi II, and became known as Qasr el-Walda ('the Mother's Palace'); it was demolished in 1947. Egyptian Arabic *dubara* means 'twine' and supposedly lent its name to the palace because of a workshop for making the latter that was located within the palace grounds (perhaps on the edge: a map of 1885 shows a small isolated building that appears to open onto Shareʿ Tawfiq Deyab) and was still in existence in 1925.

Subh, Shareʿ (Abdin)

Probably from after 1935; unidentified. Subh is a family name, perhaps that of early residents.

el-Sufi, Haret (Downtown)

'The Sufi's Lane.' Since 1887; unidentified. Now referred to informally as **Haret el-Sudaniyin** ('Lane of the Sudanese') because of the large number of Sudanese-owned shops and cafes on it. Pedestrianized.

Suq el-Tawfiqiya, Share' (el-Tawfiqiya)
'El-Tawfiqiya Market Str.' By 1912; the street contains an ancient vegetable market (largely converted since c.2000 to the sale of auto accessories) that may predate the development of the Tawfiqiya district by Khedive Muhammad Tawfiq (r.1879–92; *see* Share' 'Urabi).

El-Suyyas, Haret (Downtown)
'Grooms' Lane.' Probably from c.1887. The *suyyas* or 'syces' not only looked after horses but also ran in front of or at the stirrup of important persons when they drove or rode through the city.

T

el-Ta'awun, Share' (el-Tawfiqiya)
'Cooperation Str.' Since 1935, after Copetrol (Shareket el-Ta'awun le-l-Betrol), founded 1934, the first nationally-owned and -managed petroleum products company in Egypt, one of whose CO-OP gas stations (likely the first) occupies the entire southern side of the street. Egyptian television broadcasting began on 21 July 1960 from a suite of apartments at #38.

el-Tabbakh, 'Atfet *see* el-Tabbakh, Haret

el-Tabbakh, Haret ('Abdin)
'Cook's Lane,' or **'Atfet el-Tabbakh**, 'Cook's Alley.' By 1888 (an ancient lane and its associated alley incorporated into the Esma'iliya project); probably after el-Hagg 'Ali, cook to Mamluk ruler el-Malek el-Naser Muhammad ebn Qalawun (late thirteenth/early fourteenth century). El-Hagg 'Ali renovated the nearby mosque on Midan Muhammad Farid known as Game' el-Tabbakh ('the Cook's Mosque') and reputedly had a house here.

el-Tabban, Haret (Downtown)
By 1913, after Sheikh Muhammad el-Khudari, known as el-Tabban ('the straw merchant'), of the Sa'diya Sufi order, whose tomb is in the lane. The name **Sekket el-Sawwafa** appears to have been used of this and surrounding lanes until 1913, when it was quashed.

Taha Hesein, Share' *see* el-Duktur Taha Hesein, Share'

Taher, Share' (el-Azbakiya)

Since 1938, after Ahmad Taher Basha el-Kebir el-Arna'udi (d.1803), a leader of the Albanian Bashibazuk troops sent by the Ottomans, along with Janissaries and other troops identified in contrast as "Turkish," to re-establish Ottoman rule over Egypt following the expulsion of the French in 1801. Taher Basha seized power from the Ottoman governor when the latter failed to pay the Albanians. He ruled as acting governor for twenty-six days until beheaded by Janissaries for failing to pay them their wages. He owned the eighteenth-century palace known as el-'Ataba el-Zarqa ('the Blue Threshold'), which, after its renaming as el-'Ataba el-Khadra ('the Green Threshold'), gave its name to Midan el-'Ataba el-Khadra (*see* main entry). From at least 1905 to 1938, this name applied to a different street, that defining the southern side of the former opera house east of Midan el-Ubera and extending to Midan el-'Ataba el-Khadra; this is now considered an extension of Share' 'Abd el-Khaleq Sarwat and is in part replaced by the el-Azhar Tunnel. Some maps give the name of this street as **Share' el-Matafi** ('Fire Brigade Str.'), after the city's main fire station, which moved to its present location on the east side of this street in 1904, the site having previously been occupied by the Cairo Governorate, which moved to what is now the Central Security Directorate headquarters on Share' Bur Sa'id.

> From 1900 to 1938: **Share' el-Busta el-Gedida** ('New Post Office Str.'), after the General Post Office, which moved in 1888 from its original headquarters on Share' el-Busta, east of Berket el-Azbakiya, to a new site west of the prison for foreigners attached to the Mixed Courts Tribunal (*see* Midan el-'Ataba el-Khadra). In 1900, the prison was demolished and this street, defining the east side of the post office, was created.

el-Tahrir, Midan (Downtown)

'Liberation Sq.' Since 1954 (interrupted between 1981 and at least 1983; *see* Midan Anwar el-Sadat *below*), reflecting the ideology of the 1952 Revolution. An article in *el-Ahram* dated 24 January 1953 reporting on a "liberation festival" held the previous evening refers to the square as "a field of liberation" (*sahet tahrir*) and in the caption to a photograph of the speakers' platform describes the location as Midan el-Tahrir. Elsewhere in the article, however, the square is referred to as Midan el-Hurriya (*see below*). It seems then that the change of name was anticipated by the media before its official announcement in September 1954.

> From 1981 to at least 1983: **Midan Anwar el-Sadat**, in commemoration of President Muhammad Anwar Muhammad el-Sadat (born 1918, assassinated 6 October 1981). The change, made nine days after his death, appears to have been allowed to fall into disuse without being officially reversed, signs bearing this name being in place until at least 1983. The decree renaming the square in his honor also called for the erection of a statue of him there, but this did not happen.

> From 1952 to 1954: **Midan el-Hurriya** ('Freedom Sq.'), in celebration of the 1952 revolution.

> From 1933 to 1952: **Midan el-Khedeiwi Esmaʿil**, in honor of Khedive Esmaʿil (r.1863–79), who reactivated his grandfather Muhammad ʿAli Basha's project for the modernization of Egypt and in doing so incurred debts that led to foreign control of the country's finances and his eventual deposition and exile by the European powers, led by Britain, to Turkey. Among Khedive Esmaʿil's most significant achievements were the construction of the Suez Canal (opened 1869) and the drawing up of plans for the development of new residential and commercial districts to the west of the medieval city, districts that became known collectively as el-Esmaʿiliya and which, as originally conceived, encompassed today's Downtown, el-Tawfiqiya, Qasr el-Dubara, Garden City, el-Munira, and Fumm el-Khalig.

> From 19 November 1888 to 1933: **Midan el-Esmaʿiliya**, after the surrounding district, which took its name from Saray el-Esmaʿiliya ('the Esmaʿiliya Palace'), built in 1871 (*see* former Shareʿ Saray el-Esmaʿiliya, *under* Shareʿ el-Sheikh Rihan).

From 4 April 1887 to 19 November 1888: **Midan Qasr el-Nil**, after the Qasr el-Nil palace (*see* Share' Qasr el-Nil).

From 1871 to 4 April 1887: **Midan el-Kubri** ('Bridge Sq.'), **Midan Kubri el-Gezira** ('el-Gezira Bridge Sq.'), and **Midan Kubri Qasr el-Nil** ('Qasr el-Nil Bridge Sq.'), after the first bridge (built 1869–71) to link Cairo to the island of el-Gezira.

The exact area to which the name Midan el-Tahrir and earlier names apply is fluid, and its status as square or street has varied. While usually taken today to include the space from in front of the Mugamma' building (*see* Share' el-Mugamma') to a point immediately south of the Egyptian Museum, and the signs affirm this, the name applies more properly to the area of the traffic circle, with Share' Mirit taking over from the intersection with Share' el-Bustan and running north to Midan 'Abd el-Men'em Reyad. In the past, the stretch north of the traffic circle to the Egyptian Museum has been called:

From at least 1918 to after 1946: **Midan Mirit**, the name applying to a square (no longer recognized as such) that fronted the Qasr el-Nil Gate of the Qasr el-Nil barracks (now the intersection of Share' el-Ra'is 'Abd el-Salam 'Aref and Share' Shambuliyon with this street) but also extending south on some maps toward the traffic circle. In this application, the name apparently coexisted for a time with the following:

From 1913 to 1933: **Kemalet Midan el-Esma'iliya** ('el-Esma'iliya Square Extension').

From after 1863 to 1913: **Share' Qushlaq Qasr el-Nil** ('Qasr el-Nil Barracks Str.'), a name that also once applied to Share' Mirit from the southern end of the Museum grounds to Midan 'Abd el-Men'em Reyad.

el-Tahrir, Share' (Downtown, el-Gezira)
'Liberation Str.' Since 1954, reflecting the ideology of the 1952

Revolution. Until 1933, the names Share' el-Tahrir and Share'
el-Bustan (now Share' el-Ra'is 'Abd el-Salam Aref) were reversed
from east of Midan el-Falaki to Share' el-Gumhuriya, so that Share'
el-Tahrir exited Midan el-Falaki from its northeastern corner, while
today it exits from its southeastern corner. The evolution of the name
in the Downtown area differs from its evolution in el-Gezira.

In Downtown (from the Nile eastward):
From 1933 to 1954: **Share' el-Khedeiwi Esma'il** ('Khedive
Esma'il Str.'), after Khedive Esma'il (r.1863–79); *see more
under* Midan el-Tahrir.

From 1872 to 1933: **Share' el-Kubri** ('Bridge Str.') or
Share' Kubri el-Gezira ('el-Gezira Bridge Str.') or **Share'
Kubri Qasr el-Nil** (not to be confused with Share' Qasr
el-Nil), after the first bridge (now Kubri Qasr el-Nil), built
between 1869 and 1871, to link Cairo with the island of
el-Gezira and Khedive Esma'il's palace at 'Abdin with the
Qasr el-Nil barracks.

In el-Gezira (from the western end of Kubri Qasr el-Nil west
to Kubri el-Galaa'):
From 1933 to 1954: **Share' el-Khedeiwi Esma'il** ('Khedive
Esma'il Str.'), that is, as the rest of the street.

From 1871 to 1933: **Share' el-Kubri el-A'ma** ('Blind
Bridge Str.'), after former Kubri el-Bahr el-A'ma ('Blind
River Bridge'), which crossed the channel ('the Blind River')
separating el-Gezira from the west bank of the Nile.

el-Tahuna, 'Atfet ('Abdin)
'Mill Alley.' By 1848.

Tal'at, Share' (el-Munira)
By 1935; unidentified. Tal'at is a given name, perhaps that of an
early resident. Not to be confused with former Share' Tal'at (now
Share' Muhammad Shawqi) or Share' Ahmad Tal'at, both of which
are nearby; however, it is possible that all three names refer to the
same person.

Tal'at Harb, Midan (Downtown)
Since 1961, after Tal'at Harb (*see* Share' Tal'at Harb). The statue of
Tal'at Harb is the work of Fathi Mahmud and was erected in 1964.

> From 1912 to 1961: **Midan Seliman Basha** (*see* Share'
> Tal'at Harb). Some maps anticipated this change as early as
> 1908, though it was not yet official. The statue of Seliman
> Basha by Henri Albert Jacquemart, erected in the square in
> 1874, was removed in 1964 and re-erected at the entrance to
> the War Museum at the Citadel.

> From at least 1882 to 1912: **Midan Qaraqol** (or **Karakol**)
> **Qasr el-Nil**, after the police station (Turkish *karakol*) on
> the square. On some early maps, this square is called **Midan
> Qasr el-Nil**, though that name belonged more properly to
> Midan Mirit (*see* Share' Mirit).

Tal'at Harb, Share' (Downtown)
Since 1961, after (Muhammad) Tal'at Harb (1867–1941), early
commercial entrepreneur and nationalist who began as an industrialist, introducing modern machinery into the cotton industry
and went on to found numerous enterprises, including Bank Misr
(the country's first Egyptian-owned bank, 1920), Studio Misr (the
country's first film production facility, 1925), and MisrAir (now
EgyptAir, 1932). It was Harb's belief that "political and economic
independence are precious twins whom it is only natural that we
should furnish with strength and . . . authority." Tal'at Harb was
forced out of the directorship of Bank Misr in the summer of 1941
following a threat of default caused by a run on the bank during the
panic accompanying General Rommel's advance on Alexandria; he
died soon after.

> From 1900 to 1961: **Share' Seliman Basha**, after Octave
> Joseph Anthelme Sève (1788–1860), known as Seliman
> Basha el-Faransawi ('Seliman Basha the Frenchman'), a
> soldier of fortune and self-styled colonel who, starting in
> 1819, established a military academy to train Egyptian
> officers for Muhammad 'Ali's new, European-modeled, army.
> Sève also served Muhammad 'Ali's son Ebrahim Basha

in his campaigns in the Sudan, Greece, and Syria and was appointed minister of war, a position in which he continued to serve under Ebrahim's two successors. He converted to Islam. His daughter Nazli, by his Greek wife Maria, was the grandmother of Queen Nazli, wife of King Fu'ad and mother of King Faruq.

From 1900 to 1912 Share' Seliman Basha began at today's Midan Tal'at Harb and ran east. Late in 1912, the name was extended west from today's Midan Tal'at Harb to Midan el-Tahrir, absorbing what had previously been the northern end of Share' Qasr el-'Eini. Earlier, the name Share' Seliman Basha applied to today's Share' Muhammad Sabri Abu 'Alam; a few older sources therefore refer to this street as **Share' Seliman Basha el-Gedid** ('New Seliman Basha Str.').

el-Tarabishi, Haret (Downtown)
'Tarboosh Maker's Lane.' An ancient lane, predating and sur-viving the demolition and rebuilding of the el-Fawwala area (*see* Haret el-Fawwala). The tarboosh—a rigid, brimless, close-fitting cap with a variety of shapes and colors, of which the taller, red, kind with black tassel is the best known—is of obscure origin, but became the quasi-universal headgear for men in Egypt and elsewhere in the Ottoman Empire after reformist Sultan Mah-mut II (r.1808–39) made it obligatory wear for the military and the civil service.

el-Tarabishi, Haret (Fumm el-Khalig)
'Tarboosh Maker's Lane.' Date unknown; *see above*.

el-Tawashi, Haret (el-Azbakiya)
'Eunuch's Lane.' By 1888; *see* Haret Geneinet el-Tawashi. Also called **Haret el-Beidaq** (*see* Share' el-Beidaq) from at least 1888 until 1913, when the name was quashed.

Tawfiq Deyab, Share' (Qasr el-Dubara)
Since 2010, after (Muhammad) Tawfiq Musa Deyab (1888–1967), a journalist and publisher known for his oratory, and a member of the Arabic Language Academy. Deyab founded the newspapers

el-Diyaa' (Lights) and *el-Gihad* (The Struggle; 1931–38), noted for their criticism of the monarchy and British occupation. The British Embassy is located on this street.

> From 1960 to 2010: **Share' Amrika el-Latiniya** ('Latin America Str.'), in honor of the Brazilian Embassy, formerly located on this street. The United States embassy has also been located on this street since 1946.

> From 1954 to 1960: **Share' el-Zahraa'** (literally, 'the Radiant'). The relevance of the name is not clear (but is unlikely to be to Fatma el-Zahraa', daughter of the Prophet Muhammad). Later, this name was reassigned: *see* Share' el-Zahraa', main entry.

> From at least 1912 to 1954: **Share' el-Walda** ('[Queen] Mother Str.'), after Princess Amina Elhami (1858–1931), granddaughter of 'Abbas Helmi I Basha, wife of Khedive Tawfiq, and mother of Khedive 'Abbas Helmi II, who lived in nearby Qasr el-Dubara palace (*see* former Midan Qasr el-Dubara, *under* Midan Simon Bulifar). The princess, famous for her good works, came to be known as 'Mother of the Egyptians.' Not to be confused with Share' Walda Basha, farther south, in Garden City.

Tawfiq Dos, Mamarr (Downtown)
Since 1935, after the builder of the Doss Buildings apartment blocks on either either side of the passageway; popularly known as **Mamarr el-Jentelman** ('Gentleman's Passage') because of the concentration there of shops selling men's grooming products and accessories.

el-Tawil, Haret (el-Munira)
Date unknown; unidentified. El-Tawil (literally, 'the Tall') may be a family name, perhaps that of an early resident or residents.

Te'eima, Haret (Abdin)
By 1888; unidentified. Te'eima may be a given name, perhaps that of an early resident.

el-Tibarsi, Share' (Fumm el Khalig)
By 1918, in historical evocation of 'Alaa' el-Din ebn 'Abdallah Teibars (or el-Tibarsi) el-Khazendari (d.1319), who built a mosque in 1307 about half a kilometer to the north of this street, near today's Midan Gamal el-Din Abu el-Mahasen. El-Tibarsi was both a member of the Mamluk ruling caste and a scholar, who donated his library to the mosque of el-Azhar.

el-Tibi, Haret (Fumm el Khalig)
Date unknown, after the mosque of Sufi saint el-Sheikh Muhammad el-Tibi on nearby Share' el-Deyura (out of area).

> Date unknown: **Haret el-Sellem** ('Stairway Lane'), after the stairs that lead to this street, which runs along a crest that may be what remains of the levee known as el-Sadd el-Barrani (*see* Share' el-Sadd el-Barrani).

el-Tibi, Kubri (Fumm el Khalig)
By the 1980s; this flyover runs above the metro line and the southern section of Share' el-Sadd el-Barrani and is named after Midan el-Tibi (out of area), to which it leads (*see* Haret el-Tibi).

el-Tubgi, Haret ('Abdin) *see* el-Tubgi, Share'

el-Tubgi, Share' ('Abdin)
'Gunner's Str.' and **Haret el-Tubgi**, 'Gunner's Lane.' From at least 1888, after 'Ali Basha Reda el-Tubgi (1828 or 1829–?), whose house was here at that date. El-Tubgi ('the Gunner') had a successful career in the artillery, serving in the Crimea. He also reorganized the police force, served more than once as a governor in Upper Egypt, and ended his career as commissioner of land taxes.

Tushtumur, Share' (Downtown)
By 1912, in historical evocation of Tushtumur el-Badri the Cup-bearer (d.1342 or 1343), known as Hummus Akhdar ('Green Chickpeas') because of his love for that snack. A Mamluk of Sultan el-Malek el-Naser Muhammad ebn Qalawun who rose to be governor of Aleppo, Tushtumur died in Antioch in flight from his enemies; the street crosses that of Share' Naser el-Din, named after

the same sultan. The naming of the street may be a historical error, in that Bustan Tushtumur ('Tushtumur's Plantation') was located not here but in the Geziret Badran district (out of area).

U

el-Ubera, Midan (Downtown, el-Azbakiya)
'Opera House Sq.' Since 1954, after the Khedivial Opera House, inaugurated in November 1869 with a performance of Verdi's *Rigoletto* in the presence of Khedive Esma'il and Empress Eugénie of France, in Egypt to attend the celebrations for the opening of the Suez Canal. The opera house was lost to fire in 1971 and replaced by the Cairo Opera House, in el-Gezira, inaugurated in 1988. The site of the Khedivial Opera House is now occupied by a multi-story car park. This name was also in use earlier (*see below*).

> From 1933 to 1954: **Midan Ebrahim Basha,** after the eldest son and heir of Muhammad 'Ali, who was born in 1789 and succeeded his father when the latter abdicated in 1848 but predeceased him, dying the same year. From 1933, the street defining the square's western side was incorporated into Share' Ebrahim Basha. Plans to further widen the street between the square and today's Midan el-Gumhuriya and thus allow the statue of Ebrahim Basha to 'see' a corresponding statue of King Fu'ad (r.1917–36) were aborted by the revolution of 1952.

> From at least 1874 to 1933: **Midan el-Teyatru** ('Theatre Sq.'). The decree abolishing this name notes that the square is also known as **Midan el-Ubera** and this name (usually in the form 'Place de l'Opéra') often appears on maps from this period. The *teatro* in question may not, however, have been the Opera House, as a Teatro del Cairo had existed in the nearby Azbakiya Garden from perhaps as early as the 1850s.

'Umar Makram, Share' (Downtown)
Since 1956, after 'Umar Makram ebn el-Hesein el-Hasani el-Seyuti (1755–1822), an Azharite scholar and prominent opponent of the

return of the old order rule following Napoleon's departure from Egypt in 1801. Appointed Naqib el-Ashraf (representative of the descendants of the Prophet Muhammad) for Egypt by the Ottoman sultan in 1802, his defiance of the Mamluks helped to ensure the appointment of Muhammad 'Ali Basha as viceroy. Later, however, the latter, who regarded him as a popular leader and rival, exiled him to Damietta, and then to Tanta, where he died. The mosque of 'Umar Makram, built in neo-Mamluk style in 1951 by Mario Rossi (*see* former Share' Mariyu Russi, *under* Share' Muhammad Mazhar) and used for the funerals of the great and the good, stands on this street. A statue of 'Umar Makram was erected on Midan el-Tahrir near the mosque in 2002, sculpted by Faruq Ebrahim.

> From at least 1912 to 1956: **Share' el-Sheikh el-'Abit,**
> after the mosque and tomb of either (according to conflicting versions) Sufi saint Sheikh Saleh ebn 'Abdallah el-Geziri (d.1379), known as el-'Abit ('the Simpleton') or Sufi saint Sheikh Muhammad el-'Abit (early nineteenth century) whose reputation for foolishness was exploited by Muhammad 'Ali Basha, who sent him to mix with people and report back on their conversations. A village called Geziret el-'Abit, which extended south to at least the area of Share' el-Sheikh Yusef, was demolished by Khedive Esma'il to make way for the palace of Saray el-Esma'iliya, the mosque being incorporated into the palace grounds. In 1954, the mosque was demolished to make way for the 'Umar Makram mosque.

'Umar ebn 'Abd el-'Aziz, 'Atfet (el-Munira)
By 1935, after the eighth caliph of the Umayyad dynasty (717–20), noted for his piety. The street derives its name from former Share' 'Umar ebn 'Abd el-'Aziz (now Share' Esma'il Serri), to which it is perpendicular.

'Umara el-Yamani, Share' (el-Zamalek)
Since 1954, after 'Umara ebn 'Ali ebn Zeidan el-Hakami el-Madhhagi el-Yamani (1121–74), a Yemeni poet who was sent as an ambassador to Egypt by the ruler of Mecca, only to defect on his second visit and remain in Cairo, where he died. The naming is historically inspired, in keeping with other names in the area that

commemorate Fatimid personalities (Share' Ebn Meyassar, Share' el-Amir el-Musabbahi, both of which also date to 1954) and, farther to the west, Ayyubids (Share' Salah el-Din, Share' el-'Aziz 'Usman, etc.). The ambiguity of the Arabic spelling has led many (including the maker of the only sign on the street) to read the name as "Share' 'Emaret el-Yamani," or 'Yamani Building Str.'; however, there is no evidence that a building of that name ever existed.

> From 1913 to 1954: **Share' el-Amir Helmi** ('Prince Helmi Str.'), probably after Prince Ebrahim Helmi Basha (1860–1927), fifth son of Khedive Esma'il. The prince served in the armed forces but was exiled to England and Italy between 1879 and 1888, during which period he wrote *The Literature of Egypt and the Soudan, from the Earliest Times to 1885* (1886–88). In 1889 he returned to Egypt and was promoted to field marshal. This area of el-Zamalek—immediately northeast of Khedive Esma'il's palace of Saray el-Gezira and extending to Share' Setta w-'Eshrin Yulyu—is home to twelve streets named after princes of the ruling family. Of these, six are the sons of Khedive Esma'il (not represented were two who died young and his second son, Muhammad Tawfiq, later to become khedive and have the whole district of el-Tawfiqiya named after him) and the others his grandsons or cousins.

Umm Kulsum, Share' *see* el-Sayyeda Umm Kulsum, Share'

'Urabi, Midan or **Ahmad 'Urabi, Midan** (el-Tawfiqiya)
Since 1954, after Ahmad 'Urabi (1841–1911), a soldier of Egyptian rich-peasant background who, thanks to reforms made by Khedive Esma'il, was permitted to rise, along with others, to officer rank, breaking the monopoly of the Turco–Circassian elite. In 1879, 'Urabi participated in, and quickly came to lead, a mutiny against continuing Turco–Circassian influence in the army that developed into a broader movement against the assumption by France and Britain of control over Egypt's finances and of its ruler, Khedive Tawfiq, following the default and ousting of Khedive Esma'il. The revolt led to British military intervention in 1882 and 'Urabi's defeat at the Battle of el-Tall el-Kebir in

the same year, followed by his exile to Ceylon, from which he returned in 1901. Reviled by the British and by the Egyptian establishment of his day, a national hero to the leaders of the 1952 revolution, 'Urabi was granted posthumous revenge by the ousting of the name of Khedive Tawfiq from this street (*see below*) and its replacement by his own.

> From at least 1912 to 1954: **Midan Tawfiq**, after Muhammad Tawfiq Basha, ruler of Egypt from 1879 to 1892, under whose patronage the Tawfiqiyya district, with this square at its heart, developed. Previously, the area had consisted of swamps, farms, and palaces with their grounds.

'Urabi, Share' or Ahmad 'Urabi, Share' (el-Tawfiqiya)
Since 1954, after Ahmad 'Urabi (*see* Midan 'Urabi).

> From at least 1906 to 1954: **Share' Tawfiq** (*see* Midan Urabi).

'Usman Beih, Haret (el-Munira)
Since after 1935, after 'Usman Beih el-Bardisi (1758–1806), whose mansion was near here. El-Bardisi (whose name refers to el-Bardis in Upper Egypt, of which he was the governor and tax collector) was a Mamluk factional leader who, following the end of the French occupation, allied himself with Muhammad 'Ali, helping him drive the Ottoman governor from Damietta. El-Bardisi then took charge of Cairo but his extortionate tax demands and the unruliness of his troops alienated the population, who are said to have chanted, "What more can you get out of me, Bardisi, now that you've fleeced me?" Muhammad 'Ali took the side of Cairo's merchants and men of religion and drove el-Bardisi out of the city, thus consolidating his own rise to power. El-Bardisi died soon after of poisoning. His mansion was eventually turned into the school known as el-Mubtadayan, which gave its name to a well-known nearby street (*see* former Share' el-Mubtadayan, *under* Share' Muhammad 'Ezz el-'Arab).

Uziris, Share' (Qasr el-Dubara)
Since after 1947, after the Uziris (Osiris) Building, an apartment block whose main entrance is on Share' Lazughli and which was

built on part of the site and grounds of the Qasr el-Dubara palace (*see* former Midan Qasr el-Dubara, *under* Midan Simon Bulifar), which was demolished and subdivided in 1947.

V

el-Vatican, Share‘ *see* el-Fatikan, Share‘

W

el-Wafdiya, Share‘ (el-Munira)
'Incomers' Str.' By 1920, probably in historical evocation of the groups of Mongols who, between the mid-thirteenth and mid-fourteenth centuries, came to Egypt fleeing unrest in Mongol-held lands and were incorporated into the Mamluk army and referred to generically by this term. On one occasion, some eighteen thousand households arrived together.

Wahba, Share‘ (el-Munira)
By 1914, after Yusef Wahba Basha (1852–1934), jurist, diplomat, and economist who held a number of ministerial positions and was prime minister from 1919 to 1920. Wahba was the first finance minister to sign Egyptian banknotes, and survived an assassination attack by nationalists in 1919. The name is sometimes misspelled 'Wahbi' on maps.

el-Wahhabi, ‘Atfet (el-Munira)
Probably after 1948; unidentified. El-Wahhabi is a name that means 'related to or associated with (any person called) ‘Abd el-Wahhab' (and not necessarily 'associated with the Wahhabite movement within Islam') and may have been that of an early resident.

el-Wahsh, Haret (Fumm el-Khalig)
By 1935. Literally, 'Monster's Lane,' but perhaps a family name, that of early residents.

Y

Ya'qub, Share' ('Abdin)
By 1888, after a Ya'qub Beih Sabri, at one time governor of the Fayoum, whose house was on this street at the date given.

el-Yasmin, Share' (el-Zamalek)
'Jasmine Str.' From after 1937; one of a group of streets in the area named after flowers.

Yunes, 'Atfet (Fumm el-Khalig)
Date unknown; unidentified. Yunes is a male given name, probably that of an early resident.

Yusef el-Gendi, Share' (Downtown)
Since 1943, after Yusef Ahmad el-Gendi (1893–1941), a law student and anti-British activist who, in protest at the sentence of exile passed on Sa'd Zaghlul and his colleagues of the Wafd party on 8 March 1919, had himself declared leader of an independent republic centered on his hometown of Zefta in the central Delta. The Republic of Zefta lasted from 18 to 29 March 1919, when the town was taken over (at the third attempt) by Australian soldiers, and el-Gendi was smuggled out and hidden until the sentence on Zaghlul was lifted on 17 April 1919. In later life, he had a distinguished career as a Wafdist parliamentarian. His son Muhammad founded the well-known progressive publishing house and bookshop Dar el-Saqafa el-Gedida ('New Culture Publishing House') on nearby Share' Muhammad Sabri Abu 'Alam.

> From at least 1904 to 1943: **Share' el-Huwayati**, after a saint of that name whose tomb, now vanished, was located on the street.

Yusef Kamel, Share' (el-Zamalek)
Since after 1973, after Yusef Kamel (1891–1973), a painter of the first generation of modern Egyptian artists, considered an impressionist. Kamel studied in Rome and specialized in scenes and portraits drawn from traditional Egyptian life, rural and urban. On his return from Rome, he became the first Egyptian to teach oil

painting at the Higher School of Fine Arts. He was also first head of the Museum of Modern Art (1948–49) and dean of Cairo University's College of Fine Arts (1952–53).

> From at least 1910 to after 1973: **Share' el-Gezira el-Wusta** ('Middle Island Str.'), after an island, originally named Arawi, that appeared to the north of the island of el-Roda (out of area) in the early fourteenth century; the appearance of a second island, Halima, in 1372, to the north of Arawi, led to the latter becoming known as 'the Middle Island' (that is, the island between el-Roda and Halima). The arrival of a third island and the coalescence of the three during the nineteenth century brought into being a single land mass known until the twentieth century as Geziret Bulaq ('Bulaq Island') or simply el-Gezira ('the Island'). This street name remains in use and is found on signs.

Yusef Wahba, Share' *see* Wahba, Share'

Z

el-Za'balawi, Haret ('Abdin)
By 1904; unidentified. The name means 'the one from Abu Za'bal,' a district north of Cairo.

el-Zabtiya (or el-Dabtiya), Share' (el-Azbakiya)
'Police Headquarters Str.' From c.1867, after the offices of the Zabet, or prefect of police (literally, 'the apprehender'), a post created by Muhammad 'Ali in the 1820s in conjunction with Egypt's first modern police force. From 1848 to 1869, the name applied to the street now called Share' el-'Ataba el-Khadra (out of area); in 1895, under the new name of the Hekemdariya, police headquarters moved to their current premises on Share' Bur Sa'id, where they are now styled the Central Security Directorate, and Share' el-'Ataba el-Khadra became known as Share' el-Zabtiya el-Qadima ('Old Police Headquarters Str.').

In the early nineteenth century, and popularly until the
mid-twentieth century, the names **Share' el-Bakri** and
Share' Suq el-Bakri ('el-Bakri Market Str.') were used of
the chain of streets running between Share' Mushtuhur on
the southwest, through the el-Fawwala neighborhood, to
today's Midan el-'Ataba el-Khadra on the northeast (former Share' Rahabet el-Tebn [*see under* Share' el-Sharekat],
Share' el-Ashmawi, and Share' el-Zabtiya), in reference to
the presence in the area (between the Main Post Office on
today's Midan el-'Ataba el-Khadra and Midan el-Ubera) of
the home of Sheikh Khalil el-Bakri, a member of the influential el-Bakri family of *sayyed*s, or descendants of the Prophet
Muhammad and of the first caliph, Abu Bakr el-Seddiq.
Sheikh Khalil assumed the post of head of the descendants
of the Prophet in Egypt in 1798, after persuading the French
occupation authorities to strip 'Umar Makram of this title
(*see* Share' 'Umar Makram); regarded as a quisling, the sheikh
narrowly escaped with his life when his house was burned
and plundered during the first anti-French uprising.

el-Zahhar, Haret (el-Azbakiya)
Since at least 1888, after a certain el-Zahhar, who had a house there
at the date given.

el-Zahraa', Share' (Qasr el-Dubara)
Since 1960; literally, el-Zahraa' means 'the Radiant.' The relevance of the name is not clear (but is unlikely to be a reference
to Fatma el-Zahraa', daughter of the Prophet Muhammad). This
name, first given in 1954 to the street formerly known as Share'
el-Walda (*see under* Share' Tawfiq Deyab), was, according to some
records, reassigned in 1960 to former Share' Lazughli (former
Share' el-Zahraa' was then renamed Share' Amrika el-Latiniya).
The name appears as the successor to Share' Lazughli (*see below*)
only on certain maps and is generally unknown to residents; likewise, all the signs on the street are for Share' Lazughli. The status
of the name is, therefore, unclear.

From at least 1912 to 1960: **Share' Lazughli**, after Muhammad Beih Lazughli (*see* Midan Lazughli).

el-Za'im el-Hendi Ghandi, Share' (Garden City)

'Indian Leader Gandhi Str.' Since 1969, after Mohandas Karam-chand Gandhi (1869–1948), activist between 1893 and 1914 for the civil rights of Indians in South Africa and from 1915 leader of the non-violent protest movement that brought an end to British rule over India in 1947. He was also the founder of India's National Congress Party.

> From at least 1933 to 1969: **Share' el-Salsul** ('Spit Str.');
> the word, meaning a spit of land joining two islands, comes
> from the jargon of Nile boatmen.

Zakariya Ahmad, Share' (Downtown)

Since 1961, after the singer and composer of that name (1896–1961), who wrote (by his own count) fifty-six operettas and 1,070 songs, including sixty-five of Umm Kulsum's best-known and most innovative ballads. The choice of this street to commemorate Ahmad reflects its former glory as part of the Share' Emad el-Din entertainment district. Different sections of the street have had different naming histories:

> From Share' Nagib el-Rihani south to Share' Seliman el-Halabi:

> From at least 1920 to 1961: **Share' Galal**, after 'Ali Galal
> Basha, owner of the palace and grounds that were cleared to
> make way for the northern extension of Share' Emad el-Din.
> Not to be confused with Share' Galal Basha (farther north,
> west off Share' Emad el-Din).

> From Share' Seliman el-Halabi south to Share' Setta
> w-'Eshrin Yulyu:

> From at least 1912 to 1935: **Share' Berentanya** ('Printania
> Str.'), after the theater of that name (now the Cairo Palace
> Cinema). The change of name to Share' Galal appears to have
> accompanied the straightening of Share' Berentanya and its
> alignment with Share' Galal to the north.

Zakariya Rezq, Share' *see* el-Shahid Zakariya Rezq, Share'

Zaki ʿAli, Shareʿ (el-Zamalek)
Since no earlier than 1937, after Zaki Basha ʿAli (c.1887–1958), a lawyer and three-time minister of state, who built and lived in the building called Dar el-Salam on the corner of this street with Shareʿ Mahmud ʿAzmi. ʿAli contributed to the drafting of the Arab Feminist Union's constitutional act in 1945 and was a member of the committee of reconciliation with Hasan el-Banna, founder of the Muslim Brotherhood, formed following the Brotherhood's assassination of prime minister Mahmud el-Nuqrashi Basha in 1948.

Zeinhum, Kubri (Fumm el-Khalig, el-Munira)
Since after 2001, after a district of the same name at this flyover's eastern end. Zeinhum ('Their Adornment') is a variant of Zein el-ʿAbedin ('the Adornment of the Worshipers'), epithet of ʿAli ebn el-Hesein (659–713), a grandson of ʿAli ebn Abi Taleb and fourth imam according to Shiite belief. Zein el-ʿAbedin's head was brought to Cairo in the Fatimid period and interred in the mosque dedicated to him in Midan Zein el-ʿAbedin (out of area). In some maps, the flyover appears as **Kubri Abu el-Rish**, after the Abu el-Rish children's hospital at its western end.

Zugheib, Haret or **Zugheib, Sekket** (Downtown)
Since 1913, after Count Antoine de Zogheb, who owned property on the street, including the large Zogheb Building (rebuilt by Zogheb in its present form in 1910). The count, whose title was bestowed by the King of Sardinia, belonged to a Greek Catholic family from Damascus that had prospered in the Alexandria cotton trade. His large and celebrated neo-Mamluk mansion overlooking Midan el-Tahrir at the other end of Shareʿ Qasr el-Nil, and next to Huda el-Shaʿrawi's similarly styled home, was built in 1887 and became at one point an art museum, the precursor to today's Museum of Modern Egyptian Art; it was torn down in 1963.

> From at least 1887 to 1913: **Haret el-Kunt Zugheib**
> ('Count Zugheib's Lane').

Zugheib, Sekket *see* Zugheib, Haret

BIBLIOGRAPHY

Printed Sources

Abed, Wael. *Zamalek, My Home Island*. Cairo, 2015.

Abu Julayyil, Ḥamdī. *al-Qāhira: Shawāriʿ wa-ḥikāyāt*. Cairo: al-Hayʾa al-Miṣriyya al-ʿĀmma li-l-Kitāb, 2007.

Abū l-ʿAmāyim, Muḥammad. *Āthār al-Qāhira al-islāmiyya fī-l-ʿaṣr al-ʿuthmānī*. Vol. 1. Istanbul: Research Centre for Islamic History, Art, and Culture (IRCICA), 2003.

Abū l-Futūḥ, Ghāda Farūq. *al-Khurūj min al-aswār: taḥdīth madīnat al-Qāhira*. Cairo: Dār al-Kutub wa-l-Wathāʾiq al-Qawmiyya, 2016.

Abugideiri, Hibba. *Gender and the Making of Modern Medicine in Colonial Egypt*. Farnham, Surrey and Burlington, VT: Ashgate, 2010.

Abu-Lughod, Janet. *Cairo: 1001 Years of the City Victorious*. Princeton: Princeton University Press, 1971.

Amin, Naguib. *Cairo A–Z*. Cairo: The Palm Press, 2000.

Arnaud, Jean-Luc. *Le Caire: mise en place d'une ville moderne, 1867–1907*. Arles: Actes Sud, 1998.

Āsāf, Yūsuf. *Tārīkh ashhar rijāl al-ʿaṣr*. Cairo: al-Maṭbaʿa al-ʿUmūmiyya, 1890.

Baedeker, Karl. *Egypt, Part 1 (Lower Egypt, with the Fayum and the peninsula of Sinai)* (2nd ed.). Leipzig: Karl Baedeker, 1885.

———. *Egypt and the Sudan* (6th ed.). Leipzig: Karl Baedeker, 1908.

———. *Egypt and the Sudan* (7th ed.). Leipzig: Karl Baedeker, 1914.

al-Barbarī, Munīr. "Mashākil al-murūr bi-madīnat al-Qāhira wa-ṭuruq ḥallihā," in *Majallat al-ʿImāra wa-l-Funūn*, Issue 7–8, 1953–54, pp.17–34.

Behrens-Abouseif, Doris. *Azbakiyya and Its Environs from Azbak to Ismaʿil, 1476–1879*. Institut Français d'Archéologie Orientale, 1985.

Beinin, Joel. *The Dispersion of Egyptian Jewry: Culture, Politics, and the Formation of a Modern Diaspora.* Berkeley: Universtiy of California Press, 1998.

Berque, Jacques. *Egypt: Imperialism and Revolution.* Trans. by Jean Stewart. London: Faber and Faber, 1972.

Bosworth, Clifford Edmund. *The New Islamic Dynasties: A Chronological and Genealogical Manual.* Edinburgh: Edinburgh Universtiy Press, 1996.

Bulletin des Lois et Décrets du Gouvernement Égyptien. Cairo: Imprimérie Nationale, various dates.

Capresi, Vittoria and Barbara Pampe. *Discovering Downtown Cairo.* Berlin: Jovis, 2015.

Clerget, Marcel. *Le Caire: étude de géographie urbaine et d'histoire économique.* Cairo: E. and R. Schindler, 1934.

Cooper, John. *The Medieval Nile: Route, Navigation, and Landscape in Islamic Egypt.* Cairo: The American University in Cairo Press, 2015.

Ḍāhir, Masʿūd. *Hijrat al-Shawām: al-hijra al-lubnāniyya ilā Miṣr.* Cairo: Dār al-Shurūq, 2009.

Daly, M.W. (ed.) *Egypt, Volume Two: From 1517 to the End of the Twentieth Century.* Cambridge: Cambridge University Press, 1998.

Dalīl Tilifūnāt al-Qāhira 1973. Cairo: Sharikat al-Iʿlānāt al-Sharqiyya, 1973.

Di-Capua, Yoav. "Embodiment of the Revolutionary Spirit: The Mustafa Kamil Mausoleum in Cairo," in *History and Memory,* Vol 13, No.1 (Spring/Summer) 2001, pp.85–113.

El-Dorghamy, Yasmine, "How to Wipe Out Your City's Memory," in *Community Times,* October 2007.

———. "Champollion," in *Turath,* Vol. I, 2009.

Egyptian Census 1848 [Taʿdād al-nufūs, Maḥfūẓāt Miṣr (1264/1848)]. Cairo: Dār al-Wathāʾiq al-Qawmiyya.

Egyptian Census 1868 [Taʿdād al-nufūs, Maḥfūẓāt Miṣr (1284/1868)]. Cairo: Dār al-Wathāʾiq al-Qawmiyya.

The Egyptian Gazette.

Fahmī, Muṣṭafā. "ʿAṣr Ismāʿīl (al-quṣūr wa-l-munshaʾāt al-ʿāmma wa-l-muntazahāt)," in *Majallat al-ʿImāra wa-l-Funūn,* no. 6–7, 1952, pp.8–12.

Fahmy, Khaled. *All the Pasha's Men.* Cairo: The American University in Cairo Press, 2003.

———. "Modernizing Cairo: A Revisionist Narrative," in *Making Cairo Medieval,* ed. Nezar AlSayyad, Irene A. Bierman, and Nasser Rabat. Lanham: Lexington Books, 2005.

Fischer, Max (ed.). *The Egyptian Directory / l'Annuaire égyptien / al-Dalīl al-miṣrī*. Cairo: Imprimerie A. Leschioni (?), 1914, 1921, 1934, 1937, 1943.

Goldschmidt, Arthur, Jr. *Biographical Dictionary of Modern Egypt*. Cairo: The American University in Cairo Press, 2000.

Goldschmidt, Arthur, Jr. and Robert Johnston. *Historical Dictionary of Egypt*. Cairo: The American University in Cairo Press, 2004.

al-Ḥadīdī, Fatḥī Ḥāfiẓ. *Dirāsāt fī-l-taṭawwur al-ʿumrānī li-madīnat al-Qāhira*. Cairo: al-Hayʾa al-Miṣriyya al-ʿĀmma li-l-Kitāb, 2009.

———. *al-Taṭawwur al-ʿumrānī li-shawāriʿ al-Qāhira min al-bidāyāt ḥattā-l-qarn al-ḥādī wa-l-ʿishrīn*. Cairo: al-Dār al-Miṣriyya al-Lubnāniyya, 2014.

Halim, Hala. "Latter-day Levantinism, or *'Polypolis'* in the libretti of Bernard de Zogheb," in *California Italian Studies* 1 (1), 2010.

———. *Alexandrian Cosmopolitanism: An Archive*. New York: Fordham University Press, 2013.

Hawāss, Suhayr Zakī. *al-Qāhira al-khidiwiyya*. Cairo: Markaz al-Taṣmīmāt al-Miʿmāriyya, 2002.

Heyworth-Dunne, J. *An Introduction to the History of Education in Modern Egypt*. London: Luzac, 1939.

Hunter, Robert F. *Egypt under the Khedives 1805–1879*. Cairo: The American University in Cairo Press, 1999.

ʿĪsā, Ṣalāḥ: *Maʾsāt Madām Fahmī: ḥikāyāt min daftar al-waṭan*. Cairo: Dār al-Shurūq, 2011.

ʿĪsawī, ʿAbd al-Salām. *Jazīrat al-Rawḍa bayna-l-tārīkh wa-l-wāqiʿ*. Cairo, 2008.

Ismāʿīl, Muḥammad Ḥusām el-Dīn. *Wajh madīnat al-Qāhira min wilāyat Muḥammad ʿAlī ḥattā nihāyat ḥukm Ismāʿīl (1805–1878)*. Series: al-Qāhira. Cairo: al-Hayʾa al-ʿĀmma li-l-Kitāb, 2014.

Journal Officiel du Gouvernement Égyptien. Cairo: Imprimérie Nationale, various dates.

El Kadi, Galila. *Le Caire, centre en movement / Cairo, a Center in Movement*. Marseille: IRD Éditions, 2012.

King, Joan Wucher. *Historical Dictionary of Egypt*. Cairo: The American University in Cairo Press, 1984.

al-Kitāb al-dhahabī li-l-maḥākim al-ahliyya. Part One (1883–1933). Bulaq: al-Maṭābiʿ al-Amīriyya, 1937.

El Kolaly, Hoda Mohamed Moustafa and Hani Muhamed Moustafa El Kolaly. *Cairo City Key*. 2nd edition (2nd printing). Cairo: Cairo City Key, 2008.

Lababidi, Lesley. *Cairo's Street Stories*. Cairo: The American University in Cairo Press, 2008.

Lajnat al-Tasmiyāt, records. Governorate of Cairo, 1960–present.

Landau, Jacob M. *Jews in Nineteenth-century Egypt*. New York: New York University Press, 1969.

Lane, Edward William. *Description of Egypt*, edited by Jason Thompson. Cairo: The American University in Cairo Press, 2000.

Leaman, Oliver (ed.). *Companion Encyclopedia of Middle Eastern and North African Film*. London: Routledge, 2001.

"Liste des noms des lieux, rues, places, et monuments," in *Description de l'Égypte, ou recueil des observations et des recherches qui ont été faites en Égypte pendant l'expédition de l'Armée Française, publié par les ordres de sa Majesté l'Empereur Napoléon le Grand*. Vol. 2, 2. Paris: Imprimerie Impériale, 1809–22, pp.603–13, 625–34.

Mansfield, Peter. *The British in Egypt*. New York: Holt, Rinehart, and Winston, 1972.

McPherson, J.W. *The Moulids of Egypt: Egyptian Saints-days*. Cairo: N.M. Press, 1941.

Meisami, Julia Scott and Paul Starkey. *Encyclopedia of Arabic Literature*. 2 vols. London and New York: Routledge, 1998.

Meital, Yoram. "Central Cairo: Street Naming and the Struggle over Historical Representation," in *Middle Eastern Studies*, Vol. 43, No.6 (November 2007), pp.857–78.

Mestyan, Adam. *Arab Patriotism: The Ideology and Culture of Power in Late Ottoman Egypt*. Princeton: Princeton University Press, 2017.

Mestyan, Adam and Mercedes Volait. "Affairisme dynastique et dandysme au Caire vers 1900: Le Club des Princes et la formation d'un quartier du divertissement rue 'Imād al-Dīn," in *Annales islamologiques*, vol. 50, 2017, pp. 55–106.

Mubārak, 'Ali. *al-Khiṭaṭ al-tawfīqiyya al-jadīda li-Miṣr wa-l-Qāhira wa-mudunihā wa-bilādihā al-qadīma wa-l-shahīra*. Cairo: Maṭbaʻat Dār al-Kutub wa-l-Wathāʾiq al-Qawmiyya, 2004.

Le Mondain égyptien: The Egyptian Who's Who / l'Annuaire de l'élite d'Égypte 1939. Cairo: E.J. Blatner, 1939.

Muḥammad, Muḥammad Kamāl al-Sayyid. *Asmāʾ wa-musammayāt: min tārīkh Miṣr—al-Qāhira*. Cairo: al-Hayʾa al-Miṣriyya al-ʻĀmma li-l-Kitāb, 1986.

Mūsā, ʻĀydah al-ʻAzab (ed.). *130 ʻāman ʻalā l-thawra al-ʻurābiyya*. Cairo: Dār al-Shurūq, 2011.

Nāfi', 'Abd al-Ḥamid. *Dhayl khiṭaṭ al-Maqrīzī*. Edited by Khālid 'Azab and Muḥammad al-Sayyid Ḥamdī Mitwallī. Cairo: Maktabat al-Dār al-'Arabiyya li-l-Kitāb, 2006.

el-Nagāti, 'Umar. "al-Mamarrāt: Farāgh 'āmm iktashafathu al-thawra" (interview), in *Mantiqti*, Issue 19, January 2015, pp.9–17.

Nagati, Omar and Beth Stryker. *Cairo Downtown Passageways, Walking Tour*. Cairo: CLUSTER, 2015.

Naguib, Nefissa and Inger Marie Okkenhaug. *Interpreting Welfare and Relief in the Middle East*. Leiden: Brill, 2008.

Nicolle, David and Angus McBride. *The Mamluks 1250–1517*. Men-at-Arms Series 259. Oxford: Osprey Publishing, 1993.

"Le Palais de Justice Indigène, Le Caire 1928," in *Impressions of Egypt*, Vol. 13, October 2001, p.23.

Ordre des avocats aux juridictions mixtes d'Égypte. *Tableau de l'Ordre, 59me & 60me Année Judiciaires 1933–35*. Alexandria: Fratelli Ventura, 1934.

Poole, Sophia. *Letters from an Englishwoman in Egypt, 1842–44*. Cairo: The American University in Cairo Press, 2016.

Qāsim, Ḥasan. *al-Mazārāt al-islāmiyya wa-l-āthār al-'arabiyya fī Miṣr wa-l-Qāhira al-mu'izziyya*. Part 12: *al-Masājid al-ḥadītha al-mustajadda*, edited by Majdī 'Alwān. Alexandria: Bibliotheca Alexandrina, forthcoming.

Raafat, Samir W. "Resurrecting Street Names," in *Cairo Times*, May 2000, pp.1–5.

———. *Cairo, The Glory Years*. Cairo: Harpocrates, 2005.

———. *The Egyptian Bourse*. Cairo: Zeitouna, 2010.

———. *Privileged for Three Centuries: The House of Chamsi*. Cairo: Samir W. Raafat, 2011.

Rabbat, Nasser. "Circling the Square," in *Artforum*, April 2011.

Ramzī, Muḥammad. *al-Qāmūs al-jiyughrāfī li-l-bilād al-miṣriyya min 'ahd qudamā' al-Miṣriyyīn ilā sanat 1945*. 4 parts, plus index. Cairo: Maṭba'at Dār al-Kutub al-Mīṣriyya, 1923.

———. *Mudhakkira bi-bayān al-aghlāṭ allatī waqa'at min Maṣlaḥat al-Tanẓīm fī tasmiyat al-shawāri' wa-l-ṭuruq bi-madīnat al-Qāhira wa-ḍawāḥīhā muqaddama li-ḥaḍrat ṣāḥib al-ma'ālī wazīr al-ashghāl al-'umūmiyya*. Cairo: Maṭba'at Dār al-Kutub al-Miṣriyya, 1925.

Raymond, André. *Cairo: City of History*. Cairo: The American University in Cairo Press, 2000.

Reid, Donald Malcolm. *Whose Pharaohs?* Berkeley: University of California Press, 2002.

Sāmī, Amīn. *Taqwīm al-Nīl*. 6 vols. Cairo: Dār al-Kutub, 1928.

Samir, Salwa. "A Blast from the Past," in *The Egyptian Gazette*, 20 February 2010.

Sayyid, Ayman Fuʾād. *al-Qāhira: Khiṭaṭuhā wa-taṭawwuruhā al-ʿumrānī*. Cairo: al-Hayʾa al-Miṣriyya al-ʿĀmma li-l-Kitāb, 2015.

Seif, Ola, Rasha Azab, and Sherif Boraïe. *Downtown Cairo*. Cairo: Zeituna, 2014.

Tabar, Paul and Jennifer Skulte-Ouaiss. *Politics, Culture and the Lebanese Diaspora*. Newcastle upon Tyne: Cambridge Scholars, 2010.

El Tabbakh, May. "What's in Store for the Historic Sednaoui Khazindar Building?" in *Rawi*. Issue 6, 2014, pp.65–67.

Talaat, Amr S. "Afrah al-Anjal," in *Turath*, Vol. II, 2008, pp.78–84.

———. "Mademoiselle Garden City," in *Turath*, Vol. I, 2009, pp.68–74.

———. "Ismailia . . . Who Remembers?" in *Turath*, Vol. II, 2009, pp.68–72.

———. "Prickly Pears in al Boustan," in *Turath*, Vol. IV, 2009, pp.72–78.

Tārīkh al-ʿulūm wa-l-tiknulūjiyā al-handasiyya fī Miṣr fī-l-qarnayn al-tāsiʿ ʿashar wa-l-ʿishrīn. 2 vols. Cairo: Akadamiyyat al-Baḥth al-ʿIlmī wa-l-Tiknulūjiyā, 1993.

Taymūr, Aḥmad. *Muʿjam Taymūr al-kabīr fī-l-alfāẓ al-ʿāmmiyya*. 6 vols. Cairo: Dār al-Kutub wa-l-Wathāʾiq al-Qawmiyya, 2001.

Thābit and Anṭākī. *al-Nujūm al-zuhr fī rusūm aʿyān Miṣr*. Cairo: Maṭbaʿat al-Shaʿb, 1905.

Thābit, Yāsir. *Futuwwāt wa-afandiyya*. Cairo: Dār Ṣafṣāf, 2010.

———. *Qiṣṣat al-tharwa fī Miṣr*. Cairo: Dār Mīrīt, 2012.

ʿUmar Ṭūsūn, al-Amīr. *al-Biʿthāt al-ʿilmiyya fī ʿahd Muḥammad ʿAlī*. Alexandria: Maṭbaʿat Ṣalāḥ al-Dīn, 1924.

Viaud, Gérard. *Le secret des mystérieuses rues du Caire*. Cairo, 1990.

Vitalis, Robert. *When Capitalists Collide*. Berkeley: University of California Press, 1995.

Volait, Mercedes. *Architectes et architectures de l'Égypte moderne 1830– 1950: genèse et essor d'une expertise locale*. Paris: Maisonneuve et Larose, 2005.

al-Waqāʾiʿ al-Miṣriyya. Cairo: al-Maṭābiʿ al-Amīriyya, various dates.

Warner, Nicholas. *The True Description of Cairo: A Sixteenth-century Venetian View*. 3 vols. London: The Arcadian Library / Oxford University Press, 2006.

Waterbury, John. *The Egypt of Nasser and Sadat*. Princeton: Princeton University Press, 1983.

Zaki, ʿAbd al-Raḥmān. *Mawsūʿat al-Qāhira fī alf ʿām.* Cairo: Maktabat al-Anglū al-Miṣriyya, 1969.

al-Zirikli, Khayr al-Dīn. *al-Aʿlām: Qāmūs tarājim li-ashhar al-rijāl wa-l-nisāʾ min al-ʿArab wa-l-mustaʿribīn wa-l-mustashriqīn.* Beirut: Dār al-ʿIlm li-l-Malāyīn, 1990.

Online Sources

almasalik.com

almessa.net.eg

ar.wikipedia.org

ar-ar.facebook.com/turath.masry

benisuef.gov.eg

bma.arch.unige.it

comboniegypt.org

egy.com (Samir Raafat)

egyptedantan.com (Max Karkégi)

elbadil.com

en.wikipedia.org

facebook.com/Wa3yDamanhour

grandhotelsegypt.com (Andrew Humphreys)

Kupferschmidt U. M._Henri Naus Bey. Retrieving the biography of a Belgian industrialist in Egypt_1999.pdf (kaowarsom.be/documents/ MEMOIRES_VERHANDELINGEN/Sciences_morales_politique/ Hum.Sc.(NS)_T.52,2_KUPFERSCHMIDT) (retrieved 21 June 2017).

mantiqti.cairolive.com

maps7.com

masress.com

mobda3.net

nizwa.com

ohchr.org

royalark.net/Egypt (Christopher Buyers)

sasapost.com

startimes.com

thelancet.com/journals

today.almasryalyoum.com

treika.forum-2007.com (Muhammad Abu Tereika)

yasser-best.blogspot.com.eg

INDEX OF FORMER,
ALTERNATIVE,
AND INFORMAL NAMES

Fumm el-Ter'a el-Bulaqiya, Share' *see* 1) el-Galaa', Share'; 2) 'Abd el-Men'em Reyad, Midan
Fumm el-Ter'a el-Esma'iliya, Share' *see* 'Abd el-Men'em Reyad, Midan
Fumm Ter'et el-Esma'iliya, Share' *see* 'Abd el-Men'em Reyad, Midan
Funduq Safuy, Share' *see* Ebrahim el-Qabbani, Share'

el-Gabalaya, Share' *see* 1) Hasan Sabri, Share'; 2) Muhammad Mazhar, Share'; 3) el-Sayyeda Umm Kulsum, Share'
Galal, Share' *see* Zakariya Ahmad, Share'
Galal, Haret *see* 'Ali el-Kassar, Haret
Galal (Basha), Share' *see* 'Emad el-Din, Share'
Gamal 'Abd el-Naser, Kubri *see* Qasr el-Nil, Kubri
Game' el-'Ezam, Share' *see* Sidi 'Abd el-Qader, Share'
Game' el-Kikhya, Share' *see* Zugheib, Haret
Game' Sharkas, Share' *see* Muhammad Sabri Abu 'Alam, Share'
Gemmeiz, Share' *see* Hasan el-Akbar, Share'
el-Geneina, Share' *see* el-Fannan 'Ali el-Kassar, Share'
Geneinet el-Musallas, Share' *see* Shambuliyon, Share'
el-Gezira, Kubri *see* Qasr el-Nil, Kubri
el-Gezira, Midan *see* Sa'd Zaghlul, Midan
el-Gezira, Share' *see* el-Sayyeda Umm Kulsum, Share'
el-Gezira el-Wusta, Share' *see* Yusef Kamel, Share'
Geziret Arawi, Sekket *see* Muhammad Anis, Share'
Gohar el-Qa'ed, Share' *see* el-Rashidi Share'

Habib 'Ayrut, Share' *see* el-Duktur Ahmad Abu el-'Ela, Share'
Habib Lutfallah, Share' *see* el-Shahid Zakariya Rezq, Share'
Hadayeq el-Zuhriya, Share' *see* el-Burg, Share'
el-Hadiqa, Share' *see* el-Mustashar Muhammad Fathi Nagib, Share'
Hadiqet el-Zuhriya *see* el-Burg, Share'
Halim, Midan *see* 1) Ebrahim 'Abd el-Qader el-Mazni, Share'; 2) Madraset el-Alsun, Share'; 3) Halim, Share'
Halim, Share' *see* Muhammad Beih el-Alfi, Share'
Hammam Shenaydar *see* Bustan el-Dekka, Share'
Hammam el-'Om, Share' *see* Bustan el-Dekka, Share'
el-Hammam el-'Umumi *see* Bustan el-Dekka, Share'
Hammam el-'Umum *see* Bustan el-Dekka, Share'
el-Haras, Share' *see* el-Duktur Mahmud Fawzi, Share'
Hasan Sabri, Share' *see* 1) el-Barazil, Share'; 2) el-Sayyeda Umm Kulsum, Share'
Helwan, Share' *see* Mansur, Share'
el-Hegg, Share' *see* Muhammad Helmi Ebrahim, Share'
el-Hekr, Haret *see* el-Sha'er, 'Atfet
Helmi Pasha, Share' *see* Sa'd Zaghlul, Share'
Hod el-Laban, Share' *see* el-Sheikh 'Abd el-Latif Deraz, Share'
Hosh el-Gella, Haret *see* Hosh Qutb, Haret
el-Hurriya, Midan *see* el-Tahrir, Midan